ISBN 978-0-243-27585-4
PIBN 10271479

1 MONTH OF
FREE
READING

at
www.ForgottenBooks.com

By purchasing this book you are eligible for one month membership to ForgottenBooks.com, giving you unlimited access to our entire collection of over 1,000,000 titles via our web site and mobile apps.

To claim your free month visit:
www.forgottenbooks.com/free271479

Photographing the Invisible

Practical Studies in
Spirit Photography, Spirit Portraiture, and other Rare but Allied Phenomena

By

James Coates, Ph.D., F.A.S.

Author of
" Human Magnetism," "Seeing the Invisible,"
"Self-Reliance," "The Practical Hypnotist,"
etc., etc., etc.

WITH 90 PHOTOGRAPHS

LONDON
L. N. FOWLER & CO.
7 IMPERIAL ARCADE, LUDGATE CIRCUS, E.C.

CHICAGO, ILL., U.S.A.
THE ADVANCED THOUGHT PUBLISHING CO.
MASONIC TEMPLE

1911

MRS JAMES COATES.

Photograph by Adamson & Son, Rothesay.]   [*Frontispiece.*

It was owing to Mrs Coates's psychic impressions that Mr Wyllie was brought to
Rothesay, and to her son, Mr David A. Simpson, who passed into the higher life 25th
July 1908, whose kindly aid and patient encouragement enabled me to edit this book.

Preface

As a further contribution to psychic science I have written this work, which represents some of the results of my inquiries and personal research. In a former book, *Seeing the Invisible*, which his late Majesty King Edward was pleased to accept, I touched —among other studies—upon thought and spirit photography.

Sir William Crookes, O.M., F.R.S., the distinguished savant, commended the book most favourably :—

It is written in a fair spirit which invites unbiassed criticism. The incidents related in it and the arguments put forward are such as to demand the careful attention of thoughtful men, and the author impartially points out some difficulties and discrepancies.

In the present work I give a fuller and more complete record of spirit photography than was at all possible in the pages of *Seeing the Invisible*—I trust also in a fair spirit which invites careful reading before criticism.

Spirit photographs, spirit portraiture, and spirit writings belong to the rarer phases of psycho-physics. They are either produced by the operations of Intelligences in the Invisible—through appropriate media—or man possesses psychic faculties and powers which have not yet received the attention they demand.

Spiritualists believe that spirits can be photographed. Experts—many of whom have never investigated—declare all spirit photographs fraudulent. To both my answer is: "The evidence does not support either hypothesis, but for the fact of spirit photography it is most conclusive."

Many problems, puzzles, and difficulties met with in the course of investigation are clearly stated. I have, however, omitted all reference to the experiments of Dr Baraduc and the photographing of invisible radiations from radio-active bodies, and matters already dealt with in *Seeing the Invisible*. I have not touched upon the discoveries of Dr W. J. Kilner, by which he has been able to render visible the hitherto invisible human auras, and their relation to health and disease, as that would carry me beyond the scope of the present work. And lastly, I have not attempted to deal with the results of Dr Ochorowicz's experiments with his new apparatus, with which, it is declared, he can photograph *spirits* — I presume, "things invisible" — without the aid of a medium. The information is too late and too meagre to be considered in this book. Notwithstanding these limitations, I give a fairly comprehensive *résumé* of the phenomena of spirit photography.

In a lesser degree I deal with spirit-painted portraits. Although I have not personally investigated these, from the abundant material at my disposal I have arrived at certain deductions, and these I give.

Psychography — spirit-writing — is briefly treated, and the conclusions reached are also given.

I am indebted for some quotations to the articles by the late Mr Stainton Moses, " M.A. Oxon.," in *Human Nature*, vols. viii. and ix. (James Burns, London, 1874–5); *Chronicles of the Photographs of Spiritual Beings and Phenomena Invisible to the Material Eye*, by Miss Houghton (E. W. Allen, Ave Maria Lane, London, 1882); *The Veil Lifted*, by Andrew Glendinning (Whittaker & Co., London, 1894); *Borderland*, by W. T. Stead (London, 1894–7); *Unseen Faces Photographed*, by Dr H. A. Reid, Los Angeles, Cal., U.S.A. (1901); and to other sources mentioned in the body of the book.

I wish to express my thanks to the Editors of *Light*, London; *The Two Worlds*, Manchester, England; and the *Harbinger of Light*, Melbourne, Australia, for the use of blocks; to the subscribers to the Wyllie Fund, who enabled me to experiment in psychic photography under my own roof; and to numerous correspondents for testimony and photographs submitted. I have not been able to use all, but have edited a selection in order to present various phases of the phenomena. I now present this work to the consideration of all thoughtful persons interested in the scientific aspects of modern psychic research.

JAMES COATES.

GLENBEG HOUSE,
ROTHESAY, SCOTLAND,
  1st September 1911.

Contents

vii

List of Illustrations

Photographing the Invisible

INTRODUCTION

THE various phases of psycho-physics published under the title of this book are so puzzling, and the claims so extraordinary, and the evidence so startling, and the material at my disposal so abundant, that I have only produced a tithe of the facts, and as many illustrations as space permits.

The major portion of these pages is devoted to spirit photography; that subject calling for some explanatory notes, I think it well to give a few just now.

I view photography as applied to the visible, the material invisible, and the immaterial invisible or the psychic.

The art of photography is of comparatively recent date. With the history I do not deal, except to recall that the discovery was made in 1839, when the processes of Daguerreotyping were patented and Talbot's invention announced. Since then, the science and art of photography have made vast strides, until it has now become an art of the highest utility and widest application, not even guessed at by its usual patrons. For these it is enough that they get a "good picture," generally as flattering as the photographer's skill can supply.

That photography renders invaluable aid to the physician and surgeon, the chemist and student of physics, and others in the more serious studies of Nature's problems, is very evident.

That it should be applied in photographing the invisible, the unseen and the unknown, does not occur to the usual patron; or if so, he dismisses it with derision and contempt. Indeed, it may be said that the average photographer is not much wiser, since he does not concern himself with the laws of photography, the work done by the majority being confined to visible objects, persons or things, and mainly performed in a routine fashion. When men so trained come to say what is and what is not possible in photography, they reveal their want of qualifications and put themselves out of court as experts.

To say that the invisible cannot be photographed, even on the material plane, would be to confess ignorance of facts which are commonplace—as, for instance, to mention the application of X-ray photography to the exploration of the muscles, of fractures of bone, and the internal organs. Astronomical photography affords innumerable illustrations of photographing the invisible. In the foregoing, and analogous cases, the photographing is that of material, though invisible, objects.

Space will not admit of my dealing with the remarkable application of photography to *sound*, by which the latter can be secured on negatives, and reproduced by photo-phonographic records. Surely this is photographing the invisible. Photography, too, reveals the recently discovered " N-rays," which proceed from the human organism, and which fluctuate according to one's state of health and mental activities. These rays are invisible, but can be demonstrated on a phosphorescent screen, be photographed, and a valuable record made of them. However, important as the application is, it does not directly concern us here, except to lead us to surmise that N-rays, *i.e.* human magnetism, may be operative in psychic photography. But, can apparently immaterial (invisible) objects be photographed? Those who have investigated thought and psychic photography say *Yes*; although it is granted that many photographers who have not, say *No*. I give some facts and reasons for the conviction that *Yes* is the correct answer.

So far, reference has been made to the fact that material, but invisible, objects and substances have been photographed. I show that, in addition to invisible objects, persons—some of whom are *departed*, and hence no longer clothed in the vesture of the flesh, or existing on the present plane of sense perception — have been photographed. In *Seeing the Invisible* I dwelt on thought photography, and outlined spirit photography; but in these pages I present a greater variety of cases, supported by remarkable evidence, including the results of my own experiments.

The subject, for clearness, is divided into three natural sections :—

The Historical. Modern spiritualism made its advent in Rochester, New York State, in 1848, and the first spirit photograph was obtained by Mumler, in Boston, U.S.A., in 1861, just thirteen years afterwards. Chronological order is followed as far as convenient.

The Evidence or Statements of Reputable Persons either known to me or known to correspondents of mine.

The Results of Experimentation carried out in our home with Mr Edward Wyllie, Cal., U.S.A., with the Testimony of the Sitters and the Nature of the Tests conducted.

Where possible and permissible, photo half-tones are given in illustration. To simplify matters. I ask and answer three questions :—

(1) What are spirit photographs ?

(2) What are spirit (painted) portraits ?

(3) What are psychographs ?

In answer to the first question, I make the following citations :—

Of what is called spirit photography it is impossible to doubt that such photographs have been honestly produced or obtained by Sir Wm. Crookes, Mr Traill Taylor, Mr Glendinning, Rev. Stainton Moses, Madame d'Esperance, and others. They are of three main classes: (1) Portraits of living discarnate beings or spirits; (2) Pictures of effigies or lay figures, often

very incomplete, and not necessarily human-like;
(3) Reproductions of physical pictures, or other objects.
(D. B. M'Lachlan, in the *Journal of the S.P.R.*, Feb.
1900, p. 185.)

The following may serve as a rough classification
of what are called spirit photographs: (1) Portraits
of psychical entities, not seen by normal vision.
(2) Pictures of objects not seen or thought of by the
sitter or by the medium or operator; such as flowers,
words, crosses, crowns, lights, and various emblematic
objects. (3) Pictures which have the appearance of
being copied from statues, paintings, or drawings;
sometimes the busts or heads only. The flatness in
some photographs of this class is supposed by persons
who have not investigated the subject to be proof
that the photographs are produced in a fraudulent
manner. (4) Pictures of what are called materialised
forms, visible to normal sight. (5) Pictures of the
" wraith " or " double " of persons still in the body.
(Mr Andrew Glendinning, *The Veil Lifted*, pp. vi-
vii.)

To 1, 2, 3, and 5 most attention is given. No. 4,
while adequately testified to by Sir William Crookes
and others, does not fall under any section of Photographing the Invisible.

What are spirit - painted portraits? These are
pictures of departed and living persons, painted in
the dark or in the light by Intelligences in the Invisible, and not by the hand of a medium or other
mortal.

What are psychographs? These are portraits of
departed persons, reproductions, replicas, and writings,
*similar to what are termed spirit photographs, but
which come on the plate without the use of the*

camera and light, necessary in photographic procedure.

Psychic photographs and psychographs do not lend themselves to artistic treatment, retouching being out of the question. They are mostly inartistic, doing poor justice either to sitters or the psychic "extras." Those taken by camera are frequently over-developed to get the "extras" defined, and do not lend themselves to the making of good half-tones. There is no help for it; I can only give them as they are.

In spite of the sweeping statement made in a London paper, that, "where experiments are carried out under scientific conditions, so as to preclude any possibility of deception, spirit photographs cannot be produced," I am convinced to the contrary, and these pages contain the refutation.

I have selected the two reports on which the statement is based, issued by a "Spirit Photography Commission," for comment. A careful reading of these reports furnishes the astounding fact that *no experiments of any kind—scientific or otherwise—were carried out by this commission.* There was plenty of theorising, various meetings, much letter-writing, and quite a number of psychic photographs exhibited. The latter were extolled, defended on the one side, and condemned and refuted on the other. But there was no experimental procedure. Could there be greater folly? Yet this is loudly proclaimed as research, and on this wise basis spirit photography was condemned.

A Mr Marriott wrote a series of articles during 1910, in *Pearson's Magazine.* They were neither complimentary to spiritualists nor to the intelligence of the readers. In them we have a good deal about Mr Marriott, with many photographs of himself, and the clever things he could do and did. In delightful, egotistical fashion he dealt with spirit photography. He "assumes" and "suggests," but in no instance does he indicate a practical acquaintance with his subject. I hardly find it necessary to deal with the futility of a person dominated by "fixed ideas" of fraud and stupidity in his fellow - men approaching the study of any subject in a calm, clear-headed, and scientific spirit. I have, however, treated him tenderly and fairly. Suppose I admit that medium-photographers may be guilty of methods that are reprehensible, such procedure will not, and cannot, account for the facts. No undertaking, much less photography, could exist for months, much less years, conducted on the methods suggested. Yet, Mr Frank Forster has been taking psychic photographs for forty years; Mr Edward Wyllie for twenty years; and the late Mr Boursnell was located in one centre in London and gave his "shadow pictures" or spirit photographs for about eighteen years. The Bangs Sisters produced spirit portraits for over twenty years. The explanation of the facts is not to be found in fraud.

There is, to my mind, the possibility of self-deception being a factor in the recognition of the "extras" as portraits of departed persons. But even this will not account for the facts. It should not be more difficult to discount than those cases of mistaken identity which occur in ordinary life. Faulty memories, perversion of the judgment from some cause, may account for the recognition of some of these photographs,—not all. That's all.

Whether the psychic pictures, symbols, etc., come on the plates on, before, or without exposure, there are two constant factors present:—

(1) For every figure, image, portrait, etc., revealed by the process of development, some *unknown cause* has produced a material, chemical change in the substance of the film; and (2) through the process of developing, a further chemical change is brought about which is necessary in order to reveal the image or portrait produced by the *unknown factor or factors.*

Those who possess knowledge based on actual experiment can vouch for the genuineness of these "extras" — whether symbols or portraits — as they have carefully scrutinised all operations, from the opening of a virgin package to the finishing processes of developing and printing. I give several instances.

Sitters have chosen their own time, position, or place for operations, and yet extraneous heads, faces, and forms have appeared. At times, a clearly identifiable portrait of a departed person is obtained, of whom no similar likeness had ever been taken in life. Clairvoyants, too, have sometimes seen the spirit form in the room before it has been photographed.

By what kind of actinic rays, whether those contained in ordinary light or not, the plates have been chemically affected cannot be definitely known, but it can be stated that something has been photographed which was invisible to normal vision.

Both from personal knowledge and a calm review of the testimony of reputable persons, I respectfully aver: (1) That genuine photographs of departed persons have been taken. (2) That in a great number of instances these have been of men, women, and children unknown to the sitters. (3) That in a lesser degree many portraits have been obtained—recognisable, but unrelated to the sitter and the operator. (4) That identified portraits are obtained of departed ones related to either sitter or operator. (5) That portraits of persons unrelated and unknown to the sitter have subsequently been recognised by relatives as those of persons who had never been known to the medium, and whose spirit photograph differed from any taken in life. (6) That in many cases portraits have been immediately identified as those of departed friends – and of living persons—the double. (7) That many of the so-called unrecognised spirit photographs have been identified subsequently by persons related to *the departed*, but who neither knew the operator-medium, the sitter, nor the occasion when the same was taken; showing in many cases, at least, that the psychic "extra" was not that of a thought-form within the sub-consciousness of the medium, or the picture of a departed produced by the desire of the sitter, but rather a portrait produced—by Invisible operators—as best they could, either hoping for, or actually anticipating, recognition ultimately. This is a reasonable deduction made from several cases reported. (8) That persons thought of have been photographed, in accordance with promises made through a psychic. Some forms have come on the plate in absence of the embodied relative—as subject —and when the promise to come had been forgotten.

The term " spirit photographs " is used as being convenient, and not as either being accurate or the best term. As to the character of these " extras," especially where they are pictures of departed persons, it is difficult in our present limited knowledge to say. To assume that they are portraits of spirits in discarnate states is as absurd as the vacuous conclusion that they are fraudulently produced. Psychical research in its plodding inquiries has established, as the result of nearly a quarter of a century's labours, that which has been known all along—the possession of psychic faculty in man. These faculties have been variously labelled—clairvoyance, second sight, crystal vision, clairaudience, telepathy, and other modes of *awareness* or cognising that which exists in the Invisible, whether the same be a reflection of impressions on the super-sensitive backgrounds of sub-consciousness, or an *actual knowing* through psychic processes that the reality has been demonstrated by substantially convincing cases and by photography, etc.

The play of the psychic faculty appears to be fugitive in most cases. Some persons can recall one or two instances of psychic appearance of the dead (?) and the *double* in their lives, while others, called *psychics*, mediums, or sensitives, have had many such experiences; yet in none, as far as my studies and personal knowledge have gone, do I find the exercise of psychic faculty a continuous feature.

Not only are the psychic faculties established by scientific inquiry, but the fact of apparitions of the dead and phantasms of the living has also been. While they have occasionally and apparently been detected by ordinary vision in the experience of the persons affected, I am forced to the conclusion that all these extraordinary super-mundane appearances of the living and the dead have been observed only through the sudden functioning of psychic faculty, vision especially.

It is also clear that, while all that which is seen by psychic vision—clairvoyance and telepathic *awareness* —cannot be and is not confined to seeing apparitions of the dead, or doubles of the living, yet these have been most truly seen. These have not been hazy and illusive, but are veridical hallucinations. In other words, that which was seen had a veritable existence in the invisible.

While careful study of crystal vision reveals that there is nothing in the crystal at periods but what the mind of the scryer, or *seer*, puts into it, it must not, however, be forgotten that mind has a deeper significance than is usually attached to it.   What the seer observes is not only what is projected from self, but that which has been conveyed there by other minds—telepathy. This is not all.   Often that which is visualised is presented in the crystal by discarnate minds.   The crystal is merely the focussing centre *where the thoughts of the discarnate and the vision of the psychic meet.*

I now make a further inference from the study of psychic faculty, and that is, many of these apparitions —in or out of the crystal—are real.   They are often most correct in every detail of feature, pose, dress, and adornment, of what the originals *were once in life.* I take it to be a fact that the photographs and paintings obtained are correct, or as correct as the memory—consciously or otherwise in operation—of the departed can produce.   But they are neither photographs nor paintings of spirits in discarnate states, although it must be convincingly clear, from the evidence produced, that the departed are intelligently interested in the production of these photographs and paintings.

The fact that many, if not the most, of these photographs, portraits, and psychographs are obtained when neither the medium, sitter, nor those most interested are aware of what is being produced, points unerringly to the conclusion that, whatever part the mediums and the sitters play on the material plane, they are not the primary factors in their production.   Intelligent discarnate spirits in the

Invisible are the controlling, directing, and primary factors.

There are many puzzles and difficulties to be considered. These are not to be met by claiming too much, as, regrettably, is done by those who insist, for instance, that all these photographs of departed persons are those of spirits. There is no evidence for that; but for the production of pictures of the departed, *as they were on earth*, there is abundant valuable evidence.

Take two common cases which occur in this investigation, that of persons who have died in childhood, whose photos are those of adults—"what they would have been had they lived"—and the truly identified portraits of children who died, say, many years ago. It must be clear that the first are only imaginary portraits. Admitting their remarkable resemblance to existing members of the family, it cannot be clearly maintained—in the absence of proof—that the same are correct likenesses of the departed. As to children who passed away years ago, and whose psychic photographs or paintings correctly represent them *as they were on earth*, it is more than certain that these *cannot be likenesses of them as they are now in spirit*. But the fact remains that genuine psychic portraits of both these classes are obtained.

From the universal experience of mankind in all ages, and from the investigations of modern spiritualists and the work of psychical research, we learn—

(1) That both persons and things exist in the Invisible — outwith the range of ordinary sense-faculty.

(2) That man possesses psychic vision, and other faculties, by which the realities in the Invisible can be perceived.

(3) That some of the objects and persons perceived *are not all* hazy illusions, old memories, and mere thought-projections, but veritable things and beings existing in the Invisible.

(4) That from the number of cases given it will be seen that not a few of those invisible have been photographed or painted. Although the existence and the perception of ghosts, apparitions, doubles is not new, the idea of their objectivity in the Invisible and that they can be photographed is.

(5) That these persons, or other Intelligences, knowing what they were like during earth-life, take a lively interest in giving their photographs, psychographs, and paintings, is shown by the fact that many of these have been pre-arranged and given in accordance with promise.

(6) That in no case can these photographs and paintings be obtained except through suitable mediums—few in number.

I am compelled—slightly varying the emphatic statement of the world's greatest living scientist, Dr Alfred Russel Wallace, F.R.S., O.M.—to say: "I see no escape from the conclusion that some spiritual beings acquainted with our departed friends (during life) have produced their recognisable impressions on plates and canvas."

The foregoing constitutes my claim, which, if any weight is to be placed on human testimony, is fully substantiated in the pages of *Photographing the Invisible*.

CHAPTER I

THE FIRST MEDIUM PHOTOGRAPHER

MR MUMLER, of Boston, was an engraver by profession, who, through the discovery of spirit photography, and the subsequent inroads on his time, was compelled to become a professional medium, and he was the first—since the inception of modern spiritualism—to obtain what are called " spirit photographs."   In the following I give briefly an outline of his mediumship and the trial which specially brought his name into prominence. Owing to the extreme faintness of some of the Mumler photographs now available, I have not been able to reproduce them.   I give three.   The first is a reproduction of an old photograph of Mrs Lincoln and her husband, the late President of the U.S.A.; the second, of Mr Moses A. Dow and Mabel Warren; the third, that of Mrs Britten—then Emma Hardinge—with psychic extra, Beethoven.

When Mr Mumler, whose reputation in the early sixties for obtaining spirit photographs had created some stir among the better class of investigators, Dr (then Mr) Andrew Jackson Davies, editor of the *Herald of Progress*, engaged Mr Guay, a practical photographer, to investigate Mr Mumler's procedure. Mr Guay, in his report, says : —

16

Having been permitted by Mr Mumler every facility, I went through the whole process of selecting, cleaning, preparing, coating and silvering, and putting into the shield the glass upon which Mr M. proposed that a spirit form should be imparted, never taking off my eyes, and not allowing Mr M. to touch the glass until it had gone through the whole of the operation. The result was that there came upon the glass a picture of myself, and, to my utter astonishment—having previously examined and scrutinised every crack and corner, plate-holder, camera, box, tube, the inside of the bath, etc.—*another portrait*. Having since continued, on several occasions, my investigations, as described above, and received even more perfect results than on first trial, I have been obliged to endorse its legitimacy.

Other reputable photographers were either called in, or went into this matter on their own account, to see what they could discover about this spirit photography, and expose, if possible, the "gross fraud and deception." They obtained every facility from Mr Mumler to make their investigations, with the usual result, that there was no detectable fraud. Nay, more, if fraud there were, the investigators must have been the culprits, for in all their investigations "spirit portraits" were obtained, some of these being identified ; and this occurred when these practical photographic experts had everything their own way, and indeed were (on the visible plane) the sole and only operators, Mr Mumler taking no part, save giving the use of his studio and the fact of his presence.

The one striking circumstance which brought Mr Mumler and his mediumship into special prominence was his trial before Justice Dowling, in the Tombs Police Court, New York, on the charge of having " by means of what he termed spiritual photographs swindled many credulous persons." It would be impossible to give more than the gist of this remarkable trial. The procedure at the Tombs in those days—and I suspect even now—did not suggest that a fair trial was possible. Anyone having a " political pull "—unless, indeed, the crime was of such a character as to make hushing up impossible, and squaring and " straw bail " of no avail—could get off. In this case Mumler had no political friends, and the charge was one which, if proved, would get the defendant severely punished.

The trial lasted several days. Mr Mumler was prosecuted by Marshall J. H. Tooker, on the information supplied by Mr P. V. Hickey, of the *World*, who—by the suggestion of the Mayor—acted as the getter-up of the case. Mr Hickey, acting in the interests of truth (!), and in order to defend the credulous, assuming a *false* name, went to Mr Mumler to get a " spirit photograph," and, while he was at it, to get some copy for the *World*. He swore in court that after Mumler had taken him he showed him the negative, on which was " a dim, indistinct outline of a ghostly face staring out of one corner." Mumler told him that it represented the spirit of his father-in-law. He avowed that it was neither like the old gentleman, his relatives, nor anyone else he knew. Marshall Tooker, on these and other grounds, instructed the prosecution. The *Tribune* and other leading papers were full of the alleged swindle. The reading public was treated to striking headlines, and the veracious writers—drawing on their imaginations for their facts—were pretty certain that this latest impostor and wonder-worker would be sent to " The Island." But, so far from this being the outcome of the trial, so strong was the independent evidence of practical photographers who had tested Mr Mumler, and of leading citizens who had been photographed, many of whom had received identifiable portraits of departed friends and relatives, that Judge Dowling, having heard counsel, decided that the prosecution had not made out a case to go before a jury, and discharged the defendant.

The evidence in favour of spirit photography which was produced at this trial was overwhelming. Judge Edmonds (late Justice N.Y. Supreme Court, 1847–51, and the U.S. Court of Appeals, also a Senator for N.Y. State for many years: the learned Judge was the author of a remarkable work on *Spiritualism*, in two volumes, 741 pages, published in New York about forty years ago), who had sat to Mr Mumler before this trial, had had two photographs taken on which there were " psychic extras," or portraits of invisible persons, one of which was recognised. These were produced at the trial, and in his evidence Judge Edmonds said :—

I know a great many persons who have visited Mumler, some of whom have met with astonishing success in procuring spirit pictures of departed friends. Mr Livermore, of Wall Street, has been particularly successful. [Another photograph was shown, that of a young man sitting in a chair in pensive attitude, with his eyes cast down, and behind him was the spectral, white-clad form of a lady, with her hands resting on the sitter's shoulders. The photographers in the court declared that by no means known to them, other than the bodily presence of the lady behind the chair, could the lady's hands be produced.] Spiritualists reason that these photographs are actual pictures of disembodied spirits, but they do not know. I am not prepared myself to express a definite opinion. I believe, however, that in time the truth or falsity of spiritual photography will be demonstrated, and I therefore say it would be best to wait and see. The art is yet in its infancy.

Judge Edmonds was one of the foremost jurists in the State, and possessed an unspotted reputation both as a man and as a lawyer. It was no easy matter in those days, however convinced one might be, to risk one's good name, reputation, and position by the announcement that he believed in spirits—" for I have seen them," as his letters testify.

Among other important witnesses cited and examined was Mr C. F. Livermore, to whom Judge Edmonds referred in his testimony.

Mr Livermore, of the firm of Livermore, Clews & Co., whose evidence I condense, said :—

I went there with my eyes open, but as a sceptic. I went into the dark-room with him, and I saw him put the collodion on the plate ; and then sat down and saw him subsequently develop the plate. I looked at the glass first and saw it was clean. When he developed the picture he held it up to the light, dripping with the water. There were two pictures upon the plate, one of which I recognised thoroughly at the time. Then I had a little quarrel with Mumler. I refused to pay him, as they were so entirely unsatisfactory to me. He then said he would give me an opportunity at another time. I left the place. But, to provide against the case of substitution, I had pictures taken off the negative. I showed them to a friend of mine, Dr John F. Gray, a physician, who immediately recognised one of the pictures as a relative of his; then I recognised it myself. I then went again to Mumler's, and made arrangements to go again the following Tuesday, but went on the Monday morning following, early, so as to take him by surprise. When I went there he said that I had expressed so much dissatisfaction on the previous occasion that I might sit till I was satisfied; consequently I sat five times in succession. I think that the first two sittings amounted to nothing but a shadowy background. I made the same examination that I had previously. I accompanied him before the operation into the dark-room, and saw him pour the collodion upon the plate. *I changed my position each sitting.* This one—it showed the picture of a lady standing behind him, bearing a bunch of flowers in her right hand, which rested upon his right breast— being in the same attitude as the woman occupied upon the picture of Judge Edmonds, mentioned in last Thursday's report. He then showed another which, in answer to counsel, he said he recognised.

Continuing — I examined the camera after this, but saw nothing out of the way. I made a study of electricity and magnetism. I also made a study of the spectroscope; in these instances I did not discover any fraud or deception, or anything that looked like it.

A severe and prolonged cross-examination elicited, in addition to the amount paid to Mumler for services,

interesting facts relating to identified extras. The
witness's testimony was unshaken.

It would serve no specially useful purpose to
recall and reprint the evidence given by various
persons at this trial, all of which not only went to
prove the *bona-fides* of Mr Mumler's procedure, his
exceeding fairness, but demonstrated that there were
men of standing and ability ready and willing to
stand all the obloquy which would surely be theirs by
declaring that they sat for these photographs and had
really obtained portraits of the departed. Witness
after witness gave evidence, and all of them spoke
of pictures received of those who had passed
away, whose features were recalled by these spirit
photographs.

As to Mr Mumler, we learn from the trial three
facts—

1st. That he was not a photographer.

2nd. That he was not a spiritualist, although not
ignorant of the subject; and

3rd. That the first spirit photograph was obtained
in 1861; and that prior to this discovery he
was not aware that he possessed mediumistic
powers of any kind.

The photographs given are chosen simply because
of their interest, rather than for the evidence which
they present. Yet that evidence must be seriously
considered. Owing to the fact that the pictures are
copies of the original, but now very faint, photographs,
they do not reproduce very clearly.

MRS LINCOLN AND THE PRESIDENT

The form of the President is seen standing behind Mrs Lincoln, with his hands affectionately laid upon her shoulders. That attitude alone tells its own tale.

FIG. 1.—The remarkable photograph of Mrs Abraham Lincoln ; on which appears the portrait of her late husband, the late President of the United States, and of his son—both almost too faint for reproduction.

No similar photograph of this group was ever taken in life. This photograph was among some of the earlier pictures taken by Mumler. Mrs Lincoln, when in Boston, visited Mr Mumler, and gave the name of

Mrs Tyndall.   She was in mourning and veiled prior to being taken.   Mr Mumler did not know who she was, and had no means of knowing; but this was a frequent occurrence, and called for no special comment.   When a print was taken, Mr Mumler recognised the spirit as that of the late President.   Mr Mumler showed it to his visitor and asked her if she recognised it.   She replied that she did.   Another lady present, on seeing it, exclaimed, " Why, this looks like President Lincoln." Mrs Lincoln then said, " Yes, it does.   I am his widow."

Mr Moses A. Dow and Mabel Warren

Writing to " M.A. Oxon.," Mr Dow, whose letter I condense, says :—

Dear Sir,—Your note of the 17th inst. reached me this morning, and I will try to give you an outline of my experience in spirit photography.   There is no more important subject before the public than that of spiritualism.   I employ in my publishing office of the *Waverley Magazine* some fifteen young ladies, some setting types, some laying paper on the presses, some laying paper on the folding machines, and some are employed in mailing papers, and others in reading and preparing MSS. for the compositors.   Among the latter class was a girl who came to my office in 1861, and remained with me till 1870, when she was suddenly taken sick and died, aged about twenty-seven years.   The latter years of her stay in my office developed her into a very intellectual, amiable, and beautiful lady.   Her long continuance with me, and her unselfish interest in my welfare, created in my mind a deep interest in her, and that interest was reciprocated and several times expressed by her.

In just seven days after she died, I happened to be

in the presence of a medium, and the controlling spirit (an Indian girl) says, " You have got a beautiful lady to see you, and she has roses in her hand and they are for you, as she loved you the best of anyone, because you was so good to her." I was surprised, for I did not suppose that an earthly affection could

Fig. 2.—The photograph of Mr Moses A. Dow (who was the editor and proprietor of the *Waverley Magazine*), and psychic extra, of Mabel Warren. Done by Mumler.

ever be expressed by our friends after they had left the body. I went to Saratoga, about 150 miles from Boston, and while there met Dr Heale, the renowned medium. I had a séance with him (a perfect stranger), and he placed a common school slate under the table, which he held with his right hand, while the left one rested on the table, in contact with my own. Immediately the pencil was heard to write, and on taking it out, the words, "*I am always with you,*" and signed with her true name, were written on it.

I had sittings with Mrs Harley, in Saratoga, every week for three months, saying nothing about the picture; at the end of that time I asked her (Mabel Warren) if she was going to give me her spirit picture, when she replied that she was ready to do so. I asked her how it would be taken. "By photography," said she. "Will the same artist take it who took your earth-picture?" "No; it must be done by a medium artist." "When will you have it taken?" "I will tell you when you call next week." At the end of another week I was at Mrs Harley's.

Mr Dow had several sittings with Mrs Harley, and under directions received he went to Mumler, with whom he had several sittings, and failed to get what had been previously arranged, dress and other things which were to be given for identification. I now give in Mr Dow's own words the obtaining of this special spirit picture :—

I told him (Mumler) I had the promise of a picture, and he said he must keep trying, and sometimes he tried five or six times before he got a picture. He placed a third plate in, and I sat just five minutes by his watch, which he held in his hand, and his back towards me, and his hand resting on the camera. He took it out and went out of the room. After he had gone, Mrs M., a medium, came into the room, and seemed to be under some influence. I asked her if she saw any spirit, and she said she saw a beautiful young lady standing near me, and instantly was in a trance; and my first spirit friend said to me, "Now, I shall give you my picture; the dress will not be positively striped, but the lights and shades will imitate stripes; I shall stand by your side, with my head resting on your shoulder, and shall have a wreath of flowers on my head. I put in all the magnetism I possessed." Then Mr M. came in with the plate and said he had got a picture. I looked at the negative, and saw evidence of there being my picture, and a lady's face by the side of mine. Mr M. said he would send me a proof of it the next day. I told him to send it to my box in the P.O., directed to Mr Johnson. I did not get it till the third day.

I was on my way home at night, and called at the P.O., and found an envelope for Mr Johnson; and on opening it I found the proof. I took it home; and having a good microscope, I used it, which made it look as large as life, and I saw the correct picture of my lost friend. The thought was very exciting to my feelings. I wrote a note to Mr M., and told him who I was and that I considered him as commissioned by the angels to do this work, and that I was perfectly satisfied with the picture. My friend asked me to have it taken large, while she was in a condition to influence the medium. I urged Mr M. to throw it up, and I have it in a frame, $2\frac{1}{2}$ feet square, in a cabinet in my office. I consider it an honest and true picture; and she has often assured me that it was a truthful picture. The pictures enclosed will enable you to see if there is a likeness.—Yours for the truth,

MOSES A. DOW.

In the foregoing condensed narrative there is abundant material for thought. The departed one manifests through several mediums, giving directions, and finally appears to give her late employer and friend an identifiable portrait.

Among the many advocates of spiritualism with whom I came in contact in the early seventies was the late Mrs Emma Hardinge Britten. This lady testified to the genuineness of Mumler's gifts and sterling honesty.

I give her own statement, slightly condensed, which

FIG. 3.—Photograph of the late Mrs Emma Hardinge Britten, and the psychic portrait thereon of Beethoven. This is a rough reproduction from the original (but faint) photograph, done by Mumler.

she contributed to the *Medium* of 17th December 1871 :—

About a fortnight ago I called on Mr Mumler for a sitting. The result of my first sitting was the production of a female form, bending over me in the attitude of affection; but although the spirit bears some resemblance to a dear departed friend, it is not sufficiently obvious to constitute a likeness. At my next sitting, a large and remarkable-looking head appeared on the negative, but ere the prints were taken I could not trace clearly any well-defined likeness. I remarked to Mr Mumler that the negative appeared to present the appearance of some musical character, as there were indications of a lyre shadowed forth in the negative. Upon this, Mr Mumler immediately wrote on a slip of paper, backwards, the name of " Beethoven." When the prints were at length produced they clearly showed the portrait of Beethoven hovering over me, and holding a faintly defined musical instrument in his hands, so placed as to present the shadow *between my dress and the watch-chain which falls across it.* Now, the circumstances which render the appearance of the great musician upon my photograph singularly significant are these :— My principal occupation during my late residence in England was to write certain musical criticisms, in which the life and works of Beethoven formed the chief theme of my analysis. The very last piece of · musical writing which I executed was an essay on the Beethoven Centenary at Bonn, celebrated just as I was about to return to America. Whilst engaged in these writings, I have the best of reasons for believing that the spirit of the noble German was frequently with me, and by a variety of test-facts convinced me and others that he was interested in what I wrote, and not unfrequently suggested ideas, or dictated corrections upon points of his life and musical intentions. These circumstances considered, I think the remarkable resemblance of the spirit portrait to the well-known head of Beethoven may be taken as a striking and conclusive test of the spirit presence. A vast number of persons with whom I am well acquainted have received admirable portraitures of their spirit friends from Mr Mumler, and that they themselves were strangers to him, and that no possibility could exist of his procuring any likeness or knowledge of the spirit friends represented, is certain.

Nearly every medium photographer whose photographs I have seen appears to have some influence on the characteristics of the work turned out. It is interesting to note what were some of the special features of Mr Mumler's spirit photographs.

We learn from comments in *The British Journal of Photography*, on the evidence of Dr Child, of Philadelphia, in 1863, that he

applied to various practical operators here and elsewhere for information; and he had had prepared ghost pictures by all the well-known processes. Armed with these, and the information received with them from their makers, he wended his way to Boston. He found this medium (Mr Mumler) very willing to give him every opportunity of investigating the matter, and, as he said, earnest himself to find a rational solution of the mystery. He permitted him to watch all his operations in the dark-room and out of it; and allowed him to examine all his apparatus. Dr Child showed the pictures made at that time, while he and several friends were watching the whole process, from the plate cleaning to the fixing. He took the precaution to mark each plate with a diamond before it was used. Yet on each was a spirit image, and he failed *in toto* to discover any human agency concerned in the formation of the spirit picture. As to these, they differ very considerably from any that he had ever seen, and he knew of no way of imitating them. *The spirit is never a full-length figure, always a bust or three-quarter length ; and yet it is impossible to tell where the figure disappears.* An examination of the prints showed that some of the spirit portraits by their whiteness (high lights) were the first to be seen in developing the plates. There were general features pretty well marked, but except the very intense part of the face, the surrounding objects are distinctly seen through the image, and yet there was *none of that clearness of definition usual in under-exposed figures in* (made or simulated) *ghost pictures.*

From the foregoing, which I have curtailed, we learn :—

1st. That while every precaution was taken these " psychic extras " appeared on marked plates.

2nd. That in every case they differed materially from any " made " photograph which the well-equipped practical photographers could supply.

3rd. That the spirit picture frequently had the appearance of not being synchronously taken with that of the subject or sitter, and often not in focal relationship.

4th. All the evidence points to the genuineness of their character.

5th. Neither will - power nor any other human agency—as far as could be detected from an expert photographic standpoint—was concerned in their production.

It is reasonable to conclude or assume at this stage two things :—That these " extras " came ; and that, as no human agency was the means of their production,

*there was some other agency at work of an unseen,
unknown character,* and yet of an intelligent and
human-like nature.   In some instances, as in the
remarkable evidence of Mr Moses A. Dow, the
spirit picture came on the plate as the result of
previous declaration and appointment with one
" departed."

Of the many spirit photographs received by " M.A.
Oxon.," of which particulars were given by him in
Human Nature, I will refer only to one, and that
merely to illustrate the character of some photographs
taken at this period :—

This is a picture of Master Harrod of N. Bridge-
water, Massachusetts, and shows three spirits standing
behind him—a European, an Indian, and a Negro.
Respecting this remarkable picture, Mr Mumler
testifies :—
When the above picture was taken, the young man
and his father called and desired a sitting—not stating
who or what he desired or expected to come on the
plate.   After developing the negative I brought it
into the room.   On looking at it, Mr Harrod exclaimed,
" Mr Mumler, that is the most wonderful picture that
you have ever taken."   I asked him to explain.
" Well," he continued, " my son has been controlled a
few months, and before coming here a spirit took
possession of him, and said if he would come to your
studio three spirits would show themselves, representing Europe, Africa, and America ; and there they are,"
he said excitedly, " a European, a Negro, and an
Indian."   Subsequently the young man called upon
me for another sitting, and received on the negative
an elderly lady and gentleman, who, he declared, were
his grandfather and mother, as had been promised.

It then occurred to me to take his picture while entranced, to see if I could get the controlling power; and to that end I asked if there was any spirit present to please entrance the medium. In a few moments he threw his head back, apparently in a deep trance. I then adjusted the focus and exposed the plate, and took the picture as represented. The spirit seen here is undoubtedly "*his double*," as it is unmistakably a true likeness of himself.

The above case—if the evidence is to be relied on—throws an interesting sidelight on the phenomenon of the double. The S.P.R. of later days has established the double in its *Proceedings*, but I think that this is the first time in the history of spirit photography that the double has been photographed. The second occasion which I can recall was that of the double of Herne, a physical medium in London, ten years later. Whether the double is a factor in trance and in spiritistic phenomena—such as in the production of trance and of that which takes place subsequently to the trance—is a matter which, although suggested here, must be dealt with elsewhere. It is, however, both an interesting and legitimate subject for inquiry. We learn from these instances of spirit photography that while they are not and could not be produced by will-power, as far as those, at any rate, on this plane are concerned, it is a notable feature that some of these identifiable portraits came in response to *exchange of thought as between the incarnate and discarnate.*

I am compelled by want of space to refrain from

giving other particulars in favour of this remarkable medium, and not from want of material. All those who have testified in his favour were not spiritualists. The intelligence and position of those whom I have selected lend great weight to their evidence.

CHAPTER II

THE success of Mr Mumler's mediumship in the
United States, and the discussion of the subject
through the Press in London, led many there to have
a keen interest in the matter. I deal with some of
these early experiences in this chapter.

Mr Hudson was the first professional medium in
Great Britain to obtain spirit photographs. When
he commenced, he had a small studio in the Holloway
district of London. He subsequently moved from
there when his mediumship came into note. The
first spirit photograph taken by Hudson was on
4th March 1872. At that time, Mr Hudson—although not a spiritualist—was interested in spiritualism, and was more or less in touch with spiritualists.
Mr and Mrs Guppy were friends. He knew Herne
and Williams, who were well-known physical
mediums, but was not certain, or probably not aware,
that he had any mediumship in this direction.

In response to directions received from spirits
through table-tipping—at the home of the Guppys—
it was arranged that a sitting should take place at
Hudson's studio. Mr Guppy was the sitter in front

of the screen, and Mrs Guppy sat in an extemporised dark cabinet behind. Mr Guppy, sitting in daylight, felt a wreath of flowers placed gently on his head, and so appeared when the photograph was developed, and there was a large veiled figure standing beside him. This was the first sign of spirit photography received in this country. On the same day, and only a quarter of an hour afterwards, with the same sitter, another white figure came, but as yet no defined portraits. A third sitting gave a similar result. That was the beginning. On 7th March 1872 there were other sittings, with certain precautions taken.

Miss Houghton, the author of *The Chronicles of Spirit Photography* (to which I am indebted), was the sitter. On the first plate there was beside herself a veiled spirit form, or white-clad figure, with a hand resting on her (Miss Houghton's) shoulder. The hand was clearly defined and human to all appearance. On the second plate taken there was a spirit figure and traces of a face, and on the third and last attempt that day with Miss Houghton, there appeared a symbol of a dagger pointing towards her head.

So much for the beginning of this phase of physical phenomena in Great Britain, on which I will make three comments.

1st. The wreath which was placed on Mr Guppy's head was one of artificial flowers, which belonged to the requisites of Mr Hudson's studio. This article was lifted by invisible means and placed on his head. This indicated that either through Mrs Guppy's mediumship, or that of Hudson, there was what Sir William Crookes called "psychic force" present, or, in other words, there were intelligent spirits present, who were able to act on material things.

2nd. That before that particular sitting in which the white figure came and placed its hand on Miss Houghton's shoulder, Miss Houghton's deceased mother promised to come and be photographed. Miss Houghton says:—

While Mr Hudson was in his dark-room preparing the plate, Mrs Guppy told me that she had a message from the spirit to the effect that mamma would try and manifest herself and place her hand on my shoulder. Of course, as soon as Mr Hudson began to develop his negative, we questioned eagerly as to whether there was anything to be seen, and hearing there was, went in to feast our own eyes as soon as we could be admitted, and behind me there is a veiled figure, with a hand advanced almost to my shoulder.

In this case we have evidence of an Intelligence in the Invisible being at work, and the promise made through the lips, or from impressions made on Mrs Guppy's mind (she was a remarkable medium in private life in her day), was fulfilled.

3rd. The symbol of the dagger, when examined, was produced by a further display of unseen physical force, being nothing more or less than a dagger which Miss Houghton had in her hair being withdrawn and suspended in the air long enough to be photographed.

On another plate taken there was a brilliant light, in which there appeared two figures to the bust.

From the faintness of the figures and the brightness
of the light, they were not very well defined. On
careful examination with a powerful glass, Miss
Houghton was able to distinguish and identify them
as her father and mother.

I summarise from Miss Houghton's letter, 14th
March 1872, to the *Christian Spiritualist* the
following :—

I have just returned from Holloway, after another
attempt. While Mr Hudson was taking the first
negative, I felt the signal by which my dear nephew
Charlie Warren (who was lost in the " Carnatic "),
makes his presence known, and some little distance
above my head appears his hand, quite perfect, with
a glimpse of the wristband ; the thumb is bent across
the palm, as if pointing to the ring on his little finger,
which had been papa's diamond ring, that we had
reset for Charlie, after papa's death.   On the second
plate, just above my head, is a small hand holding a
leaf ; it is the same little hand that withdrew the
dagger from my hair on a previous occasion.   While
the third negative was in progress, I felt something
on my head for a moment, and then a young rabbit
(from Mr Hudson's rabbit-hutch in the garden wherein the studio is built) was placed in my lap, where it
did not remain very still, so that it is not very clear,
but sufficiently to show what it is.   There is a male
figure behind, stooping slightly forward ; but having
had to move in consequence of the vagaries of the
rabbit, it is of course hazy.

The editor of the *Christian Spiritualist*, commenting, adds :—

Copies of the photographs to which the letter
refers have been received by us. They certainly do

illustrate, in a striking manner, Miss Houghton's narrative, and we should strongly advise persons interested in the subject to put themselves into communication with Mr Hudson, the photographer, or with Miss Houghton, or better still, with both.

From this time onward there were greater successes. The veils which obscured the faces of the figures became thinner, so that the features could be discerned, and latterly the veils were dispensed with altogether. There was naturally great excitement. It soon became evident that the claims made for photographing invisible persons — especially those who had departed this life—must be thoroughly investigated. The first competent expert to do so was Mr Thomas Slater, optical and philosophical instrument maker. His letter (owing to its importance, the ability of Mr Slater, and the early day of his inquiry) I give in full. It will be remembered that the first spirit photographs were obtained in March, and as Mr Slater's investigations were in the early days of May, not much time was lost in putting the matter to test. Mr Slater's letter, which appeared in the *Spiritualist*, 15th May 1872, says :—

I visited this artist (Mr Hudson) and told him my object in calling. He took a negative of me, and it turned out to be a very good one, viz. a clear, sharp negative—nothing more. I requested him to try another, which he did, taking one indiscriminately from some *previously used* and dirty plates. After cleaning it in my presence, he poured on the collodion and placed it in the bath. I remained in the dark-room all the time the plate was in the bath. I saw it put into the camera frame and then into the camera, which had been previously focussed to me, and all that Mr Hudson did was to draw up the slide and uncover the lens. I saw the slide drawn up, and, when sitting, saw the cap or cover of the camera removed, and, after the usual exposure, replaced on the lens. I then accompanied him into the dark-room, and saw the developing solution poured on the plate, but not a vestige of anything appeared, neither myself nor background, but a semi-opaque film all over the plate, as if it had been somewhat over-exposed. I then asked for another attempt, which was carried out under precisely the same circumstances, viz. that I witnessed the whole process from beginning to end. I asked, mentally, that if it were possible the spirit of my mother would come and stand by my side, and portray her presence, to do so. On the plate is a fine female figure, draped in white, standing before me, with her hand resting on my head. The drapery nearly covers the whole of my body, leaving only the side of the head and one hand visible. I am certain Mr Hudson played no tricks on this occasion.

Having read in the *Journal of Photography* that the editor thought it very unlikely that he would get any spirit picture if he took his own instrument and plate, I took the hint and did as he suggested. I made a new combination of lenses, and took a new camera and several glass plates; and I did, in Mr Hudson's room, all the looking on, focussing the instrument to the sitter, and obtained, in the same manner as before, a fine spirit-picture.

This was repeated with another sitter, and with like success. Collusion or trickery was altogether out of the question. After the last attempt I felt further induced to carry out the optical arrangement for the spiritual photography; and, knowing, as most scientists do, that the visible end of the spectrum is the actinic, I resolved to exemplify to sceptics that, with such an instrument as I now had made and would use, we could take portraits of sitters, although the colour of the glass was such as only in the strongest light you can see the sitter at all. And no one was more astonished than Mr Hudson, after seeing me focus the instrument to a lady sitting in the chair, to find not only a sharp, well-defined negative, with good half-tone, but also that standing by the lady was a fine spirit-figure draped in black and white. Nor was the exposure any longer than with the usual lenses of same aperture and focal length, namely 2½-in. lenses with 2-in. stops, the focus from the back lens 5 in.

We tried another with, if possible, better success. The sitter was a little child belonging to the lady just alluded to, and the result was a female figure standing by the child.

I think Mr Hudson was quite satisfied that other persons' instruments and plates answer the purpose just as well as his own; and if he is not satisfied on that score, I am; for not a move did he make, nor a thing did he do to these, *my own plates*, unobserved by me, and there is no room for any transparency to be placed in the frame of the camera; nor was there any other device used on these occasions.

I may now ask the sceptical if they can explain why we are able to take portraits of persons through instruments that exclude so much light that the sitter is scarcely visible; so that, in fact, you can no more discern with human eyes the details of the features or the dress of the sitters than you can discern the disembodied spirit. When the scientists explain this they perhaps may also explain why and how it is the spirit-dress—which is also material yet intangible—impresses itself so vividly upon the photographic plate.

I am now carrying on experiments on this part of

the spectrum, and am convinced that much may and will be discovered that is useful in photography by making use of invisible light.   THOMAS SLATER.

19 LEAMINGTON-ROAD VILLAS,
  WESTBOURNE PARK, W.,
    May 7, 1872.

It will be noted also that two or three things happened :—

1st. Sometimes the sitter is not photographed; something obscures the sitter, and *that something* evidently comes between the sitter and the lens, and cuts off the usual rays of light by which an ordinary photograph is taken.

2nd. That genuine psychic photographs can be obtained by other cameras, etc., than that of the photographer.

3rd. That while not absolutely necessary to the manipulation of the camera and the processes of photographing, the *presence* of a specially gifted medium is necessary.   No spirit photograph or psychic " extras " can be obtained without such a sensitive being in the room.

The following is an extract from a letter written by Mr Howitt to the *Spiritual Magazine*:—

DEAR SIR,— . . . . During my recent short and hurried visit to London, I and my daughter paid a visit to Mr Hudson's studio, and through the medium-ship of Mr Herne—and perhaps of Mr Hudson himself — obtained two photographs, perfect and unmistakable, of sons of mine, who passed into the spirit world years ago.   They promised to thus show themselves if possible.

These portraits were obtained under circumstances which did not admit of deception. Neither Mr Hudson nor *Mr Herne knew who we were*; *Mr Herne*,[1] *I never saw before.* I shut him up in the recess of the back of the studio and secured the door on the outside, so that he did not—and could not—appear on the scene. Mr Benjamin Coleman, who was with us, and myself, took the plates at haphazard from a dusty heap of such; and Mr Coleman went into the dark chamber with the photographer, and took every precaution that no tricks were played there. But the greatest security was that, not knowing us, and our visit being without previous announcement or arrangement, the photographer could by no means know what or whom we might be expecting. Mr Coleman himself did not know of the existence of *one* of these children. Still further, there was no existing likeness of one of them.

On sending the photographs to Mrs Howitt, in Rome, she instantly and with the greatest delight recognised the truth of the portraits. The same was the case with a lady who had known these boys most intimately for years. A celebrated and most reliable lady medium whom they had spiritually visited many times, at once recognised them perfectly, and as resembling a spirit sister, whom *they told her* had died in infancy long before themselves, which is a fact.

I had written a letter to state these particulars publicly, when a friend, who mixes much with London spiritualists, assured me that to his knowledge Hudson and Herne had played tricks. On hearing this, as I had no means and no leisure, during my

[1] Mr Herne was then a well-known physical medium, a professional. Mrs Guppy was also a remarkable medium, but non-professional. At this period of experimenting in Great Britain it was thought necessary to have a physical medium present in the studio, hence Mr Herne's presence as narrated.

J. C.

short and fully occupied stay in England, of ascertaining what was really the truth, I kept back my letter, reluctant to sanction fraud should it by any possibility exist; but on all the occasions I have stated, so far as I was concerned, the result of my visit to Mr Hudson was a perfect success.

It was my full intention to have made another experiment with him, but found it impossible, much to my regret. I feel it, however, only due to Mr Hudson, and to the cause of spirit-photography, to say that my visit to him was thoroughly satisfactory —that by no earthly means could he have presented me with the photographic likenesses which he did; and that I, moreover, feel an inward and strong conviction that he is an honest man. Were he otherwise, he would, in fact, be a very great fool, since my own experience with him is proof positive that he can and does produce realities.

I may add that the two portraits in question are the best and the most clearly developed of any I have seen, except that of Annina Carbomi, obtained by Chevalier Kirkup, in Florence.—Yours faithfully,
WILLIAM HOWITT.
DIETENHEIM, AUSTRIAN TYROL,
    August 10, 1872.

At this early stage of the manifestations in Great Britain of this special phase of physical phenomena, it was not at all surprising, owing to the very nature of the claim -- so extraordinary—that the spirits of the departed could be photographed, that the easy and ignorant cry of " fraud " was so soon raised.

Mr Howitt, whose eminence as a thinker and writer, and reputation as a man of honour, must be at once conceded, in his letter reveals something of the clamour which was already gathering to a head against Hudson, and furnishes the best possible answer of *a something superior to all tests*, viz. that of receiving two clearly identifiable portraits. Not only that, but these portraits were received as the result of a previous promise obtained from the departed through a sensitive. Here we have evidence for a super-normal intelligence at work in the production of the pictures.

(*a*) The departed spirits suggest through a medium, and induce their father to go and have a sitting, that they may appear if the conditions are at all favourable.

(*b*) They succeed in appearing and are photographed, and of one of them no portrait was ever taken in life, and of the other no similar picture or photograph ever existed.

(*c*) The intelligences testify to their resemblance to a spirit sister who had passed on long before themselves, which was a fact.

(*d*) The conditions under which these photographs were obtained, even though the operators and the sitter were disposed to connive at fraud—which was impossible,—were such that the proceedings would not account for the results.

About this time there were others besides Mr Hudson by or through whom these photographs were obtained. I only briefly notice these, if for nothing else than to emphasise the rarity of the mediumship. Chevalier Kirkup, of Turin, had been getting some, indeed many, well-defined portraits, some of which were recognised. The spirit Annina had appeared in circles in which materialisations took place, and was the spirit to which Mr Howitt referred in one of his letters.   Others nearer at home who obtained photographs at this time were Mr Guppy, Mr Jones, Mr Beattie, a retired photographer at Clifton, who, in conjunction with a Dr Thomson, obtained phantasmal figures, human-like, but, so far as I am aware, nothing in the way of recognisable portraits.

When in London, in the year 1875, acting as *locum tenens* for Dr Mack, in Southampton Row, I had a sitting with Mr Hudson.   I was accompanied by the late Dr James M'Geary (Dr Mack) for that purpose.

From a psychic standpoint, Mr Hudson was a puzzle, that is to say, this mediumship came to him late in life.   (His first picture came in 1872.)   At the time I visited him I should think he was about sixty years of age.   Mumler and Parkes were much younger men, more in their vital prime, and better able to throw off that X aura or nervauric atmosphere which is the special endowment of these mediums, and without which spirit photographs cannot be obtained.   Possibly financial cares, which his mediumship provoked, contributed to his aged and careworn appearance. He was most certainly not a man of astuteness, or competent to deceive the ablest photographers in London.   We were greeted openly, and would have been afforded every opportunity for investigation, had we had the time at our disposal.

The spirit photograph received by Dr Mack was that of the face and the upper half of a male form

draped in white nebulous stuff, the lower part of the
figure disappearing, leaving the background clearly
visible below.   On my own was a somewhat similar
figure, showing a three-quarter dark face, with
aquiline nose, mouth invisible, hidden with moustache
and a dark, pointed beard.   The head, shoulders, and
the body were clothed in more opaque white, as if a
tablecloth had been utilised for the purpose.   Dr Mack
appeared to recognise the spirit photograph which he
had obtained.   As to the one which I received, I have
never been able to obtain a clue as to who it was.   I
regret I have had no further opportunities of sitting
with Mr Hudson.

While I did not test Mr Hudson's mediumship, I
knew a large number of discerning and well-known
persons who had had spirit photographs with Hudson
under satisfactory conditions.   Of these I will mention
a few in addition to those to whom reference has already
been made : Mr and Mrs James Burns, 15 Southampton Row; Mr Wm. Tebb; Mr E. T. Bennett, editor,
Christian Spiritualist; Mr Thomas Shorter, the
author; Mr Guppy; Dr George Sexton; Mr C. W.
Pearce; and Mr Thomas Blyton, London; Mr John
Lamont, Mr Archibald Lamont, and Mrs A. Lamont, of
Liverpool; Mr T. Martheze, of Brussels, then in
London, a very able and enthusiastic investigator.
This able man spent a very great deal of time and
money in his careful research.   He was delighted in
getting, among others, a clearly identifiable photograph
of his mother.   He told me the whole story, but I

am indebted to Miss Houghton's *Chronicles* for the
portrait which is given here.   Mr Andrew Glen-

FIG. 4. —The photograph of Mr T. Martheze, with the
psychic full-length figure of his mother thereon.
From Miss Houghton's collection.

dinning [1] was among those who obtained some of these
photographs with Mr Hudson; Dr Thomson, who, like

[1] While revising the MSS. I learned that this veteran reformer
had passed into the land of spirits, in his eighty-fourth year, on
the 25th October 1910.   He was an esteemed correspondent for
whom I had great reverence.

Dr Alfred Russel Wallace, obtained the picture of his mother; Mr Beattie, Mrs Everitt, and Mr Adshead.

The wife of Mr Desmond Fitzgerald, M.I.C.E., an eminent electrical engineer in London, and at one time on the Council of the then National Association of Spiritualists, obtained a fully identified portrait of her own father. The lady went to Hudson, with her daughter, for a spirit photograph, but she did not tell the photographer either what she wanted or the special character of the picture she expected to receive. She thought of her father, and longed, naturally, to have his photograph. She hoped that if he came he would appear wearing the old black cap which he had been accustomed to wear in his last illness. She neither told her daughter, who was with her, nor the photographer of this test. It was not until the plate was developed and the clear features of her father revealed, that she made known the test which was in her mind. This particular spirit photograph was published in the *Daily Graphic* in June 1892, and was reproduced in Mr Glendinning's interesting work *The Veil Lifted*, now out of print.

DR ALFRED RUSSEL WALLACE AND HIS MOTHER

Owing to the importance and unique standing in science and literature of this eminent naturalist, I give Dr Wallace's own account,[1] slightly abbreviated, of this remarkable photograph :—

[1] *Miracles and Modern Spiritualism.* By Alfred Russel Wallace, D.C L., LL.D. F.R S. George Redway, London. Footnote, pp. 196, 197, and 198.

4

On March 14th, 1874, I went to Hudson's by appointment. I expected if I got any spirit picture it would be that of my eldest brother, in whose name messages had been received through Mrs Guppy. Before going to Hudson's I sat with Mrs G., and had a communication by raps to the effect that my mother

Fig. 5.—The photograph of Dr Alfred Russel Wallace,
and the spirit picture of his mother, copied from
Miss Houghton's collection.

would appear on the plate if she could. I sat three times, always choosing my own position. Each time a second figure appeared on the plate with me. The first was a male figure, with a short sword; the second a full-length figure, standing a few feet, apparently, on one side, and rather behind me, looking down at me, and holding a bunch of flowers. At the third sitting, after placing myself, and after the prepared plate was in the camera, I asked if the figure would come close to me. The third plate exhibited a female figure standing *close* in front of me, so that the drapery covers the lower part of my body. I saw all the plates developed, and in each case an additional figure started out the moment the developing fluid was poured on, while my portrait did not become visible till, perhaps, twenty seconds later. I recognised none of these figures in the negative; but the moment I got the proofs, the first glance showed me that the third plate contained an unmistakable portrait (fig. 5) of my mother—like her both in features and expression; not such a likeness as a portrait taken during life, but a somewhat pensive, idealised likeness—*yet still to me an unmistakable likeness.* The second figure is much less distinct; the face is looking down; it has a different expression from the other, so that I at first concluded that it was a different person. On sending the two female portraits to my sister, she thought the second was much more like my mother than the third, was, in fact, a very good likeness, though indistinct, while the third seemed to her to be like in expression, but with something wrong about the mouth and chin. This was found to be due in part to the filling up of spots by the photographer; but when the picture was washed it became thickly covered with whitish spots, but *a better likeness of my mother.* I did not see the likeness in the second picture till I looked at it with a magnifying glass, and I at once saw a remarkable special feature of my mother's natural face, an un-usually projecting lower lip and jaw. This was most conspicuous some years ago, as latterly the mouth was somewhat contracted. A photograph taken twenty-two years before shows this peculiarity very strongly, and corresponds well with the second picture, in which the mouth is partly open and the lower lip projects greatly. This figure had always given me the impression of a younger person than that in the third picture, and it is remarkable that they correspond respectively with the character of the face as seen in photographs taken at intervals of about twelve years, yet without the least resemblance to these photographs either in attitude or expression.   Both figures carry a bunch of flowers exactly in the same way ; and it is worthy of notice that while I was sitting for the second picture the medium said, " I see someone and it has flowers," intimating that she saw flowers distinctly, the figure only faintly.   Here then are two different faces repre- senting the aspect of a deceased person's countenance at two different periods of her life.

Dismissing as untenable the probability of Hudson getting access to portraits of the deceased, and using them, he says :—

I see no escape from the conclusion that some spiritual being, acquainted with my mother's various aspects during life, produced these recognisable im- pressions on the plate.

The doctor sent a copy of the third print—as repro- duced here—to his brother in California, and received the following reply :—

" As soon as I opened the letter I looked at the photograph attentively and recognised your face, and remarked that the other one was something like Fanny (my sister).   I then handed it across the table to Mrs W., and she exclaimed at once, ' Why, it's your mother ! '   We then compared it with a photograph of her we had here, and there could be no doubt as to the general resemblance, but it has an appearance of sickness or weariness."   Neither my brother nor his wife knew anything of spiritualism, and both were prejudiced against it.   We may therefore accept their testimony as to the resemblance to my mother, in confirmation of myself and my sister, as conclusive.

Concerning the next picture, the late editor of *Light* wrote Mr Hudson the following:—

FIG. 6.—Photograph of "M. A. Oxon.," and psychic portrait of a friend, taken from Miss Houghton's collection.

June 2, 1876.

DEAR SIR,—You ought to know that the photograph taken of me three weeks ago is a remarkable instance of a recognised portrait of a personal friend. You will find it described by me at length in *Human Nature* of this month, and it forms the subject of a Spirit Teaching which I am about to forward to the *Spiritualist*. It is the first case in which I have secured the likeness of a friend, though I have several times succeeded, under test conditions, in getting "spirit pictures" in your studio. The present picture is by no means one of your best; indeed, the image is rudely made, and the photo is not good. But the face is there, and that makes it valuable. I am glad to add this testimony to that which I have already printed in your favour.   "M.A. Oxon."

Mr J. Traill Taylor's Testimony

A gentleman who went to Mr Hudson obtained a spirit photograph, and, having recognised the spirit portrait, he published an account of it; and, being much elated, he showed it to Mr John Beattie, of Clifton, Bristol. That gentleman pronounced it to be a fraud, and Mr Hudson got into much disfavour in consequence. In June 1873 a gentleman called on Hudson to have sittings. He wished to go through all the processes of photography himself, and to this Mr Hudson consented. In a few days afterwards Mr Hudson received a letter signed "John Bruce Beattie," saying that the spirit picture was that of a nephew, and that he had sent it to the mother for identification. He subsequently sent a long account of the whole procedure to the *British Journal of Photography*, and as a result he obtained several *portraits*, by which he was convinced, in addition to his experience elsewhere, of

the possibility of photographing forms invisible to ordinary eyesight, and forms which indicate the presence of unseen, intelligent beings of some sort controlling the forms so photographed.

Further than this I do not propose to quote the long article. I will, however, reproduce—somewhat summarised—the comments of Mr J. Traill Taylor, then the editor of that journal. Both Mr Beattie's article and Mr Taylor's remarks appeared in the issue for August 1873. The editor says:—

The main facts once admitted, the question arises: By what means are these figures formed upon the collodion film? The first impulse is to attribute it to a double exposure on the part of Hudson, the photographer. But here a difficulty interposes—Mr Hudson need not be present at all; indeed, it is but an act of justice to that gentleman to say that when we were trying experiments in his studio to determine the truth of the "so-called spirit photography," we obtained entire possession of his dark-room, employed our own collodion and plates, and at no time during the preparation, exposure or development of the pictures was Mr Hudson within ten feet of the camera, or the dark-room. Appearances of an abnormal kind did certainly show on several plates, by whatever means they were caused. The photographer had nothing whatever to do with their production. Neither will the "previously used plate" theory apply in this case, for the plates were quite new, and were obtained a few hours before they were used; and apart from the fact of their never having been out of our possession, the package was only undone just before the operations were commenced.

In closing this chapter, I have dealt pretty fully with the evidences in favour of spirit photography at this period. Mrs H. Sidgwick—without personal knowledge—ridiculed Professor Wallace's account of getting his own mother's photograph, maintaining that

Hudson certainly produced bogus spirit photographs, giving as an instance of " fraud " the fact that a spirit picture was no other than a photograph of Herne, the medium, dressed for the part.   In a similar way, this eminent psychical researcher condemned Mumler, as the portrait of a living man appeared in one of Mumler's Boston photographs as an " extra."   Actual experience and reliable testimony of competent experts go for nothing because this clever woman assumes fraud.   " Phantasms of the living " existed before they were established by the Society for Psychical Research.   " The double " has been photographed. Herne was not dressed and posed as a " spirit " for someone else, but was photographed while in trance, and his " double," in auric garments, appeared (as the " extra ") standing by his side.

CHAPTER III

As we have seen, when dealing with Mr Hudson's mediumship, there were others at this period who succeeded in obtaining, by the aid of spirits, photographs of men and things. In fact, there was a little "boom" in spirit photography from 1872 till 1877. Among the accredited were Messrs Parkes and Reeves. Both were contemporary with Hudson, Beattie, Thomson, Slater, Jones, and Mr and Mrs Guppy, in England; Mumler, in the States; and Buguet, in France, besides a few others of lesser note.

Neither was a professional medium. I did not know either personally, but I knew several who had sittings with them. Mr James Bowman, a well-known photographer in Glasgow, whom I knew, and whose skill in photographic matters could be fully depended on, was among those who tested Mr Parkes, and was fully satisfied.

I can only make a few extracts from the statements of Mrs J. W. Jackson, wife of the eminent anthropologist; Dr Sexton; "M.A. Oxon."; and Mr E. W. Wallis, the present editor of *Light*, all of whom I knew, and in whose testimony I have the fullest confidence.

Mrs Jackson, writing to the *Medium*, 24th May, 1872, says :—

MY DEAR MR BURNS, — I went to Mr Reeves, in York Road, who is not a professional photographer, and therefore has no interest or motive for producing astounding results. When the very simple arrangements were made, I sat down, and in a few seconds longer than his usual for ordinary photos, I distinctly recognised the face of my husband standing over me. The expression and the chiselling of the features, contour of the head, the curling length of beard, and outline of form, were as perfect as when he was on earth. There could be no imposition in this instance, for Mr Reeves never saw or knew anything of my husband during his life.

A few days afterwards I took a lady friend, who sat for her photograph also, a stranger to our kind friend Mr Reeves. On the other side of the small table at which the lady was seated, when the plate was taken from the camera, there appeared two spirit forms, which were immediately recognised as two of my friend's ancestors who had left this earth many years ago.   E. B. JACKSON.

I suppose the latter were identified from family portraits, but Mrs Jackson would not have made this statement except on good grounds.

For a time Mr Parkes and Mr Reeves experimented together, uniting their mediumship to get results. Mr Reeves emigrated to Canada, and Mr Parkes continued to take pictures. He had sometimes the presence of other mediums, but as often as not proceeded without such aid. The photographs obtained, when these two earnest men were together, were in many ways different in style from those afterwards secured. Without the presence of Mr Reeves, or his own wife, Mrs Parkes, Mr Parkes could not get full form and clearly defined pictures, only white patches and cloudy appearances, like the Clifton photos of Mr Beattie.

Dr Sexton (who obtained through Mr Parkes, too, " a likeness of the late Mr J. W. Jackson, who had passed away just before ") gave the following account, in the *Christian Spiritualist*, January 1875 :—

As a dark-room is indispensable in photography, and as in the case of spirit photographs there appears to be a necessity for the photographer to have the plate in his possession in some such room, for the purpose of magnetising it previous to its being placed in the camera, a suspicion naturally arises that this offers an opportunity for playing a trick, and thus imposing upon the sitter. Mr Parkes had an aperture made in the wall of this room through which the spectator can see the plate through its entire process. A few days since, we selected a plate from a packet ; this we marked to be used on the occasion, and never lost sight of it up till the time that there appeared upon it, in conjunction with our own portrait, that of a spirit figure. As to the camera, it remained in the room all the evening, and was open to the inspection of anyone. We may remark here that, being evening, the portrait was taken by means of a magnesium light, which was found to work admirably on the occasion. Spirit photography is, therefore, an established fact, beyond the possibility of dispute, and Mr Parkes is one of the most successful mediums by means of which this wonderful phenomenon is now accomplished.

Mr Parkes not only magnetised the plates but the camera. He did this in consequence of the directions which he had received. It appeared to be one of the conditions necessary. He had evidently great faith in the process. So we see that, at this early stage of spirit photography in the United Kingdom, " magnetising " was one of the processes which was adopted and one of the conditions to be obeyed in order to get these photos.

Among those who wrote to " M.A. Oxon." was the father of Mr Parkes. This gentleman was opposed to both spiritualism and the spiritistic theory concerning these portraits. I give an extract from his letter, which appeared in *Human Nature*, 9th February 1875 :—

I freely admit that I was, and probably still am, an unbeliever in what may be said to be comprehended in *spirit* photography. I cannot believe in the presence of spirits, but that the likenesses of the departed are produced and faithfully represented I have *now* not the least doubt.

This was followed by his opinion as to the character of his son, and testimony to the fact of having himself sat, and obtained the likeness of his father :—

There is no mistaking the likeness, and my family all immediately recognised it. Others of our kindred sat, and similar results have followed.

Dismissing the thought of trickery, he concludes :—

I look forward with some interest to the time when

the subject will be well ventilated, and which I think will end in a *natural* solution.

It will be well to bear this shrewd observation in mind later on.

" M.A. Oxon.," who examined 110 of these photographs, of which he gives a full report in *Human Nature*, says :—

A considerable number of the earlier pictures taken by Messrs Parkes and Reeves were allegorical.   One of the earliest, taken in April 1872, shows Mr Reeves' father holding up a cross above his head, and displaying an open book on which is written, " Holy Bible." Another shows a cloud of light covering two-thirds of the picture, and made up of the strangest medley of heads and arms, and flashes of light, with a distinct cross in the centre.   Another, in which Mr and Mrs Everitt are the sitters, taken June 8, 1872, is a symbolical picture of a very curious nature.   Mr Everitt's head is surrounded with a fillet on which " Truth " is inscribed, while three pencils of light dart up from it. There are at least two figures in the picture which blot out Mrs Everitt altogether.   In a later photograph, in which Mr Burns is the sitter, is a giant hand of which the thumb is half the length of the sitter's body.   It is just as if a luminous hand had been projected or flashed on the plate without any regard to focus.   Another very startling picture is one which shows on a dark background a huge luminous crucifix. Then we have angels with orthodox wings hovering over some sitters.   One is a very striking model : the face of great beauty and of pure classical design. The figure floats with extended arm over the sitter, and below it, almost on the ground. appear nine faces, and, strangest of all, close by the the sitter's head, a large eye, with beams of light proceeding from it. The eye is larger than the head of the sitter, and the whole picture presents a most curious appearance. Some show mere faces; some, heads; some, again, whole bodies floating in the air; and some, partially formed bodies projected on the plate, apparently at haphazard.

At this early stage in spirit photography, it dawned on some of the leading thinkers and investigators concerned, that while Intelligences in the Invisible have been at work—as claimed by them, through mediums—the psychic "extras" thus projected, or which came on the plates, were not the photographs of spirits, but rather of plastic designs, crude portraits or paintings, scrolls, and other more or less weird fancies. Amid all this experimenting, with most conclusive evidence of genuineness, *there were, however, obtained many identifiable portraits of the departed, as they once appeared when in the body.*

As I have known Mr Wallis (secretary of the London Spiritual Alliance), who is a well-known lecturer and writer on spiritualism, for over thirty years, I thought it best to elicit his opinions and experiences —if any—in connection with psychic photography. In reply, dated 12th September 1910, he says :—

The most satisfactory instance of spirit photography that I have been associated with occurred with Mr Joseph Cotterell. He was instructed by automatic writing— through his own hand—to go to Mr Parkes, who was at that time obtaining spirit photographs, as his departed wife desired to give him her picture. An appointment was made without divulging to Mr Parkes what was expected. When the day arrived, it was very foggy, and Mr Cotterell was disinclined to make the journey from Vauxhall to Bow. I urged him to keep his appointment, and suggested that by the time he reached his destination the fog might lift. On his arrival the weather had much improved, and several photographs were taken, one of which Mr Cotterell recognised as the portrait of his departed wife. He wrote to each of her three sisters, then living in different parts of the country, and—without comment—enclosed with each letter a print of the spirit photograph. From each sister he received answers, and they all desired to know how he obtained the picture of their sister— thus admitting the recognition; but when he explained how it was taken, they were equally unanimous in expressing the opinion that it was the devil's work— forgetting that in that case their beloved sister must be acting as his Satanic Majesty's agent!

It has always seemed to me that the real value of spirit photographs is in the recognition—provided that there is no possibility of faking up an already existing portrait. In Mr Cotterell's case no such portrait existed.

This is a case where the sitter was influenced—in fact, directed—by an Intelligence in the Invisible to go and be photographed, with the result that he obtained his late wife's picture. In this and in similar cases we get a glimpse of the directing powers behind—shall we say ?—these psychic phenomena; and with this I conclude my references to Messrs Parkes and Reeves.

BUGUET MEDIUMSHIP

In dealing with M. Buguet, I am compelled to rely on the experiences and the opinions of others. I knew Mr W. H. Harrison, editor of the *Spiritualist*, as a man of scientific attainments and an expert photographer.   Most of those to whom he refers I knew by reputation, as among the most sincere, intellectual, and careful investigators of psycho-physics at this period. Mr Harrison, 26th June 1874, says:—

On Thursday, last week, I was invited, with other friends, to observe the manipulation in the studio of M. Buguet, spirit photographer, of Paris, who is taking pictures at 33 Baker Street.   Mrs Macdougall Gregory, Mrs Ross Church, Mrs Showers, Mr Coleman, Mr Ivimey, Mr Martheze, and other friends were present.
I offered to take the negative myself, be merely standing by to get the influence of his mediumship upon the plate.   This he declined, saying that the manifestations were more likely to be successful if he handled the plates and the chemicals throughout.
After trying one picture, on which no spirits came, he began to take another as follows:—He cut a corner with a jagged fracture off a bare plate of glass, and handed the little piece to the sitter, who was a friend of Mr Coleman.   The object of cutting off the piece was to show, by the separated corner afterwards fitting the plate with its finished picture, that the plate had not been changed during the operations.

From this point, preparation in dark-room, its examination, and all procedure to putting the plate in the dark slide, which he "had previously opened and examined," are graphically described by Mr Harrison.

I examined the camera and the lens thoroughly, taking them to pieces to a considerable extent.   I took part in the focussing, and saw only the sitter on the ground glass—no spirits.
During the exposure of the plate, M. Buguet stood near the camera, with his head leaning against the wall; he seemed to go into semi-trance.

Afterwards I followed him, with the dark slide in his hand, to the developing-room, saw the plate removed from the slide, the developer immediately poured over it, and two spirits made their appearance on the plate behind the sitter. Their features came out distinctly; it was not a good photograph, artistically speaking; the chemicals were working badly, and threw down much loose silver deposit.

The operations all through lasted from seven to ten minutes.

Invisible pictures may be painted on a background with sulphate of quinine, æsculine, or other fluorescent substance, which invisible pictures can be photographed so as to appear in any negative taken before that background. The photograph now under notice was not one of that nature.

The background was the ordinary wall-paper of the private room in which the photographs were taken. The spirits on the negative and the finished prints have not been recognised.

Obviously, it is not possible to say much about spirit photography on the slender experience of one experiment, but I do not know how to produce by artificial means a similar picture under like conditions.

In the foregoing we have all the watchful procedure of a skilled scientific observer, recorded with modesty in statement. Before passing away from Mr Harrison's testimony as to the apparent *bona-fides* of M. Buguet's mediumship, under careful test conditions, let it be noted, although two psychic " extras " were on this occasion obtained, they were " not recognised." No amount of testing will, or has ever, produced an identifiable portrait of a departed. The tests adopted, few or many, may go to demonstrate that the

5

medium's secret methods, if any, have not been detected, and the experts are baffled—that's all. The identifiable portrait is the crux of the whole matter. Neither testing nor fraudulent procedure can produce these. They often come when least expected, and present their own—which is the best—evidence.

Out of the many identified "extras" obtained through this medium I produce one.

Lady Caithness, formerly of Barragill Castle, Wick, Scotland, but who principally resided in Paris, sent an account of her experiences to the *Spiritualist*, 24th July 1874, from which I summarise the following :—

I experience so much happiness every time I look at the photograph obtained through the celebrated French photographer, Monsieur Ed. Buguet, that I feel bound . . . to make the fact known.

One lady in Edinburgh to whom I sent copies has written me : "I recognised everyone; darling Ellen (my sister) is most wonderful, and your late husband and father not less so." . . . Percy came to me at four o'clock in the morning, saying, "I cannot sleep for thinking of those photos"; I truly echo the words and endorse them.

I went with my son, Count de Medina Pomar, both of us perfect strangers to Mons. Buguet, and found him as courteous and amiable as Mr Burns had described him in the *Medium*.

After describing the almost empty room and the procedure of posing and taking the sitters, Lady Caithness says :—

After a short absence from the room, at the close of every pose, Mons. Buguet returned, bringing the negatives for our inspection; he had an anxious, concerned look, until rejoiced by our recognising, even on the glass, some dear and well-remembered features long passed away from our midst. Sometimes no

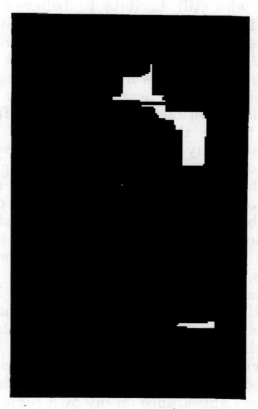

Fig. 7.—The Count de Medina Pomar, with the psychic portrait of his father, General the Count de Medina Pomar. The above is reproduced from *Human Nature*.

spirit form whatever was visible on the glass, but between my son and myself we were successful thirteen times; and out of the thirteen *we distinctly recognised the spirit forms of five dear ones whom we had never hoped to see again on earth.* One of these, my father, appears no less than three times; once with my son, once with me, and once as if floating over us both, and enveloping us with part of his fluidic drapery. Strange to say, in order that there may be no doubt about the identity of my late husband, he brings in his hand the family crest and emblem.

To those who still hesitate to believe . . . I will only point to this extraordinary and beautiful test, and to these perfect likenesses, *recognised by each and every 'friend who has seen them,* and again bid them remember that we were perfect strangers to the medium, who had never heard of us before.

I must also mention one other wonderful circumstance, and that is the appearance of the late Allan Kardec on one of my *cartes.* This is most satisfactory to me in more ways than one, as it also gives me a proof that he is near, and watching over me in the work I have undertaken, of translating one of his wonderful books, *La Genèse,* into English, and in making known his other works in England and America. I have formed a large collection of spirit photographs, commencing last year in America, through the aid of Mr Mumler, and have now completed the album with those of Mons. Buguet. Amongst the latter I have five others of Allan Kardec —three with his widow, one with Miss Blackwell, and one with the celebrated French astronomer and talented author, Mons. Camille Flammarion. Allan Kardec's appearance on my own *carte* forms the sixth. . . . The test I allude to is most conclusive, for *each is perfectly distinct* in appearance and position from the other, yet all perfect likenesses of the great philosopher.   MARIE CAITHNESS.

Lady Caithness, Countess de Pomar, was a woman of marked ability, author of several works of psychical interest, and her *salon* was the centre to which flocked the brilliant intellects of Europe. In the palace there was a large lecture-hall, in which

Mrs Emma Hardinge Britten, as well as many able men and women, delivered inspired and cultured lectures. Owing to her culture and eminent position, I have given prominence to her testimony.

Among the well-known writers of this period, Mr S. C. Hall, F.S.A., stands in the first rank. For many years he was editor of the *Art Journal*. Besides being an authority on art, literature, science, and philanthropy, he was well able to write on spiritualism, which he investigated with care. He wrote to the *Medium and Daybreak*, 4th September 1874, and from his contribution—which I have curtailed—I take the following :—

I wish to state a simple fact. . . . While Mr Buguet was in London I sat to him. I was not only not expecting any result, I was more than suspicious. He produced of me three photographs ; in each there was a form besides my own. There was no medium [1] present. I watched his proceedings narrowly.

Of the three, I could not help recognising my father; I will tell you why. The face is so obscure, that I cannot determine the likeness by the features; but the face is round, the head bald, there is neither beard, moustache, nor whisker. That was exactly my father's head. But there are thousands of heads to which a similar description would apply. There was one peculiarity, however, which not one in a thousand could have had; I explain it. My father, Colonel Hall, was an old officer, and he wore the *queue* up to his "death"; it was buried with him. That was in his time, sixty or seventy years ago, the "common

[1] With Hudson, Messrs Herne and Williams, sometimes Mrs Guppy, and other mediumistic persons were present at sittings. —J. C.

head costume" of soldier officers, but it has long gone
out. Now, in the photograph to which I refer, this
queue is perfectly distinct—as clear as if a brush had
painted it in; white (he was a very aged man when
he died, and had been an officer more than sixty
years), and proceeding from the back of the head down
the back of the body—standing out indeed, and apart
from the shoulders. I ought to add that on another
of the photographs the features are much more
distinct; but that is a full face, and of course the
queue is not seen.   S. C. HALL.

In the foregoing, Mr S. C. Hall obtains two photographs, which he identifies as those of his father:
first, from the form, the pose, and the *queue*, the
features not being distinct; second, from a full-face
photograph in which the features were quite distinct.
The late S. C. Hall had the eye of an artist and the
judgment of an intelligent man, and as such could
not be classed with those who would recognise "a
broom and a sheet" photographed for the present-
ment of a relative.

Mrs H. Sidgwick, in her article on spirit photographs, in the *S P.R. Proc.*, p. 280, in her anxiety to
make a case, ignores the second photograph, and
assumes that Mr Hall was deceived in basing his
recognition on the pigtail, the *queue*, "practically the
only point of identification." This procedure —
whether deliberately or unintentionally carried out—
was a suppression of the truth, and an omission of a
most important statement of the late S. C. Hall. One
has to ignore the writings of persons posing as
scientifically fair, yet so misleading in statements.

The same lady condemns another photograph as fraudulent — it might be, for all I know—as the "extra" therein was either that of, or resembled, a living person. That it resembled a living person there is no doubt. *All doubles* are photographs of living persons. In this case it was a matter of disputed identity in which one of the groups concerned was mistaken. "Mistaken identity" is no new thing.

This French medium obtained, among other recognised "extras," fully identifiable portraits of "the double." I give the account here, as well as the evidence of the Rev. Stainton Moses as to the fact of his own double being photographed by Mons. Buguet, summarised from *Human Nature*, vol. ix., 1875 :—

HOTEL DE L'ATHENÉE, RUE SCRIBE, PARIS.

I, the undersigned William Julian, Count de Bullet, certify to having obtained at M. Buguet's, photographer, Boulevard de Montmartre, by ordinary methods of photography, at several sittings, the following portraits :—

1. The double of my sister, now living at Baltimore, U.S.A. 2. My uncle. 3. M. de Layman, an intimate friend. 4. One of my aunts. In assurance of which I freely sign the present attestation.

G. J. DE BULLET.

PARIS, *Dec.* 10, 1874.

"M.A. Oxon." was so much interested that he sought information on the following points : 1. Whether the sister was asleep at the time the photograph was taken; 2. Whether he had seen the double at any time; 3. Whether the likeness was recognised by others; 4. Whether he had ever tried to impress his thoughts on his sister by will-power; 5. Whether the phenomenon occurred more than once.

To the foregoing questions, I summarise the Count de Bullet's replies, which were dated Paris, 13th January 1875 :—

1. It is probable that my sister was asleep. I calculated the hour.

2. I have never seen her double at any time, although I have felt her impression by intuition, *always at a time when she would be likely to be asleep.*

3. The likenesses are so striking that everyone who knows her has instantly recognised it. I have had her likeness in eight different positions. There is not the slightest doubt about the likeness.

4. I have never tried to impress thoughts on the mind of my sister. Between her and me since childhood there has always existed the deepest affection.

5. When I pose before the camera I simply put the question I wish, and ask her to come if possible. On one plate she comes with card in her hands, with her answer to me written quite distinctly. The writing is in French, except when she does not want M. Buguet to know; then it is in English.

The foregoing was followed by a long account full of interesting details giving procedure at Buguet's, and the obtaining of these remarkable photographs of persons living 1200 miles away.

With regard to the photographing of the double of " M.A. Oxon.," I would gladly give his account in full, not only as testifying to the fact of the double being photographed at a distance, but owing to the great value and high esteem in which the late " M.A. Oxon." is held by all spiritualists at home and abroad ; but space forbids.   From his own articles in *Human Nature*, vol. ix. pp. 97–99, I summarise the following :—

The action of the incarnated spirit beyond the limits of the body which it occupies is a familiar fact to me. . . . *It seemed then that a plan might be arranged to obtain on the sensitised plate a permanent record of the presence of an embodied spirit, apart from its physical body.* [Italics are mine.—J. C.] Such an arrangement was actually made by my friend Mr Gledstanes, of Paris.

As the outcome of this arrangement, Mr Gledstanes posed in M. Buguet's studio, Sunday morning, 31st January 1875, at 11.15 a.m., or 11.5, London time.

On the first plate exposed appeared a faint and indistinct image of my face.   A second exposure produced a perfect result.   The first half of the plate contains a decided likeness of me ; the second half, one of an old man with a very striking head and commanding figure.   The portrait of me is quite unmistakable ; no one who has seen me in the flesh could fail to recognise it.   The eyes are closed and the face bears the indefinable look of trance. The body is shrouded in fluidic drapery.   The only persons present in M. Buguet's studio, besides himself, were Mr Gledstanes, the sitter, and the Count de Bullet.

I turn now to my own part in the experiment.   At the time when the photographs were taken I was lying in bed in London, in a state of deep trance.   I had a

half-consciousness of awaking at 10.25 a.m.   I fell
into a state of dreamy listlessness, between sleep and
waking.   The sound of the church bells fell upon my
ears, and I had a flash of recollection of the experiment
proposed for eleven o'clock.   Complete unconscious-
ness supervened before that hour.   When I regained
consciousness it was 11.47 a.m.   About this interval
I have no recollection whatever.   It is an absolute
blank, as is all the time during which I am completely
entranced.   So it was on this occasion.

"M.A. Oxon." had other experiences of a similar
kind, which I will not reproduce, but conclude this
part with a few words of his succinct claim :—

I have recorded with literal exactness the facts
connected with this remarkable phenomenon.   All
comes to this.   *Here is the photograph of the spirit of
a living person taken in Paris while the body in
which it is incarnated is in London.*   I may be excused if I estimate highly the value of this experiment.
I may lay personal stress on the evidence, which, so
far as it concerns this world, is perfect, and which, so
far as it concerns the invisible operators, is assured
to me by those whom I have never found tripping
yet. . . .   That *it is a fact* I am as certain as I am of
anything.

I cannot conclude these testimonies without emphasising the fact of the " double," which, as we have
seen, has been a feature in the photography of Mumler,
Evans, Hudson, and Buguet.   Mumler left Boston
owing to the picture of a living man appearing as
an " extra."   Evans was " suspect " owing to the
" double " of a gentleman asleep by a stove, and out
of reach of the camera, being photographed; Hudson,

for the double of Herne; and Buguet, for the photograph of a living person, which was taken as the spirit picture of one M. Edouard Poiret.

Of 120 photographs examined by " M.A. Oxon.," he furnishes evidence of the recognition of forty. He could have given many more, but from the nature of the photographs and the standing of the witnesses, so to speak, forty attested photographs would be most convincing to those who really understand the value of evidence.

In M. Buguet's case, we have the fly in the ointment, the counterfeit among the coins. His conduct is among the causes which help the man in the armchair, who has never experimented, to say: " All the ointment is bad, all the coins are counterfeit; all your psycho-physical phenomena are fraudulent, and all your mediums are impostors." As to others, whose *bona-fides* we have no reason to doubt, the charges of fraud came from those who assumed fraud as an hypothesis; but when it came to evidence before the courts, as in Mumler's case, the hypothesis and the facts *did not square.*

Mediumship neither implies manliness, honesty, nor spiritual worth, and in this case Buguet's mediumship did not save him from being a worthless fellow. Still, I am sorry for him, as he is an outstanding instance of how the weak and the foolish are exploited, and how the lust for gold—with the hope of salvation thrown in — has tempted men not so innocent and inexperienced as our father Adam to put expediency before principle.   This self-confessed knave *could not* and did not explain how all his spirit pictures were obtained, and his demonstrations only went to show how some could be made.

The photographs which " M.A. Oxon." had dealt with were within two classes, all others being rejected. The first consisted " of those only recognised by one or more persons (generally more than one) as portraits of friends who had departed from this life." The second " included only pictures taken under test conditions." The latter were valuable only so far as the testing conditions met all the requirements of skilled photographers.

When the history of Buguet's " confessions " and trial and subsequent repentance is fully considered, it will be found that he was more fool than knave. That he was both needs not to be denied.

The *Revue Spirite* had flouted the Catholic Church in the person of the Archbishop of Toulouse, as perhaps spiritualistic organs everywhere are liable to flout priestly intolerance and theological tyranny of all kinds, irrespective of the particular creed or Church to which the priests belong.   Such insult by the *Revue Spirite* was not to be tolerated by an all-powerful Church, and that in a country where—at this time— the whole civil and military forces were at her command.   M. Leymarie, the editor of the paper, was tried and condemned.   Buguet was a pawn in the game for the double purpose of inflicting injury on spiritualists, and punishing the editor as well, who was condemned and sentenced, equally with Buguet, to twelve months' imprisonment.

These trials were organised by the emissaries of the then State Church of France. Buguet's trial did not and could not efface the facts of genuine psychic photography. Still, it must be admitted that his confession vitiates all that can be said in favour of even those pictures recognised as genuine. But as no reference to the subject of spirit photography could be complete without calling the attention of the reader to M. Buguet, his pictures, the class of people who testified to them, and the trial in which he stood as a self-condemned trickster, I feel it my duty to give an outline of the whole miserable business.

Of him, " M.A. Oxon.," in a letter to *Human Nature*, 20th August 1875, says :—

The poor wretch was bribed by promises of immunity, and told his tale. His judges had not even the honesty to keep faith with him, and he found himself in a dungeon, in spite of his false swearing.

Since the trial of M. Buguet, the authorities of the Holy Mother Church, through various agents and in the press, have acknowledged the genuineness of spiritistic phenomena, but condemn both the practice and their investigation outside the pale of the Church.

CHAPTER IV

MR DAVID DUGUID'S MEDIUMSHIP

IT would be impossible, within my limited space, to do justice to either Mr Duguid or his mediumship. He was born in 1832 and died in 1907. I became acquainted with him in 1878, shortly after *Hafed* had been published. I knew not only Mr Duguid, but all the members of the " Hafed Circle," and have been several times witness to his trance painting gifts. Out of the hundreds who could bear testimony, I have selected a few, and these mainly from those whom I knew as possessing undoubted authority and fitness. My remarks are confined to spirit photography, which was only one phase out of the psycho-physical phenomena which took place in his presence. The characteristic feature was not so much the number of identifiable psychic portraits as the evidence—scientifically demonstrated—of the fact of spirit photography. In addition to this, through him were obtained the clearest possible cases of what are called in these pages " psychographs," *i.e.* pictures obtained without sunlight, *phos*, lens, or camera.

In giving this original and hitherto unpublished photograph, I do so not only because of its genuineness, but of its history. No one can say whether it is a true likeness or not of the reputed Hafed, seeing

FIG. 8.—Photograph of the late Mr David Duguid, the Glasgow trance painting medium, at the age of sixty-two, taken after a series of test experiments conducted by Mr J. Traill Taylor, in London.

that this spirit claims to have lived in the body when Jesus lived and taught on earth.

Mr David Duguid was not a cultured man; that

cannot be denied. Of the volumes of information which fell from his lips, *Hafed, Prince of Persia*, is a notable instance, unique in literature. The contents

FIG. 9.—Photograph of Mr Andrew Glendinning and Mr James Robertson, and psychic portrait of "Hafed," taken on marked plates supplied by Mr Glendinning.

of the volume and the manner of its production, and the "direct" illustrations, were undoubtedly beyond the intellectual capacity of the medium, and are striking evidence of the existence of Intelligences in the Invisible.

Mr James Robertson, being present at, and taking part in, the majority of cases when Mr Duguid took psychic photographs, is my first important witness.

Writing me on 6th August 1910, from 5 Granby Terrace, Hillhead, Glasgow, Mr James Robertson says :—

DEAR MR COATES,—I may not be able to comprehend the process by which spirits are able to impress their forms or thoughts on a sensitive plate, but as I believe the spirit body is a substance, and substances can be photographed, I have no difficulty in accepting the fact that eyes do not catch all this universe presents—we have neither the microscopic nor the telescopic power—but who would deny what these discoveries have brought to view. We see in the process of materialisation solid forms built up, which we can touch; at other times these forms are vapoury and we can see through them, and so by degrees our sight fails to take in all there is. What to our eyes becomes invisible is caught up by the more subtle eye of the instrument. All this will be found to be in harmony with the laws of Nature, and experiments made outside the domain of the psychic will come into touch and accord with what has been done by us. In David Duguid we had a rare instrument for giving forth that aura through which the unseen world could manifest. He readily lent himself to all experiments which were suggested, and took as deep an interest as anyone. The phenomena in his case gradually developed. There were but hints at first, some vague markings it may be, but sufficient to show that something was added from an external source. The success was so limited at first that the matter was discarded for some years, till the arrival of a friend from New Zealand, who was an ardent investi-

6

gator, and this gentleman induced Mr Duguid to sit with him.   The experiment was made in my dining-room, and a form came clearly on the plate.   The face

FIG. 10.—Photograph of Mr James Robertson and Mr Andrew Glendinning, and the earliest *test* psychic portrait of the "Cyprian Priestess," taken in Glasgow.   Mr Robertson was present, but is cut out of the print.   Both Messrs Robertson and Glendinning superintended the experiment, Mr Duguid merely making the exposure.   Two other test pictures of this "extra" are produced further on.

was quite distinct, though the drapery was shadowy, and we could see through it the knobs of the shutters in front of which the plate was exposed.   A new interest was created after this, and several experiments were made in my garden with good results. I can remember the fervour with which I witnessed the development of the plates, and the satisfaction when we were rewarded. My old friend, Mr Glendinning, was soon informed of our success, and he eagerly entered with us on our investigations. All these were made with the greatest carefulness, not that we had any doubt of Mr Duguid's *bona-fides*, but that we wished to be in a position to speak positively that there was no room for fraud. The same care we took was afterwards carried through by Mr Traill Taylor when he was asked to give the weight of his authority as to the genuine nature of psychic photography. Nothing more forcible could be penned than Mr Taylor's report, which was reproduced in Mr Glendinning's *Veil Lifted.*

When carrying out these experiments, Mr Duguid did not complain much of loss of power, but ever after there seemed to be a great drain on his constitution when he lent himself to these sittings. It seemed to me that his "controls," after Mr Taylor's scientific report, felt that he need not give himself more to this work. His honesty and the facts of psychic photography had been established.

One of the most effective tests of spirit power and spirit identity given through Mr Duguid's mediumship was obtained by a well-known legal gentleman in Edinburgh, who had long desired the portrait of his deceased son. Nothing could be more satisfactorily attested. The parents ever spoke in the highest terms of gratitude for the blessing granted to them. As years went on they were again and again favoured with other pictures of the boy, grown-up, but still revealing the features so loved. This stands out as *one* clear bit of evidence that the dead, so-called, can make their impress on the sensitive plate. The gentleman who got the picture was no weak-minded enthusiast, but a man of culture, trained long in criminal investigation. Mr Taylor's support built up to the full the great fact that in the presence of some human sensitives it is possible for those gone on to give consolation to those left behind.

Mr David Duguid was in my service for over twenty years. I knew the man thoroughly ; a more honest, modest person—with ideals of truth and right—I never met.—Yours fraternally,   JAS. ROBERTSON.

I have known Mr James Robertson intimately for thirty-three years, and can safely say that no man is better known throughout Scotland as a shrewd, far-seeing man of business. For nearly forty years he has been an investigator of modern spiritualism, wields a vigorous pen, and has never hesitated to advocate whatever he knows to be true. He has found leisure, amid his great business concerns, to lecture and write on spiritualism. His latest work is entitled *Spiritualism : the Open Door to the Unseen Universe*.[1] In journalistic circles he is held in high esteem. Were it not for the facts of modern spiritualism, Mr James Robertson would have been a hard-headed, dour Scotch agnostic—a materialist—without guile. No one living is better qualified to testify to Mr Duguid's character and gifts.

Mr Andrew Glendinning, to whom Mr James Robertson refers, was a man among men, who lived a full and strenuous life. I knew of no one in connection with spiritualism who possessed his ripe experience. He was a lifelong total abstainer, and

---

[1] Messrs L. N. Fowler, Publishers, London.

advocated temperance when to do so was not fashionable.   As a friend of William Lloyd Garrison, and of
Elihu Burritt, the learned blacksmith, he was an anti-
slavery man in 1850–60, when it was fashionable to
find excuses for slavery.   He waged war not only on

Fig. 11.—My copy of the enlarged psychic portrait
of the "Cyprian Priestess," from *The Veil Lifted*.[1]

[1] Concerning this portrait I take from p. 92 of *The Veil Lifted*
the following, contributed by Mr James Robertson :—" It was the
good fortune of Mr Glendinning to get beside us on one occasion
a most exquisite face of a lady, full of each charm and grace that
make up the womanly character.   The term 'angelic' might be
applied to it.   Such a face the seraphic painters have ofttimes
drawn ; a Raphael might have painted it.   From somewhere
must have come this form.   And spiritualism demonstrates what
Mr Justice Groves, in the *Co-relation of Physical Forces*, gives as
a probable theory—myriads of organised beings may exist, im-
perceptible to our vision, even if we were among them."

negro slavery, but on the white man's slavery to intemperance, debasing passions, intolerant theology which made infidels, on materialism, then fashionable in scientific circles. Over thirty years ago, he and another were pioneers of the vegetarian and fruitarian restaurants in London, which helped to familiarise thousands with the physical benefits and economies of reformed diet. Amid his many interests in life, he found time to investigate spiritualism, which came to him forty-seven years ago in Scotland. When satisfied he had found something real, he did not hesitate to state the facts as he knew them.

In his letter to me, dated Dalston, 23rd April 1910, giving me permission to use certain extracts from *The Veil Lifted*, he authorised me to say he had nothing to withdraw as to his good opinion of the late Mr J. Traill Taylor and Mr David Duguid, the thoroughness of the London test experiments; and said : " When I reprint, I shall put emphasis on this." Our friend did not live to carry out this proposal. Writing on 19th August 1910, and thanking me for a number of the Parkes and Duguid photographs which I submitted to him, he says :—

It may interest you to learn that at a private séance here, on 17th inst., Mr J. Traill Taylor materialised, also my wife, my daughter, and many other friends. The Rev. Haraldiur Nielsson, of Reykjavik, Iceland, was with us, and he conversed in the Danish language with one of the materialised forms, who was known to him in his earth-life.

The Rev. Mr Nielsson visited Mr Wyllie and got a

photo, on which is the face of his uncle, the late Bishop Savinsson. This was in fulfilment of a promise. The face of the Bishop is quite distinct. Mr Nielsson has kindly given me a print of it.

The foregoing were among the last letters received from Mr Glendinning, who passed into the Higher Life in October 1910.

FIG. 12.—The original photograph of Mrs J. N. Anderson and Mrs Andrew Glendinning, and the psychic portrait of Mr and Mrs Anderson's child ; Mr David Duguid, medium.

Referring to the above photograph, Mr Andrew Glendinning, in *The Veil Lifted* (pp. 143–144), says :—

. . . Another child's portrait was got *unexpectedly* at a test séance in April 1892. The arrangements and operations were under my superintendence. I invited a lady (Mrs J. N. Anderson) to take a place near the sitter, in order to try whether her mediumistic power would aid in the experiment.

I was vexed at not getting the result I wanted, but soon I had cause for gladness in the joy which the portrait obtained brought to the hearts of the child's father and mother. The child's dress exhibits what was not known to any person outside of Mr Anderson's family. That test is of a kind to impress the mother's mind. Previous to the child's departure, he was lying cold in bed, when his mother took from a drawer a nightdress of one of her older boys and put it on the ailing child. This nightdress had a certain kind of frill round the neckband, and that nightdress, with its long frill and long sleeves, is represented in the photograph. There was no picture in existence from which the photograph could have been copied. The likeness is not only attested by the parents, but by friends of the family, and by Mr James Robertson, who had often seen the boy.

Someone may ask, How was the photograph of the child obtained, seeing he was too young to come unaided to stand before the camera? An interesting question, no doubt. To it I reply, I do not know; I am stating facts, not trying to explain.

The facts concerning the above were well known in Glasgow, where Mr and Mrs James Anderson resided. I wrote Mr Robertson, who not only sent me the original print produced above, but the statement: "This was taken in my dining-room in Glasgow, and is the portrait of Mr James Anderson's child, whom I knew. It is a good likeness."

This is one of the many well-substantiated cases obtained through Mr Duguid in the months of April and May 1892, when several sittings were held in Glasgow, under strict test conditions.

Mr J. Traill Taylor was fortunate enough to have Mr David Duguid introduced to him by Mr Andrew Glendinning, who was, in fact, one of the "two extremely hard-headed Glasgow merchants, gentlemen of commercial eminence and probity," mentioned as among the witnesses present. Mr James Robertson, of Glasgow, was another, when Mr Taylor conducted his experiments. So struck was Mr Taylor with the results of these with Mr Duguid, that he read a paper on "Spirit Photography, with Remarks on Fluorescence," before a meeting of the London and Provincial Photographic Association. The lecture, and discussion which followed, were printed in full in the *British Journal of Photography* (vol. xl., No. 1715, 17th March 1893), and afterwards in Mr Glendinning's work, *The Veil Lifted*, published in 1894.

While the paper is of deepest interest, much of it was really intended for the consideration of practical photographers, and need not be repeated here. Mr J. Traill Taylor was admittedly head of the profession in his day. He *had* investigated psychic photography with mediums, and speaking with the authority of one who *knew*, says:—

My conditions were exceedingly simple. They were that I should use my own camera and unopened packages of dry plates, purchased from dealers of repute, and that I should be excused from allowing a plate to go out of my own hand till after development, unless I felt otherwise disposed; but that, as I was to treat them as under suspicion, so must they treat me, and that every act I performed must be in presence of two witnesses; nay, that I would set a watch upon my own camera in the guise of a duplicate one of the same focus—in other words, I would use a binocular stereoscopic camera and dictate all the conditions of operation.   All this I was told was what they very strongly wished me to do, as they desired to know the truth and that only.   There were present during one or other of the evenings when the trials were made representatives of various schools of thought, including a clergyman of the Church of England; a practitioner of the healing art, who is a Fellow of two learned societies; a gentleman who graduated in the Hall of Science, in the days of the late Charles Bradlaugh; two extremely hard-headed Glasgow merchants, gentlemen of commercial eminence and probity; our host, his wife, the medium, and myself.   Dr G. was the first sitter, and, for a reason known to myself, I used a monocular camera.   I myself took the plate out of a packet just previously ripped up under the surveillance of my two detectives.   I placed the slide in my pocket, and exposed it by magnesium ribbon, which I held in my own hand, keeping one eye, as it were, on the sitter, and the other on the camera. There was no background.   I myself took the plate from the dark slide, and under the eyes of the two detectives placed it in the developing dish.   Between the camera and the sitter, a female figure was developed, rather in a more pronounced form than that of the sitter.   The lens was a portrait one of short focus; the figure, being somewhat in front of the sitter, was proportionately larger in dimensions. I do not recognise her, or any of the other figures I obtained, as being like anyone I know, and from my point of view, that of a mere investigator and experimentalist, not caring whether the psychic subject were embodied or disembodied.

Many experiments of like nature followed; on some plates were abnormal appearances; on others, none. All this time, Mr D., the medium, during the exposure of the plates, was quite inactive. If the precautions I took during all the experiments are thought to have been imperfect or incomplete, I pray of you to point them out.

The psychic figures behaved badly. Some were in focus, others not so; some were lighted from the right, while the sitter was so from the left; some were comely, others not so; some monopolised the major portion of the plate, quite obliterating the material sitters; others were as if an atrociously badly vignetted portrait, or one cut oval out of a photograph by a can-opener, or equally badly clipped out, were held up behind the sitter.

It is due to the psychic entities to say that whatever was produced on one half of the stereoscopic plates was reproduced on the other, alike good or bad in definition. But, on a careful examination of one which was rather better than the other, I deduce this fact, that the impressing of the spirit form was not consentaneous with that of the sitter. This I consider an important discovery. I carefully examined one in the stereoscope, and found that, while the two sitters were stereoscopic *per se*, the psychic figure was absolutely flat. I also found that the psychic figure was at least a millimetre higher up in one than the other. Now, as both had been simultaneously exposed, it follows to demonstration that, although both were correctly placed vertically in relation to the particular sitter behind whom the figure appeared, and not so horizontally, this figure had not only *not* been impressed on the plate simultaneously with the two gentlemen forming the group, but had not been formed by the lens at all, and that, therefore, the psychic image might be produced without a camera. I think this is a fair deduction. But still the question obtrudes: How came these figures there? I again assert that the plates were not tampered with by either myself or anyone present. Are they crystallisations of thought? Have lens and light really nothing to do with their formation? The whole subject was mysterious enough on the hypothesis of an invisible spirit, whether a thought projection or an actual spirit, being really there in the vicinity of the sitter, but it is now a thousand times more so. There are plenty of Tycho Brahes capable of supplying details of observations, but who is to be the Kepler that will from such observations evolve a law by which they can be satisfactorily explained.

I read in *The London Magazine* a statement to the effect that Mr J. Traill Taylor, shortly before he died, withdrew from the position he had taken as to spirit photography. This I am in a position to deny *in toto*. In the first place, Mr Taylor—while admitting the fact of psychic or spirit photography—never stated that the "extras" obtained were those of spirits; and, secondly, Mr Taylor was thoroughly convinced there were no errors in his experiments, and of the fact that these psychic figures came on the plates outwith the ordinary laws of photography. Both Mr Andrew Glendinning and Mr James Robertson were, among others, in touch to the last with Mr Taylor. So far from denying the genuineness of the phenomenon, he eventually became thoroughly convinced that our spirit friends did affect the plates, even to the extent of producing identifiable portraits.

With the questions raised by Mr Taylor at the conclusion of his paper I do not propose to deal. It is, however, interesting to note :—

1. Psychic pictures are obtained under scientific conditions.
2. "The psychic figures behaved badly"; in a word, looked fraudulent, were genuinely produced.
3. While Mr David Duguid was present, he had nothing whatever—photographically—to do with the results.
4. That psychic images might be produced without the camera.

THE TESTIMONY OF "EDINA"

"The gentleman who . . . was no weak-minded enthusiast, but a man of culture, trained long in criminal investigation," referred to by Mr Robertson, was no other than the late Mr Duncan Antonio, a legal luminary whose figure, for forty years, was well known in the Court of Session, Edinburgh. As "Edina," he was a frequent contributor to *Light* and other publications. His testimony to Mr Duguid's gifts and to psychic photography was of the most valuable and convincing character. With reference to obtaining the psychic photograph of his son, "Edina" says :—

It has been with considerable reluctance that I have alluded to so much that is sacred and personal in our family, but in the interests of spiritual truth, and for the sole purpose of showing that spirit photography, by an honest medium like David Duguid, is possible, I have deemed it necessary to give the facts, and they have been stated with all the care and minuteness of detail in my power. We are certainly under a deep debt of gratitude to Mr David Duguid for the beneficent use of his mediumistic powers in literally " giving us back our dead," or rather showing us our dear one, clothed as he now is, in his spiritual body, as on the other side. These are the consolations of spiritualism, which the uninstructed cannot understand or appreciate. In my humble judgment spiritualistic research should be prosecuted in the *home*, as there only results will be got of the best and purest kind. That at least has been our experience, and we gratefully acknowledge the mercies bestowed upon us.

Owing to the standing of the writer, I give the above. I have been privileged to see the psychic photograph of this child alluded to. I regret I did not succeed in getting permission to produce it in this work.

The Puzzling Reproduction called the " Cyprian Priestess "

Many were the pictures obtained of this lady, of whom two photographs have already been given. I produce two more, which a tyro in psychic photography would denounce as fraudulent. Before giving " Edina's " evidence (summarised from pp. 439–463, *Light*, vol. xvi.), I wish to state that this gentleman (who was an expert amateur photographer) and a friend, Mr G., an accomplished photographer, who is not to be confounded with the late Mr Glendinning,

three years after the conclusive tests of Mr J. Traill
Taylor, had a series of test sittings with Mr Duguid
in May 1896.   The test procedure was simply effective.
The plates were purchased in Edinburgh by Mr G.,
who there loaded his camera with twelve plates.
These were brought to Glasgow, and except when
Mr Duguid was asked to take off the cap and make
an exposure, the same was untouched by him. *The
camera was never for a moment out of sight while
the experiments were conducted.* The plates (with
the camera) were taken back to Edinburgh and
developed there.   Concerning the results, some plates
revealed nothing, but on three were distinct " extras,"
one being Mr G.'s brother Alexander, who had already
shown himself to his surviving brother, at Cecil Husk's,
in Peckham ; one of an old lady, identified by a lady
in Edinburgh as her mother; and the third was the
reproduction of a female, similar to one obtained three
years previously.   This séance thus gave two identifiable portraits and one replica.

At the test séance held in June, Mr G.'s brother
Alexander came again, and the portraits of a military
man and of two females unknown.   I wish to
emphasise that neither Mr nor Mrs Duguid, who
were present, saw or handled the plates, which were
developed in Edinburgh and prints taken off them
there.

At further test sittings, held in July 1896, with
similar precautions by these honourable men, Mr David
Duguid, Mrs Duguid, and a niece of Mrs Duguid were

present.   Sometimes G., Mrs Duguid, and her niece sat as subjects.   The plates were brought from Edinburgh,

Fig. 13.—Photograph of Mrs Duguid, and psychic photograph of the so-called "Cyprian Priestess."

and taken back there for development.   Neither Mr nor Mrs Duguid nor the niece saw or handled them.
What were the results ?

The first psychic photograph was that of the so-called "Cyprian Priestess" (see figs. 10, 11, 13, 14). Although the face is distinct, the drapery is different from that in former photographs, but reveals, in quite a natural position, a plump hand and arm held across

Fig. 14.—Photograph of the foregoing "Cyprian Priestess" magnified, showing the inartistic joining of the head to the body.

the lower portion of the chest. On another plate of Mrs Duguid's trio, there was a reproduction of a spirit face obtained by Mr G. four years before. Of the three plates where Mr G. was the sitter, one was blank. On one was found the "Cyprian Priestess," and on

the third the face and form of a lady clad in modern
costume. She stood by Mr G.'s side, clasping his arm.

I have called the "Cyprian Priestess" a reproduction, for whether, as represented, it is the photograph
of a spirit who manifested in the Duguid circles or
not, one thing is now clear, that before this photograph
was obtained there was in the possession of Mr Brodie
Innes, an Edinburgh solicitor, a photograph of a
German picture called "Night." The discovery was
made, I believe, by Madame de Steiger, F.T.S. Upon
examination, the face and head in "Night" and on
Mr Duguid's photographs and psychographs were
found to be identical. Great publicity was given
to the matter at the time, and five, among other,
things are clear :—

1. Mr Brodie Innes, W.S., was not a spiritualist,
   and Mr Duguid neither knew of nor ever had
   access to the portrait.
2. With all the publicity in *Light* and *Borderland*,
   which raged for several years, and search in
   Great Britain and Germany, neither the original
   painting nor a copy of it has been obtained.
3. Under the strictest test conditions, both photographs and psychographs of this reproduction
   have been obtained by experts, including Mr
   J. T. Taylor.
4. To the very last, Mr David Duguid believed in
   her reality as a spirit, and those most familiar
   with the Hafed and other circles were impressed
   by the story that in earth-life she was dedicated

to the Temple of Venus in Cyprus.   I cannot recall when she was called the "Cyprian Priestess,"
but this name was given to her by the habitués
of Duguid's circles.

5. The critical investigators, even those who were
   non-spiritualistic, upon a crucial examination
   of the whole circumstances, acquitted Duguid of
   dishonest procedure.

Mr A. J. Riko, editor of *The Sphinx*, The Hague
(who at one time made a thorough study of these productions, wrote a critical article and severe condemnation of them), sent Mr W. T. Stead the following *amende*
(which appeared in *Borderland*, p. 179, vol. iv.):—

Your readers remember my article on " The Cyprian
Priestess." . . . I need not say that I wrote so in perfect good faith, as I do now.   Well, I have since then
followed with attention all that has been written on
the same subject by my old acquaintance, Mr Glendinning, by " Edina " and others, and I frankly confess
that my suspicions are greatly shaken, and that now
I admit also the most perfect honesty at least of the
operators on this side, Mr Duguid and consorts.   On
the other side there remains, however, still, I will not
say fraud, but an amount of mystery in relation to
that perfect beauty of the " Priestess, whom I offer my
homage."

THE HAGUE, HOLLAND,
      February 1897.

I have given this as the most striking and inexplicable case of reproduction in the history of spirit
photography.   It is another illustration that spirit
photographs are not necessarily photographs of spirits.

Mr W. T. Stead and his son, Mr William Stead, experimented with Mr Duguid later on, but in a very hurried manner. The results were neither of a test character nor conclusive. With Mr Duguid's stereoscopic camera and magnetised plates, Mr William Stead developed one plate and Mr Duguid the other. A female form was obtained. This was submitted to Mr J. Traill Taylor, who said :—

The figure of the female was not, as on some spirit photographs, the result of photographing a plane surface. The photograph indicated the existence of a body with sufficient substance to indicate rotundity and solidity. The pictures were stereoscopically correct.

Attempts made by Mr William Stead to get psychic pictures with his Frena kodak failed. Notwithstanding this, Mr Stead says :—

I know that Mr Duguid is a thoroughly honest man. It was my own fault that the photograph was not taken with my own plates. Mr Duguid assented to my conditions, and was annoyed that I had no time to carry out test experiments. It was only at my suggestion and with much reluctance he consented to use the only two plates of his own which he had left in the house.

Had Mr Stead brought plates and been able to give a few days to these experiments, so as to place himself in touch and sympathy with the medium and his surroundings—as Mr Taylor, Mr Glendinning, and "Edina" had done—no doubt better results would have been obtained.

I have frequently come into contact with Mr Duguid, and also with many who were familiar with the man and his varied gifts of mediumship. I had evidence of his psychic powers in having photographic plates impressed while in his hands, the experiments being carried out in Glenbeg House. The plates were bought by me from Mr Jamieson, chemist, Rothesay, wrapped up in pairs, film to film, as taken out of original packet, and after they were held, I took them away and had them developed for me by Mr Howie, photographer, Rothesay. All the plates held presented indications of the abnormal—but not due to light. On two of these plates were portraits, one a positive and the other a negative. One of the faces I knew, but the history is not of sufficient importance to have a half-tone produced for these pages. Other plates were held by friends, while Mr Duguid was present. He had nothing to do with the plates. On one pair, held by Mrs Coates and Mr Auld, there was a long message written on the plates. This was in accord with a message which Mr Auld had received some three months previously to making our acquaintance. Unfortunately, the plates taken under the above circumstances were accidentally broken by Mr Howie, photographer. Upon plates held by Mrs Coates and Mr Duguid there were two imperfect forms, one said to represent "Silver Eagle," a Blackfoot Indian, who was one of Mr Duguid's controls, and the other that of the late Professor Blackie, whom I knew personally. The psychic impressions were valueless from an identification standpoint, *but from the standard of test and scientific inquiry, most valuable.* We had in our home many other such experiments, but never had anything like the results obtained with Mr Duguid, when that gentleman and his good lady were our guests at Glenbeg House. I may say, in passing, that the experiments with Mr Duguid were suggested by me, and the matter was spontaneously entered upon. There was no pre-arrangement. That Mr Duguid was a medium —among other things—for psychic photography I can endorse. I think, however, that the testimony of Mr Traill Taylor, Mr Andrew Glendinning, "Edina" (the late Mr Duncan Antonio), Mr W. T. Stead, and Mr James Robertson, a group of shrewd, independent investigators, is much more important than anything which I can advance myself.

THE late Mr R. Boursnell, who passed away in December 1909, and who had been taking psychic photographs in London for about twenty years, was the last of the British professional mediums to do so. He was not a cultured man, and as a photographer did not rank higher than Hudson, but as a psychic he was a man of many gifts. No man has been more discussed, and certainly none have been able to give consolation to thousands more than he. With the materials at my disposal, I should be compelled to issue another book to place the facts and the controversies before the public. I, however, confine myself to a few cases, out of many, given me by correspondents and friends upon whom I can rely, and introduce some facts as they relate to myself.

It appears that, before Mumler got his first picture in 1861, Mr Boursnell got curious appearances on his plates, not only spoiling them, but leading to disagreements with his employer, who accused him of not cleaning the glass properly. These splotches came at intervals. For a long time there was a lull. Boursnell was a medium; that was the trouble. He was influenced by one "Tulip." I do not know who "Tulip" is or was, but I do know that her picture frequently came on the plates, and that under test conditions.

Mr H. Blackwell, a first-class amateur photographer, had over fifty sittings with Mr Boursnell, and frequently brought his own plates, marked them, filled the *single slide*, and developed each plate after exposure, invariably getting something. Not a few of these were identifiable portraits. I also know that many others did so. Reproductions and duplications were common, and threw unmerited suspicion on Boursnell's work, especially from spiritualists and others ignorant of the elementary facts of psychic photography. One day Mr Boursnell informed Mr Blackwell: "There is an old gentleman here who says you have a painting of him at home in your dining-room, near a bookcase." Mr Blackwell sat, and obtained a capital likeness of his grandfather, wearing the white stock as in the portrait at home, the photograph not being that of a spirit, but of the figure in the old oil-painting. Another feature of his mediumship was that many departed ones were either described by Mr Boursnell or by some clairvoyant prior to exposure and development of the plate. The descriptions were sometimes accompanied by the name of the original of the "extra."

In reply to me, Mr H. Blackwell was good enough to send me a number of cases, but of those sent I select the following as being specially interesting:—

LONDON, 9/10/09.

DEAR MR COATES,—In August 1901, at a sitting in Glasgow with Mrs Stevenson, to whom I was a complete stranger, the medium said: " First comes to you a little girl with blue-grey eyes. She has on a light holland dress, trimmed with braid, a kind of belt, and little shoes. She says she will show to you like that when you get back to London." Then followed other

2   1   3

FIG. 15.—1. Photo of little Louie taken in life at four years of age. 2. Psychic picture taken in 1902. 3. Another psychic photo taken with her mother in 1903. Copies of the originals by Mr H. Blackwell.

descriptions which proved quite accurate. Soon after my return to London I had a sitting with Mr R. Boursnell, taking my own plates and, being an amateur photographer, assisting in the development. A clairvoyant who accompanied me saw a little girl posing for her picture, and the plate when developed showed that my niece had kept the promise given in Glasgow. The dress and sash were remembered by her mother, with whom she has since been photographed (3, fig. 15).   About fourteen months later I was again at Mr Boursnell's, accompanied by a lady who is a fine clairvoyant.   She noticed a little girl holding out her hand to me, and this was endorsed a moment later by Mr Boursnell, who, on entering the room, said: "Why, there is your little niece, and she is holding out her hand to you.   Be quite still and we'll try to take her."

This photograph (2, fig. 15) is an extraordinary one, as she has come in the same dress as before, with the folds only slightly altered, but the position of the arms and hands is quite different.   This was on one of my marked plates, and I assisted in the development.   She has been taken with me on several other occasions, and has materialised both in London and New York through four different mediums.   The only portrait taken of her when in earth-life, about this age, is reproduced; the next one was about six years later. This is but one of the many instances known to me where the spirit friends have redeemed their promises, made in some cases thousands of miles distant, through the wonderful gift possessed by Mr Boursnell.   His work is known in all parts of the world, and has been of immense value in introducing and proving the truths of spiritualism.   H. BLACKWELL.

Although I withhold Mr H. Blackwell's London address and the mother's address from publicity, they can be obtained privately.   I am much indebted to this gentleman for the amount of valuable information placed at my disposal during the last three years, and for lending me out of his large private collection so many spirit photographs.   Of that collection I prize most those of his niece, and have reproduced two of them.   No man living is in a better position to testify to Mr Boursnell's *bona-fides* than he. Some of the most interesting cases I have to withhold, since, as Mr Blackwell says in his letter dated London, 9/7/09, "it is very difficult to get people to allow their photographs and names to be published." I know this to be too true. Therefore I appreciate Mr Blackwell's photographs and testimony all the more.

Mr A. W. Jones, in his account of the photograph, fig. 16, says :—

LONDON, 10*th October* 1909.

In January 1904, through the introduction of a friend, I went with my wife to the well-known spirit photographer, Mr R. Boursnell, for the purpose of getting a spirit photograph. We arrived at the house at 12.30 p.m., and were invited into a front parlour and sat down and chatted for a few minutes with the photographer, who was advanced in years, but a very genial old gentleman. Then, with but little arrangement, he proceeded to take a photo of my wife After exposing and developing three plates, he said that there appeared something on the negative, and that he would send prints of same in a few days. My wife had quite decided in her mind that if a spirit photo was obtained it would, of course, be that of her mother, who had passed over a few years previously, and of whom she thought a great deal.

Upon returning from business a few evenings later, my wife said to me: "The photos have come, and my mother's portrait is not upon them, but a man's face." Her disappointment was great, and I just glanced at the photo and then threw it aside. Later in the evening, whilst my wife was out, I took up the photo, and was examining it closely when my wife returned;

and as soon as she came into the house she said to me :
" Do you know that whilst walking along a sudden
impression came to me" (she is highly sensitive) "that

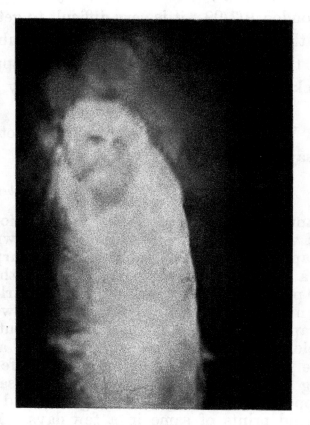

Fig. 16.—The photograph of Mr A. W. Jones, who is cut
out of the print, and the psychic picture of his father.
(I have seen two other photographs of this spirit-form
in imperfect states of development, as if the same
were being photographed in the process of building
up before the camera. I have produced the one
identified, sent by Mr Blackwell.)

the photo of the man is that of your father." Now,
my father had been dead forty-five years, and I was
about eight years of age at the time of his death, so
that my recollection of him was not vivid, but upon

looking closely at the photo, I was able to recognise the likeness.

Having two brothers and three sisters older than I am, I decided to put the photo before them and hear what they had to say. My eldest sister calling upon us a few days later, was told by my wife that she had got a spirit photo, but that she was disappointed, as it was not that of her mother, but the photo of a man whom she did not recognise. Thereupon she showed the photo to my sister, who immediately said : " Why, Jessie, that's a portrait of my father; wherever did you get it from ? " She was most startled at the great likeness, as she knew that my father had never been photographed in his life, and she did not believe in spiritualism.

Not being at home at the time of this visit, I was at home when she called again, and our conversation turned upon the photo, and I then asked her to take a good look at it, and if she had any doubt about it, I begged she would express it, and revoke her previous decision. She then said : " The more I look at it, the more convinced I am that it is the portrait of my father." Now, this lady is a most sceptical individual, especially with respect to the existence of spirits, and is of such a practical nature that she fails to see the use of spirits returning, even if it were her own husband, unless he was able to pay her rent and other incidental expenses.

One of my brothers and the other two sisters also considered it a striking likeness of my father.

A. W. JONES.

Mr Jones's present address is 29 Parkhurst Road, Holloway, London, N., he having removed to it since the foregoing account was written. This gentleman and his good lady knew little Louie well, as only those familiar with the child from earliest days could.

Mr Blackwell, in sending me the next photo, says: "I had pleasure later in the same year of giving a copy of it to a Presbyterian minister in Newfoundland, who was delighted to receive a spirit portrait

FIG. 17.—This photograph of Mr H. Blackwell and the late Professor Blackie was taken by Mr Boursnell on 21st May 1901, but was not recognised at the time by either Mr Blackwell or Mr Boursnell.

of his old Professor. It may have been given for that purpose." As Dr Wyld, Professor Blackie's brother-in-law, was one of my oldest correspondents, not only in psychic matters, but on hygiene and smoke abatement, over twenty-five years ago, and as Professor Blackie himself had been an esteemed guest of ours when we resided in Crosshill, Glasgow, the photograph possesses for us a double interest. Possibly to Scotchmen at home and abroad the portrait of this virile and truly noble, if somewhat eccentric, scholar may be of interest too, and for that purpose I add it to my collection.

I give with pleasure the testimony of Mr Elliott, London and Trinidad, who believes with the poet Whittier—

> I have friends in Spirit-land,
> Not shadows in a shadowy band,
> Not others, but themselves are they.

This gentleman, who paid me a visit in November 1910, prior to his return to Trinidad, told me of his experiences in spirit photography. During a visit to England he had a sitting, on the 3rd of March 1903, with Mr Boursnell. When he saw the plate—which was developed immediately after exposure—it had, in addition to himself, the spirit form of a female friend. Two days later he went to a séance—Mr Husk's — during which several faces came and were recognised by the sitters. Three came to him. The first was that of his father; the second he did not know; and the third was the psychic face of the original of the photograph. "I knew her at once," he said, and added: "Mr Boursnell did not know, and I did not know either, that I should be at this séance. At this time the photographs were not printed."

About a week later, *i.e.* 12th March 1903, he went again. This time he had the photograph of this spirit friend in his pocket, a fact only known to himself. There were the usual phenomena. Several new faces came and were recognised by the sitters. Two—whom he recognised on the first occasion—came to him. One of those was his friend of the photograph. For several minutes they conversed together, and he had ample opportunity of examining her features, which were also seen by several persons present. After the sitting was over, he showed the photograph to these, and all immediately recognised the (materialised) face from the photograph. As links in the chain of evidence, one is that of obtaining a spirit form of a female on a photograph; of obtaining a written description of her on the same day by automatic writing; of seeing the original—in materialised form—twice in subsequent séances, and having the spirit identified by several other persons, from the photograph which he had in his pocket. He was so convinced that he sent a full account (with a copy of the photograph) to *Light*. He had several other photographs taken by Mr Boursnell—one of which was that of his own father—and these he took with him to Port of Spain.

He left England to resume his duties in Trinidad, and for some months thereafter—for reasons I can well appreciate—he said nothing about these photographs. On showing them to some friends, one was recognised by Miss Cathie M'Kay as that of an intimate acquaintance, not only of herself, but of Mr Learmond's family, in Demerara, where she had resided. The original of the psychic picture had not only passed away four years previously, but had since frequently controlled a member of Mr Learmond's household. Miss M'Kay sent a copy of the photograph to Demerara, and Mr Elliott saw the reply, stating that they all recognised " Pat's " picture, before they read her letter which accompanied it.

It is interesting to note—taking for granted that the statements of this clear-headed gentleman are correct — that Mr Boursnell, about four thousand miles away, produced an identifiable photograph of a departed who had lived and died in Demerara, and of whom the sitter had no knowledge. Mr Elliott was a stranger to Mr Boursnell. This psychic picture might to this day have been marked " unrecognised," had Mr Elliott not taken it to Trinidad. Acting on the information given me, I looked up the file of *Light*, and found that Miss Cathie M'Kay, 70 Oxford Street, Trinidad, Port of Spain, in her letter dated 8th April 1904, certifies to the photograph, adding :—

He had always promised us his photo, but we did not know at what time or place he would " sit." We are all very pleased to have the photo, and will always treasure it as a precious souvenir.

Owing to Mr Elliott's official position, I have not given his designation and address, but these can be supplied, if desired.

THE REPRODUCTIONS PUZZLE

By *reproductions* I mean pictures of material objects produced by psychic or occult processes.

I am indebted to Mrs Annie Bright, the able editor of *The Harbinger of Light* (Melbourne, Australia), for this interesting case of *reproduction*, and the cuts which illustrate it.

Mr F. C. Barnes, a well-known business man of Brisbane, Australia, had occasion to visit London, and availed himself of the opportunity to investigate spiritualism, and therewith spirit photography. We learn that in the year 1908 a friend lent him *The Martyrdom of an Empress*. This book deals with the life and assassination of the Empress of Austria. The frontispiece is a portrait of this beautiful woman. Mr Barnes *often thought of this picture and the Empress*, after he returned the book. He says:—

Before I left Brisbane, my wife, speaking through a medium, told me to go to England to a spirit photographer, and she would try to reflect herself.

When in London, I went to Mr Boursnell. . . . As he was old and had given up practice, it was with much difficulty that I persuaded him to give me a sitting. Two others were present at the first sitting, which took place in an ordinary drawing-room, with two windows. Behind me was a wall covered with a black cloth as a background. Mr Boursnell said: "There is a spirit of a beautiful lady here, who seems in a very bright light, and suffered greatly on earth." I concluded at once that it was my wife, and on receipt of the proofs was greatly disappointed to find it was not. I asked those present if they could recognise it.

"No," said the lady, "but it looks like royalty." This was inexplicable. Then the impression came to me that it might be the Empress of Austria.

FIG. 18.—Portrait of Elizabeth, the Empress of Austria.

On arriving at this conclusion, Mr Barnes took the trouble to get several books, in the hope of getting a portrait of her. He also ordered a copy of the book

which he had read in Brisbane, from *The Times* Book
Club.   On comparison, it is clear that the spirit photo
was a reproduction of the portrait in the frontispiece
referred to.

Fig. 19.—Photograph of Mr Barnes, and the psychic *reproduction* of a
portrait of the Empress Elizabeth of Austria.

Mrs Bright, commenting on the case, says :—

The most surprising thing to myself, and which
opens a large subject as to reflected thought forms,
is the absolute identity of the spirit photo with the
one in the book, even the cross worn there. . . . In

the late Mr E. G. Bennett's valuable book, *The Direct Phenomena of Spiritualism*, he gives side by side illustrations to *Hafed, Prince of Persia*, given under the mediumship of David Duguid, as " Direct Spirit Drawings," and copies of almost identical pictures from *Cassell's Family Bible*. This caused a great stir at the time, and caused the withdrawal of the first edition of *Hafed*. It does not necessarily show that David Duguid's mediumship was fraudulent, *but simply that we do not know how the image of a picture may be retained in the mind, and reproduced, unknown to the medium.*[1]

Mr Duguid had probably seen the illustrations, and they would naturally impress his mind. This is the direction in which modern scientific research is tending. The "facts" are accepted. Our task lies in the future in their interpretation. . . . It may be mentioned that at a second sitting with Mr Boursnell, when Mr Barnes was accompanied by two of his children, a remarkable series of spirit photographs were produced, including those of his wife and sister.

In the experiences recorded of Mr Barnes, a shrewd, energetic Antipodean, we glean that the intelligent operators in the invisible, working within the mediumistic aura of the late Mr Boursnell, and that of his sitter, evidently reproduced a face which they found easiest to secure, and having succeeded, were then able at the next sitting, when Mr Barnes brought his two children (making still more favourable conditions) to give him the photograph of his late wife, and thus redeem the promise made to him by her before he left Australia. *The power by which* the reproduction of the Empress's portrait was made, was

[1] Italics are mine.—J. C.

also *the power by which* Mr Barnes was enabled to get the identifiable photographs of his wife and sister. That is the central fact.   It was singularly appropriate that the reproduction of the Empress should be given to the one man who had such a special interest in her life.

The conclusion appears to be this—that we have as much evidence for the psychical reality in the *reproduction*—which is not the photograph of a spirit but of an earthly object—as we have in the identifiable portraits of the departed produced by similar or psychical means.

THE SPIRIT PHOTO OF PIET BOTHA

Mr W. T. Stead's article, "How I know the Dead Return," in *The Fortnightly Review* (January 1909), bears testimony to some interesting facts in the author's experience as to spirit return and spirit photography.   He tells—among other cases—how he obtained the photograph of Piet Botha; the description of the fierce-looking old Boer, the name, etc., all of which were given to Mr Stead by Mr Boursnell, before the exposure of the plate.   Mr Stead knew several Bothas, but none of the name of Piet.   The medium was doggedly firm, and insisted, "That's what he says," meaning the name given by the spirit. Mr Stead kept the matter to himself till the conference held in London after the South African War. The photograph was sent to General Botha, and it was recognised by a relative and several of the late commandant's confrères.

FIG. 20.—The photograph of Mr W. T. Stead, and the psychic picture of Piet Botha, taken by Mr Boursnell in 1902.   The above is my copy of the much-handled original in Mr Stead's possession.

The statements made by Mr Stead in *The Fortnightly Review* were not long unchallenged. Mr J. N. Maskelyne, of Egyptian Hall fame, did so in a journal called *The Magic Mirror*. The redoubtable Dr Andrew Wilson rescued Mr Maskelyne's criticism from obscurity. To be perfectly fair, I quote the exact words. Both Maskelyne and Wilson have the usual qualifications of "experts." They possess no knowledge whatever of the subject, but make up for this with abundant animus. Neither of these qualifications is helpful in scientific research, nor do they justify confidence in their conclusions. Dr Wilson, in the *Illustrated London News* (5th March 1909), says :—

With Mr Stead Mr Maskelyne deals very effectively. One of the series of spirit photographs was claimed by Mr Stead to be that of Piet Botha, a Boer commandant killed in the war. It was alleged that no one has had access to a real portrait of Piet Botha, Mr Stead saying that "no one in England, so far as I have been able to ascertain, knew that any Piet Botha ever existed." Critically regarded, Mr Stead's spirit-photograph was obviously a reproduction, not a direct, photograph. Mr Maskelyne states that Botha was killed at the siege of Kimberley, on October 24, 1899. Four days later the news of his death arrived in England, and on October 28 the *Daily Graphic* published a portrait of the deceased. The value of Mr Stead's assertion regarding the impossibility of a photograph having existed, and that nobody knew of Botha's existence in England, may be judged from the foregoing details, and also from the fact that, as Piet Botha was one of the first Boer commandants slain in the war, his name and identity were made familiar to the whole world.

This great authority modestly adds :—

I have often urged the extreme importance of every statement made regarding occult matters, from dreams and apparitions to spirit photography, being thoroughly tested by the rules of ordinary and expert evidence. *Few of us have the opportunity to undertake such a task,* but when it has been accomplished the result is invariably the same—the relegation of the marvellous to the domain of the commonplace or that of fraud. [Italics are mine.—J. C.]

I wrote Mr Stead in March 1910, calling his attention to the Wilson-cum-Maskelyne explanations (?), and asking for a reply, which I now submit in full :—

BANK BUILDINGS,
KINGSWAY, LONDON, W C.,
16th *March* 1910.

DEAR MR COATES,—You ask me for my testimony about spirit photography, especially the photograph of my late friend Mr Boursnell. What I have to say is very brief, but I hope it is to the point. I have always in discussing the question of spirit photography admitted more than is necessary to the adversary for the sake of argument. I say I am quite willing to admit, if they like, always for the sake of argument, that it is absolutely impossible to prevent a clever photographer, who is also a skilful conjurer, producing faked photographs which have the appearance of spirit pictures. I am also willing to admit, although it is quite contrary to reasonable commonsense, that even if you take your own plates, place them yourself in the camera, and afterwards develop them yourself, without allowing a photographer to have any access to them, it is still possible that the spirit picture which appears on the negative may be the result of fraud.   But when all that is said and done, my faith in the reality of some spirit photographs is invincible, and for this reason.   Fraud can do many things, conjurers can deceive the eye of the most vigilant observer, but there are limits to fraud and conjuring, and this limit is reached when a photographer is confronted without notice by a sitter, who asks him to take a photograph and produce the portrait of a deceased friend or relative on the same plate.   The photographer has no means of knowing whether the relative desired is a man or woman, adult or child. If in these circumstances the photographer can then and there produce an authentic portrait of the spirit form of the deceased friend or relative of his unknown sitter, then I say that such occurrences cannot be explained by any conceivable hypothesis of fraud or conjuring.

Such spirit photographs have repeatedly been reproduced by Mr Boursnell, and the portraits of the spirit people have been so clear and unmistakable as to be instantly recognised by the sitter.   The ablest conjurer in the world may safely be challenged to produce such likenesses with his own camera in his room, when he has had ample notice and been afforded every facility for using the tricks of his trade, but he cannot do it.   Mr Boursnell did do it.   Hence, whatever may be said about many of the pictures of Mr Boursnell which were not recognised, there remains a sufficient number of those which were instantly recognised to entirely preclude the notion that spirits cannot be photographed, or that Mr Boursnell did not photograph them.

The story of the Piet Botha photograph is well known.   When I went to sit with Mr Boursnell I did not know that Piet Botha was dead.   He appeared much to Mr Boursnell's surprise in the studio, was photographed standing behind me, and when asked by ·

Mr Boursnell, at my suggestion, what was his name, he said it was Piet Botha. Subsequent research proved that a Botha, whose name was not given as Piet, had been killed at an early period of the Boer War. A portrait of this Botha had been published in a London illustrated paper. It bore not the least resemblance to the Piet Botha on the Boursnell picture. I kept the print until the end of the war, and then submitted it to the Boer delegates who came to London after peace had been made. It was instantly recognised as a striking likeness of Commandant Pietrus Johannes Botha, who was the first Boer commandant killed at the siege of Kimberley. It was recognised by his own relative, one of the Free State delegates, and by others who had served with him during the war. At the time the portrait appeared on the plate, and as far as I know, up to the the present time, no photograph of the living man has been seen in London. I was not expecting any such picture, and his relatives were furious at the appearance of his portrait in the background of my portrait. They did not believe in spiritualism, and they said it must have been produced by some fraud, but they did not dispute the authenticity of the likeness, nor could they dispute the accuracy of my statement as to how it had been procured.

There is much that can be said on this subject, but I forbear.—Yours sincerely,   W. T. STEAD.

That the psychic portrait of Piet Botha was not a reproduction of the one which appeared in the *Daily Graphic* (28th October 1899) is clearly seen by placing the two photographs together, a method which might have occurred to gentlemen accustomed to test reported facts " by the rules of ordinary and expert evidence." Possibly, as these experts did not want "the opportunity to undertake such a task," they assumed, conjectured, and decided what they thought must be the case, in the absence of evidence. Had the portraits been produced side by side, it would have been seen there was no resemblance between the two to stamp the Boursnell photo "a reproduction." Had it been, however, that would not prove it to be fraudulent, as in scientific investigation of spirit photography we are perfectly familiar with reproductions, duplications, and other puzzles; and we can testify to their genuineness.

Since the receipt of Mr Stead's letter, another Solomon has come to judgment in the person of Mr Wm. Marriott. In his article on "Spirit Photographs," in *Pearson's Magazine* (August 1910), he is much more interesting than Maskelyne, and writes a better article than Dr Wilson. He is "an expert," for, whatever qualifications he possesses, he is quite pleased with himself, and says:—

The famous spirit photograph of Piet Botha, taken during the Boer War, was recognised by those who knew him in South Africa. This seems curious at first sight, but the mystery vanishes on consideration. Piet Botha was recognised, *after his death*, in Boursnell's picture. A glance will show that this might be due to imagination, as the spirit face is exceedingly fuzzy and indistinct. But let us go a step further. The spirit face does bear a striking resemblance to the face of Boursnell himself.

Mr Marriott gives his readers the benefit of his gifts as a conjurer, and illustrates his article with a very

" fuzzy and indistinct " face of the Boer general—in
no way like the original photograph—and then produces an equally indistinct face of Boursnell, adorned
with a false beard, and the addition of some drapery,
by which he assumed Mr Boursnell was enabled
to convert himself into a tolerable likeness of Piet
Botha :—

" My strong suggestion is that this was, in effect,
Boursnell's method in this case."

If Mr Maskelyne was right in asserting that this
Boursnell photograph of Piet Botha was a reproduction of a *Daily Graphic* print, then Mr Marriott
is wrong in his " strong suggestion."   Before accepting
Marriott's " fuzzy and very indistinct " pictures, and
equally lucid explanations, it would have been
better had these two eminent conjurers and experts
compared notes before sending their articles to the
press.

Mr Marriott's luminous remark that " Piet Botha
was recognised, after his death, in Boursnell's picture,"
is very subtle and mysterious, and worthy of " an
expert."   But having no sense whatever in it, it
may be taken as a fair specimen of the conjectures and
inanities by means of which this writer exposes—
himself.

The spirit photograph was recognised by the
personal friends and by a relative of the late Boer
general, who could not be deceived by a " fuzzy and
indistinct " faked picture of Boursnell, not even if

they were presented with it, backed by **Mr Marriott's** "strong suggestion." These men were in a better position than anyone else to recognise Piet Botha *after his death*, seeing they *knew him in life*. Neither Maskelyne, Marriott, poor Boursnell, nor his intrepid defender, **Mr W. T. Stead**, possessed that knowledge. *To suppress the truth and suggest that which is false*, has ever been " the guiding rules of ordinary and expert evidence " of the Cagliostros of the stage. In this case, Marriott's evidence (?) breaks down under cross-examination.

I sent the foregoing account to **Mr E. W. Wallis**, author and journalist, who (like **Mr Stead** and a host of others) knew **Mr Boursnell** well. Commenting, in *Light*, **Mr Wallis** says :—

The two suggested identifications would destroy one another even if both were not equally fantastic. Again, portraits can be converted almost *ad lib.*; and we are no more likely to see the features of Mr Boursnell in the "fuzzy and indistinct" photograph of Marriott's alleged concoction than we can in the other much more definite and striking face of Piet Botha, in the print sent us by Mr Coates. The recognition of the deceased commandant by his relative and friends in a photograph obtained by a process which they designated as "superstitious," and apparently regarded with the utmost distrust, is a proof of identity which it will need much more than the "strong suggestions" and suppositions of the Maskelynes and Marriotts to overthrow. The whole attitude of the Free State delegates, as described by Mr Stead, was that of men who were forced to admit the fact of identity in spite of their own strong religious presuppositions as to the impossibility of any such photograph being taken in England.

We do not see that anybody can go behind such testimony, as it is not that of persons predisposed in favour of spiritualism.

I will conclude by pointing out that Mr W. T. Stead's account of the Piet Botha spirit picture, and his published interviews with Mr Fischer, Mr Wessels —Piet Botha's relative—and the other Free Staters, have now been before them for several years, and none of these gentlemen have denied the identity of the original in the photograph, or repudiated the statements which they are said to have made.   I have taken some trouble to get at the facts.   This is my case.

CHAPTER VI

MR R. BOURSNELL'S MEDIUMSHIP—*continued*

MR ROBERTSON, in his testimony to the facts of spirit photography and the genuineness of Mr Boursnell's mediumship, wrote me (5th August 1910) to the following effect :—

When Mr Stead, in the pages of *Borderland,* began to write about the work of Mr Boursnell, I was deeply interested, as was also Mr Duguid. As usual, a large amount of criticism of the usual snarling kind followed Boursnell. I first saw him after a series of cruel stabs, the majority of which came from those who had not studied the mysteries of mediumship; those who ever look for fraud, and at once assert that "honesty and truth do not belong to the persons with medial gifts." I took with me on that occasion a packet of marked plates. (Though my feeling is that all this careful testing rarely brings satisfaction to the mind. Better to go in the spirit of trust and await results. If what is obtained lacks something in the nature of a crucial test, then wait till something which gets beyond all possible tests is presented.) Mr Boursnell had been so oppressed by the burden of assaults made upon him, that he declined my request to experiment with my plates. I did not feel in the least annoyed. I recognised how readily the sensitive can be affected by the thoughts of others, and sat chatting with him for an hour or so. He evidently felt that I was an honest truth-seeker, with some ideas of what the conditions of mediumship required, because he said at parting that if I came the next day he would try and meet me. I weighed the man up, and felt convinced that he belonged to the great group of in-

Fig. 21.—Photograph of Mr James Robertson, and the psychic portrait of the late Mr John Lamont, Liverpool, who was an ardent spiritualist, and a lifelong friend of the author.

struments I had met with, men and women who could not explain themselves, but only knew that certain phenomena transpired in their presence. I was out the next morning, with my marked plates, and was rewarded to the full, some five forms appearing on the six plates I had brought. I did not recognise any of the figures, but there was much evidence of a collective kind which followed the showing of the pictures, which I need not particularise. I was given the fullest opportunity to follow all the processes, including development, and seeing the full results; but all this is of little value to those who have a bias against the honesty of mediums. The test has to transcend all observation of sitters. I have seen several hundreds of the Boursnell pictures. I have had strong assertions of men, clear-headed, scientific in the best sense, who vouched that amongst these were the veritable portraits of their deceased friends. Men and women in position do not care about associating their names with a subject which the world has not come in line with, hence I cannot use their names. All over the country I have been shown pictures which had brought cheer to the hearts of those who got them. Year after year they were turned out, and though the same psychic form might be seen on the plates of different persons, yet there were hundreds, nay, thousands, quite original.

The picture (fig. 21) of John Lamont, of Liverpool, a man loved and admired in the ranks of spiritualists, appeared on a plate beside me at one of my sittings, when Mr Boursnell said: "This man says he is going to be with you when you lecture to-night." I scarcely think the remark had any impression upon me, as I had no thought it would be corroborated. The next day I called upon a well-known medium, Mrs Manks, who said at once, when I came into her presence: "I see a man who gives the name of John Lamont. Why," she said, "I saw this man standing by your side last night while you were speaking!"

Mr James Robertson, writing to me at my request, says:—

The case of Janie Dewar, whom I knew well in the body, is one of those authentic bits of evidence revealing identity from which there is no getting away. There she is (fig. 22) by her brother, the veritable form that I had followed to the grave years before.

Fɪɢ. 22.—The photograph of Mr John Dewar, Glasgow, and the psychic portrait of his sister Janie.[1]

[1] "Mr John Dewar, junior, went to Mr Boursnell's, hoping to get a picture of his mother, but received instead a good portrait of his deceased sister Janie.   Last month Janie materialised at my family séance, stood beside me and kissed me.   I went twice with Mr Dewar to Boursnell's, Mr Dewar taking his own plates with him.   Mr Boursnell invited Mr Dewar to examine the camera and also invited us both into the dark-room, and requested Mr Dewar to put the plates in the slides.   After exposure of the plates in the camera, Mr Boursnell asked Mr Dewar to take the slides to the dark-room, to remove the plates and to develop them.   I was with

However often I look at it and recall the features, there comes with greater force and conviction that this girl (from the knowledge of spiritualism received on earth) used her opportunity, after the change, to let her friends know that she was still awake in that other life.

The story was told by me in the pages of *Borderland,* and had I no other bit of evidence, I would bring this to my mind as something authentic from the land of spirits.   No doubt in some future year, someone will gather together the scattered evidences of Mr Boursnell's gifts, and many will wonder that such a thing did exist and so many remained in ignorance.   The most transcendent of facts has been obscured by the politics and the gossip of the hour.   I hold the man in reverence that he worked on amid the calumny which assailed him, and was content to scatter what blessings he could among mortals.   A poor, illiterate man no doubt, but one of those instruments whom the spirit people recognised had the highest virtues.

Mr Archibald M'Arthur, Laurel Bank House, Crow Road, Partick, who is a shrewd business man and is well known in engineering and shipbuilding circles on the Clyde, bears somewhat similar testimony to Mr Boursnell's *bona-fides* and courtesy.   Not only did Mr M'Arthur watch all the processes carried out with his own plates, but was fortunate to receive the undoubted likenesses of departed relatives.   Mr and Mrs M'Arthur had several sittings at different periods with Mr Boursnell, and are emphatic in their testimony as

them in the dark-room during the process of development and fixing.   Others were privileged in the same way when Mr Boursnell felt certain that they were honest and earnest."—Mr Andrew Glendinning, in special letter written to Mr J. J. Morse, Manchester, and reproduced in *A History of Spirit Photography,* 1909.

to the genuineness of Boursnell's mediumship, and as to the identification of psychic portraits received.

Mr Duncan Mackintosh, 2 Royal Terrace, Springburn, Glasgow, brought for my inspection three photographs done by Mr Boursnell, for Mrs Shaw, 303 Sauchiehall Street, Glasgow. (Mrs Shaw is the lady with whom Mr Wyllie obtained the second and much better picture of Mrs Coates's daughter, described elsewhere.)

Mrs Shaw states that on the occasion when these photographs were taken Mr Boursnell was in a more or less trance-like state, and in every instance he gave a full description of each Invisible before the exposure.

Concerning portrait, fig. 23, Mrs Shaw says :—

I was only six years of age when grandma died, so that my recollection of her would not be thought of sufficient weight by itself, but all who knew my grandmother have recognised this spirit picture of her. Mr Boursnell, the photographer, was unknown to me before I sat in his place. I know of no means by which he could have obtained and produced for me this fully identified picture of my grandmother, whom I so well remember.

In addition to this statement by Mrs Shaw, I asked for corroboration. Mr Duncan Mackintosh (date 8th October 1910) writes :—

The people who recognise the " extra " as Mrs Shaw's grandmother are Mrs Shaw's own mother and her cousins in Halifax, Yorkshire. When Mrs Shaw's mother first saw the photograph, she exclaimed : "I hope that you have not disturbed mother in her grave ! " I called the other evening and spoke to the lady herself. She admitted that these were the words she used. This lady is a fresh, keen, critical sort of person, and not likely to make a mistake in recognising the portrait of her mother. Other members of Mrs Shaw's family recognise the psychic picture of

FIG. 23.—The photograph of Mrs Shaw, and the psychic
picture of her maternal grandmother.

her grandmother, but as they are so averse to spiritualism, they will not give their names for publication in your book.

I again wrote Mr Mackintosh, and said that I considered the testimony of Mrs Shaw's mother more important than her own. In his favour of 14th October 1910 I received the following :—

I authorise you to say that the spirit face which appears on the photograph of my daughter, Mrs Shaw, is that of my mother, Hannah Kaye, who died 27th December 1874.

She is also recognised by Mrs H. E. Shaw.

SARAH ANN EASTON.

37 NEWCOMEN TERRACE, COATHAM, REDCAR, YORKS.

I know Mr Mackintosh personally, and several good people who know Mrs Shaw, and all testify to the latter's good repute. As to those who recognise the spirit photograph, but decline to give their names, I can only say this is a common experience. It is not surprising, as we find that many convinced spiritualists do the same, although the motives may be different.

The second photograph—not reproduced—is that of Mrs Shaw and a young woman, with flowers round the head and what are said to be coral beads around the neck. Mrs Shaw says:—

This photograph was taken at the same sitting. The spirit is described to be that of my sister Nancy, who died thirty-one years ago, at the age of fourteen months. She comes back with the appearance of what she would have been had she lived. She is so like my sister Mrs Pretty, now living in Wales, that it might be taken as a photograph of her. The coral beads are like those which she wore as a baby girl. Not only from these means of identification, but from the fact that she has been described by clairvoyants and has communicated, I am convinced that this is her portrait.

I have seen the photograph of Mrs Pretty and compared it with her spirit sister, and their features are wonderfully alike. I might add that Mrs Pretty was not in London, and the psychic picture is not a copy of herself.

The third psychic picture is that of the head and bust of a female, surrounded by nebulous stuff. It is claimed that this is the portrait of an Egyptian spirit guide of Mrs Shaw; for, being a spiritualist, she believes in guides. This spirit has been· frequently described as being in the surroundings of Mrs Shaw before and subsequently to being photographed by Mr Boursnell.

Whatever, then, may be thought of the second and last, as being outside ordinary and expert evidence, it must be borne in mind that these photographs were taken at the same sitting and under similar conditions to those under which the fully attested psychic picture of the grandmother was obtained. Unsupported, not of much value as evidence, yet, in connection with other evidence, most important to be considered.

THE AULD PHOTOGRAPHS

Mr John Auld visited the late Mr Boursnell in the hope of obtaining the photograph of his wife. Instead, he received two prints of a man and that of two females as "extras," and none of these were recognised by him. Of these three, that of the man is, I sincerely believe, the psychic portrait of my own father. That named Lizzie represents one whom I knew for many years. The second female, not recognised by Mr John Auld, has claimed to be a relative, and is certainly remarkably like a daughter of hers now living. I produce the attempt of the Invisibles to give me the psychic portrait of my father, who entered the higher life twenty-five years ago.

At my time of life, my relatives are few in number and are non-spiritualists. I sent the photograph to

FIG. 24.—Photograph of the author is introduced for comparison with the assumed psychic picture of his father.

three. One would not look at a psychic picture. Another said: "Yes, we know who you think it is. It is physiognomically and ethnologically correct." A third was of the opinion that I must have used my will-power and in some way caused the portrait to come on the plates. Strangers to the original, resident here, who have known me for the last twenty years, are all struck with the likeness of the psychic picture

to myself. My relatives are agreed that I am very
like now what my father was. The evidence which

FIG. 25.—The photograph of Mr John Auld, and the psychic
portrait of the author's father.

I offer is very meagre, and my readers can judge for
themselves by examining the two photographs given.

I have not been in London for thirty odd years. I
neither knew nor sat with Mr Boursnell. No similar
photographs have been in existence. Why these

"extras" came on the plates with Mr Auld, I can only surmise — which is neither ordinary nor expert evidence—but my surmise is that the Intelligences in the Invisible took advantage of the opportunity to have these psychically — produced — faces photographed. Mr John Auld and I have been associated for years in the study of the psychic.

I give extracts from Mr Auld's letter of 1st July 1909, in further substantiation of the foregoing :—

DEAR MR COATES,—In September 1908, while visiting London, I embraced the opportunity of calling upon Mr Boursnell and got my photograph taken, in the hope that some psychic figures might come on the plate. Mr Boursnell met me at the door and escorted me upstairs to a large room, apparently a dining-room, with two windows facing the street. Before taking my photograph, he said there were three psychic forms present in my surroundings, a man and two ladies. He also got the name of "Lizzie." In broad daylight, he exposed two plates in succession, withdrew the slide and put in a fresh one, and the plates in this were rapidly exposed. On the receipt of the cabinets I found on two the face of a gentleman about seventy years of age; snow-white hair on head, silvery whiskers, moustache, and beard; expressive eyes, a countenance of much refinement, glowing with intelligence and advanced spirituality. On the other two plates were two ladies, unknown to me.

Mr James Robertson, who has an extensive collection and has seen hundreds of psychic photographs, says they are new to him. Mr Robertson has obtained, through Mr Boursnell, photographs of departed friends under conditions beyond cavil. Mr Wm. T. Stead, of the *Review of Reviews*, and Mr John Lobb, editor of the *Christian Age* for over thirty years, have had speaking likenesses of departed friends; and from other sources of testimony, together with my own favourable impressions on seeing Mr Boursnell, I did not think it necessary to have my photographs taken under test conditions.   JOHN AULD.

Mr A. Mackellar, 17 Calderwood Road, Merrylea, Newlands, Glasgow, whom I know as a man of integrity and sound judgment, having considerable experience in psychic photography, wrote me (29th May 1910) in response to a note I sent him. He enclosed a large parcel of prints and negatives for inspection, including the identified photographs of a sister, a daughter, and of a late family doctor, well known to some of us in Glasgow, and said :—

My own photographs are very faded, and they cannot be of any weight for your book, as they were not taken under conditions that would satisfy the sceptics. This is very unfortunate, as I have no doubt of the genuineness of the one selected [the doctor.—J. C.], and I am not at liberty to give the names for publication.

This shows the inherent fairness of the man. He, as well as I, knows that Boursnell could not produce the identifiable photographs of persons unknown except under mediumistic conditions. Out of Mr Mackellar's large collection, I produce one and refer to two others.

Mr Mackellar's account is accompanied by a photograph of his daughter taken in life three or four years before she passed away. The hair, nose, lips, and eyes present, by their strong resemblance, evidence of

the correctness of the father's statement. Relatives
and friends recognise the psychic photograph, and it
was because I knew Florrie in life, and had seen her
photograph at a previous time, that I wrote Mr
Mackellar for particulars.

The psychic photographs of Mr Mackellar's sister,

FIG. 26.—The photograph of Mr A. Mackellar and his daughter
Florrie, done by Boursnell.

while quite recognisable, are too faded for process
blocks. I regret this, as the evidence is equally good
and is supported by a photograph taken in life. I
did not know this lady.

As to the doctor's psychic photograph, I cannot do
better than reproduce, summarised, Mr Mackellar's
account :—

I called on Mr Boursnell, along with my daughter

Nan, in the hope that I would get a photograph of my late wife (her mother). I had previously received very remarkable spirit photographs from Mr Boursnell, and hoped that on this visit I would be successful, from the fact that my wife in her lifetime was a splendid medium. I was on holiday and in the best of spirits, but when I sat down before the camera a severe depression came over me, and an irresistible inclination to weep, which, however, soon passed off.

Mr Boursnell described the spirit (a clergyman), with whom, he said, I had been associated in my earlier days. I did not recognise the description. *When I received the print, I at once recognised the striking photograph of the family doctor who had attended me from childhood until well on in life. He had attended a daughter of mine constantly for over a year* [the italics are mine.—J. C.], in which the subject of spiritualism often came up. I showed the photograph to his son (also a medical man in the city), who admitted it was a remarkable likeness of his father. Dr L. is not a spiritualist, but I have reason to know he was much impressed with it. That Mr Boursnell described him as a minister is easily accounted for by the fact that the late doctor had quite a clerical appearance. This to me is one of the points that tell, along with others, as it showed Mr Boursnell was describing what the spirit seemed to be.

I have shown this photograph to others, and also to a doctor who knew Dr L. in London. He did not recognise the likeness. Here is a photograph recognised by his son and not a spiritualist, and not recognised by a colleague, a spiritualist, whom one would expect to know.

As to the depression I experienced at the time of sitting, I have since learned it was due to the disappointment of the spirit who wanted to show herself, but was unable--from some cause not understood—to manifest.   A. MACKELLAR.

The evidence in these cases is excellent, although not sufficient for a sceptic ignorant of the facts and having no personal experience of a like character.

I wrote to Mr John Lobb, F.R.G.S., F.R.Hist.S., who had been for thirty years editor and proprietor of the *Christian Age*, and who had not become less Christian, but more so, from his investigations of spiritualism. His testimony I esteem of value, he being a man of affairs, having an outstanding reputation in London as journalist, author, and lecturer; a man honoured by Her Majesty Queen Victoria, and by his fellow-citizens.

THE TESTIMONY—SLIGHTLY CONDENSED—OF MR JOHN LOBB TO SOME EXPERIENCES IN SPIRIT PHOTOGRAPHY

In the year 1904, I was introduced to the late Mr R. Boursnell, the well-known medium, of 15 Richmond Road, Shepherd's Bush, W. I was startled by his clairvoyant and clairaudient powers. While sitting in front of the camera, he described the spirit forms of old friends with whom I had been associated in public life, and some of them appeared on the sensitive plates. Up to the time of his passing, on 21st December 1909, hardly a week passed but I had to meet the wishes of bereaved by an introduction to the dear old, simple, unpretentious mediumistic photographer, for the portrait of their dead, who for upwards of twenty years dried the tears and lifted sorrow from aching hearts. On Friday evening, 3rd May 1907, the beloved wife of Mr Andrew Glendinning, the editor of *The Veil Lifted*, manifested to Mrs Lobb and myself, and urged that we both visit Mr Boursnell on the following Tuesday, 7th May, and we were to insist that Mr Glendinning go with us. Neither

Mrs Lobb nor myself knew that that date was the birthday of her husband.   She came, and, to the delight of husband, children, and friends, her sweet face appears on the sensitive plate, with others, from the spirit world.   After nine months in the spirit life, the beloved wife returns and is photographed on her husband's eighty-first birthday.[1]   (Photograph enclosed.)

The power of spirits to cause representations of their forms to be impressed upon the sensitive surfaces of chemically prepared plates of the photographer has, like other psychic powers, been denied and ridiculed, but the possession of this power is now a well-

---

[1] In confirmation of the above, my late much-esteemed correspondent, Mr Andrew Glendinning, correcting an error of mine, referred me to a communication of his published in *The Two Worlds*, in 1909 :—

"I fear I am sending too long a letter, so now I pass on to mention the crowning glory of my life, so far as regards spirit photography.   This is a wonderful — very wonderful— portrait of my dear wife, obtained through Mr Boursnell nine months after her translation to the higher life.   It is quite different from all the photographs of her taken during her earth-life, and yet it is her very image as she was shortly before and during her last illness.   When my family saw an enlargement of it they were all so delighted with it that I had to get seven copies made so that each might have one to frame.   The doctor who attended her gazed at the remarkable photograph and asked how I got it.   He not knowing of spiritualism, I did not try to explain, but merely said, 'You see it is my wife's portrait.'   He replied, 'Yes, and it is an excellent likeness.'

"She always materialises at our family séances, is very frequently with me, and says she will be until I pass on.   She says to me, 'I am not separated from you as you are from me.'   Such are the joys and comforts of spiritualism.   Those called dead still live and love us.   They can and do return to cheer, to guide and bless us.   ANDREW GLENDINNING."

They are now no longer separated by the veil of time and sense, and seeing no longer as through a glass darkly, they pursue the pathway of eternal progress, illuminated by the love of God, which united them on earth.

established fact. Dr Alfred Russel Wallace, O.M., F.R.S., the famous scientist, and collaborator with Darwin in establishing the doctrine of evolution, in his famous book, *Miracles and Modern Spiritualism*, pp. 188–205, deals with spirit photography scientifically, supplying an accumulation of indisputable evidence of the fact that spirits from the unseen world do materialise for their portraits, and are identified by their friends. Sir William Crookes, F.R.S., etc., an expert with the photographic camera, has in his possession forty-four negatives. Others, both in England and abroad, possess numerous portraits of their departed friends. "Doubtful Thomas" has seen his own plates used, and seen for himself the operator develop his sensitive plate on which one or more of his loved ones show themselves.

The portrait of my sister, after a residence in spirit life for many years, returns as she now appears in spirit life. She was my only sister. She died young ; I attended on her in her dying hours, and she touchingly recalled incidents. Dear C. H. Spurgeon, my old and valued friend of thirty-five years' close connection in religious work, constantly seen with me on the platform, after fourteen years and five months in spirit life, materialises for his photograph. . . .

So sorry to have forgotten your request, but so many callers keep me busy. Mrs Lobb joins me in loving thoughts and prayers for the dear Master's blessing on you and yours.—Sincerely yours,

JOHN LOBB.

In Mr Lobb's postcard, dated 5th January 1911, he states in the most matter-of-fact way :—

DEAR FRIENDS,—Mr Andrew Glendinning appeared here at 6.30 this evening, smiling. . . .

JOHN LOBB.

Considering I have recorded the passing away of

Mr Glendinning in October 1910, the statement is arresting.

Mr Boursnell took three photographs of Mr Charles Davieson, and the "extras" on these were two females

FIG. 27.—The photograph of Mr Charles Davieson, and the psychic picture of his brother, Mr Edward Davieson, done by Mr Boursnell.

and one male. The two former were not recognised. They are well-defined, full-length figures. The latter was Mr Davieson's brother, between whom and himself there was a strong attachment. The evidence consists of the recognition of the spirit photograph by Mr Charles Davieson, who resides at Leipzig House, 22 Church Road, St Leonards-on-Sea; by Dr David Davieson, another brother, at present in practice at South Broadway, St Louis, Mo., U.S.A.; by his surviving sister, Mrs Fred. Simpson, Beech Hurst, Preston Road, Chorley, Lancashire; and by Mr Ruben Jordon, 28 Drayton Road, Harlesden, London, all of whom knew the late Mr Edward intimately. He passed away twenty years prior to the photograph being taken. Mr Charles Davieson is a son of Dr Davieson, Liverpool, an able medical man —himself a Jew—having a large practice there some years ago. Mr Davieson is of the Jewish persuasion (a descendant of Mendelssohn) and a musician, having graduated at the Conservatorium in Leipzig. Mr Davieson became interested in spiritualism through the force of facts, and is a most competent witness to psychic experiences. He testifies to the remarkable mediumship of Mr Boursnell.

THE TESTIMONY OF A. P. SINNETT,
THE THEOSOPHIST

I thought I should like to obtain the opinion of a leading theosophist on what is termed spirit photography, and as Mr A. P. Sinnett, author and journalist, and editor, at one time, of a prominent magazine, is one of the best known and most advanced theosophists in the world to-day, I wrote to him on 20th August 1910.

69 JERMYN ST., LONDON, S.W.,
1st September 1910.

DEAR SIR,—I received your letter of the 20th ult. I send you a photograph done by Boursnell, but on a plate of my own, taken from a new packet, opened by myself in his dark-room, and put by me into a dark slide and used in a camera I have examined, which was certainly free from tricks. I sat as you see— went back with Boursnell into the dark-room and saw the plate developed. I do not see how I could be cheated under these conditions.—Yours very truly,

A. P. SINNETT.

As Mr A. P. Sinnett had not only taken an active part in, and was in fact the initiator of, the *Daily Mail* Spirit Photography Commission, and once wrote a paper about "Photographing the Unseen," I further addressed him, sending him the above summary of his letter, which I proposed to publish. I inquired whether he had any experience with other mediums, had he recognised the psychic portrait, and what was his opinion as to the nature of these "extras." I give his characteristic reply :—

69 JERMYN STREET, S.W.,
6th September 1910.

DEAR SIR,—I have no objection to your proposal to publish my former letter, as enclosed. I have had no experience of any other photographic mediums besides Boursnell. I do not recognise the figure on the print I send you—nor do I attach any importance to the circumstance when such figures appear to resemble persons known to the sitter. Entities on the astral plane seem to have the power of personating others to an unlimited extent.—Yours truly,

A. P. SINNETT.

Mr Sinnett (whose experience with Mr Boursnell was by no means confined to the obtaining of the test recorded) is convinced of the genuineness of the medium and of psychic photography, but not,

FIG. 28.—The photograph of Mr A. P. Sinnett, and psychic "extra," unrecognised by the sitter, taken under the test conditions detailed in letter.

as it will be noted, that these spirit photographs are the portraits of departed persons. I give Mr Sinnett's opinion as a side-light on the subject. But whether "entities on the astral plane have the power of personating others to an unlimited extent," I confess I do not know, and regret that my ignorance has to be confessed.   Mr Sinnett requires no introduction to the reading public.   His testimony to the *fact* of psychic photography is deemed by me of sufficient importance to produce here.

Owing to the pressure on my space, I have had to rule out many interesting cases, and would merely mention in conclusion that in many instances, of late years, Mr Boursnell declined to submit to the proposals of "experts."   In this he was quite right.   There is no doubt his identifiable spirit photographs furnish their own best evidence.   At the same time it is due to him to state that he frequently submitted to be tested—and under these conditions "extras" were obtained, hundreds of which were identified.

CHAPTER VII

SOME AMERICAN CASES

In this chapter I give a few unrelated cases, ranging from the days of Mumler to the present time. I regret I have none of those taken by Drs Hausmann and Keeler, of Washington, U.S.A.

The late Professor Gunning, one of the ablest geologists in America, sent a long and interesting letter to the *New York Tribune*. Although it was written just about the period (1872) when experiments in spirit photography were first attempted in Great Britain, the thoughts suggested are as appropriate now as then.

Space will not admit the production in full of the letter. After contrasting the treatment and dismissal of psychic facts by Mr Herbert Spencer on *a priori* grounds, with that of his friend Dr Wallace, "one of the first naturalists of Europe," he gives the results of his experimentation—assisted by a competent friend —with a photographer on four afternoons, when they obtained several times the psychic form — bright though vapoury—of a woman: duplications of the same form which came on his plates when having an ordinary sitting with the same photographer a short time previously. The operator in this instance was a

FIG. 29.—Photograph of Mr F. Rice, Greigsville, Livingstone Co., New York
U.S.A., with several psychic portraits, showing the advance made from M
time.   Mr Rice was a friend of the late Mrs Emma Hardinge Britten.
above was intended for the *Encyclopedia of Spiritualism* which tha
prepared for publication.   Mrs Wilkinson, of Stretford, Mrs Britten's
ing sister, presented it for this work.   I put it in for her sake.   The
graph is credited to Mr Frank Foster.

non-spiritualist, and had a horror that his name should be mixed up with spiritualism in any form. Professor Gunning states that this photographer gave the use of his rooms, chemicals, and time without charge; that he (Professor Gunning) and his expert photographic assistant took every precaution to prevent and detect trickery. Throughout their careful experimentation this psychic form persisted.

In the same letter he gives a long and carefully detailed account of a psychic picture obtained under remarkable circumstances. The sitter, a young lady, as well as the operator was a non-spiritualist. Photographing the young lady on a new sheet of tin, giving eight portraits, there were on the plate, and on each portrait, a pair of hands clasped round the sitter's neck, the right hand coming on the chin and the left partly thrust under the girl's collar. The hands are shown up to the wrist, and then fade away. Professor Gunning had the utmost confidence in the photographer. In his case, as in the former one, these so-called spirit pictures occasionally came, and the photographer had no control over the phenomena.

His deductions from these experiments, and from the evidence produced at the Mumler trial, are :—

First. — That the sensitive plate may be more sensitive to light than the human eye.

Second.—That men and women — spirits, but not incorporeal — can, under certain conditions, clothe their persons with elements of sufficient substance to reflect light.

PHOTOGRAPH OF THE DOUBLE

In the account given by "M.A. Oxon." of how his "double" was photographed, he stated that he was asleep, in London, at the time when his "spirit" was photographed in Paris. He was a medium and accustomed to go into trances, and the photograph represents him in a state of trance, or at least with his eyes closed. In the following account the tale that is told is more prosaic.

In the early winter months of 1875, Mr Evans, a spirit photographer, was taking pictures in the studio of a Mr A. C. Maxwell in New York City. A Mr Demarest called in the hope of getting a spirit picture. The proprietor, Mr Maxwell, was sitting asleep by the stove, which was situated some ten feet in rear of where the camera stood. Mr Evans, after making the usual preparations, posed Mr Demarest and "took his picture." When the plate was developed there was on it, beside the figure of the sitter, an "extra," not of a departed, but of the face and full form of Mr Maxwell—the man dozing by the stove. Mr Demarest was not only annoyed but very suspicious when he saw the purported spirit beside him. It was, in his opinion, none other "than the picture of Mr Maxwell, produced by some hocus-pocus on the plate." The latter demurred, and declared that he did not know, and could not tell, how his profile, face and figure, got on the plate. All he knew was that he had been dozing at the stove at the time

when Mr Demarest was taken.   Being confused and
surprised at the charge, Mr Maxwell took the plate
and showed it to his wife—whose room was adjoining
the studio—and asked her, " Whose likeness is that
beside Mr Demarest ? "   She said, " Why, yours, to be
sure."   Mr Maxwell was more confused than ever, and
returning the plate to Mr Demarest, declared that he
(Maxwell) knew nothing about it.   The curiosity was
shown to Mr Fanshaw, artist, and he concluded that
it was a repetition in New York of the phenomenon
of the " double," as reported in the attestations of the
Count de Bullet as having taken place in Paris.

   After weighing all the statements which are given
in this case, and which I do not propose to quote at
length here, it is clear—to use the words of the narrator
—that while Mr Maxwell, the mortal, was dozing at
the stove, his dual existence, his spirit, was having its
likeness taken with that of Mr Demarest on the
photographic plate.   If we substitute " double " for
" spirit " in the above, I think the statement would be
more accurate.   In our present state of knowledge we
do not really know what our spirit friends in discarnate states are like, but we do know that in all
cases " the double " is as like the man in the flesh as
two peas are like one another.   I am not in a position
to vouch for the accuracy of the account sent from
New York, 8th July 1875, to *Human Nature*, but I
can believe the incident to be possible, as other cases
previously stated indicate.   When dealing with Mr
Ed. Wyllie, medium photographer, I gave a case of

the photographing of " the double " of a little girl well known to us, for which there is no explanation.   This is equally true whether the extra be that of one in the

FIG. 30.—Photograph of Mrs Flood, and the psychic pictures of friends, done by Mr Evans.

body or that of a person departed.   The facts are there. The why and how do not meet with a ready solution.

I am indebted to Mrs Wilkinson, of Stretford, near Manchester, for the above early example of Mr Evans' work.   The subject of the photograph is her own mother, Mrs Flood, who accompanied them to the United States, as related in the *Autobiography of Emma Hardinge*

Britten, her sister.   Mrs Flood is seen surrounded by
several " extras."   Who these are, Mrs Wilkinson—
now a very old lady—does not remember, except one.
This is the lowest one on the left, concerning which
she often heard her mother declare that it was the
spirit picture of her old nurse.   The case is given not
so much as evidence, but as an illustration of one of
those early psychic pictures.   In this we see a departure from the flat, full-form " extras " of Mumler,
the three-quarter length sheeted forms of Hudson,
the scrolls and crudities of Reeves, etc., to the American
type of psychic photograph which obtains to-day, viz.
a face, or groups of faces, sufficient for identity, the
whole suggesting that the spirit workers in the
Invisible had, as the result of experimenting, decided
on a policy of concentrated effort to produce identifiable faces only, and at the same time economising
energy and psychic force.

THE CINCINNATI PHOTOGRAPH

This account is summarised from the *Cincinnati
Enquirer*:—

Mr Jay J. Hartman has been producing "spirit
pictures" at Teeple's Gallery, No. 100 West Fourth
Street.   He has been bitterly denounced as a fraud
and trickster by the sceptics and unbelievers.   Although he gave private "test sittings" that seemed
satisfactory, yet even many of his friends began to
doubt him, until he, last week, published a card that
on Saturday morning, December 25th, he would give
a free public investigation addressed to the public
generally, and to the photographers especially ; stat-

ing that it would pass all the arrangements in the hands of those taking part in the investigation; they to choose the room where the test was to be held; bring their own marked plates, furnish their own camera, chemicals in fact everything. Hartman simply

FIG. 31.—An old woodcut of Dr Morrow, and psychic picture of young lady, taken under test conditions by Mr Jay J. Hartman, in Cutter's studio, in Cincinnati, in March 1876.

asking to manipulate the plates in the presence of practical photographers, to show that he used no fraud or trickery. Christmas morning came, bright and cheerful, and found sixteen gentlemen, five of them practical photographers of this city, assembled at his rooms. Putting the question to vote, it was decided to adjourn to the photograph gallery of Mr V. Cutter, No. 28 West Fourth Street, Mr Cutter being an expert in detecting the "spirit-picture trickery," and, as Mr Hartman had never been in his gallery, he would be at the double disadvantage of being in a strange room, surrounded by sceptics and practical men quick to detect fraud.

I do not propose to detail the nature of each experiment; of these there were several, and all failures except the last, when, to the surprise of the sceptics and the ijoy of the medium's friends, "there was a picture!" The report states:—

Hartman had never touched the plates or entered the dark chamber during the manipulation! How it got there he didn't know; there it was! While Messrs Cutter, Murhman, *et al.*, do not admit the "spiritual" origin of the form on the plate, yet they all agree that Mr Hartman did not and could not, under the circumstances of never touching the plate or entering the dark-room, produce the "spirit-picture" by fraud or trickery. There is the face of Dr Morrow, with the face of a young lady, with something resembling a wreath arching over their heads! Whence came it? If it is not what it purports to be, a "spirit form," what is it? And how came it there? All finally agreed to sign the following certificate:

"We, the undersigned, having taken part in the public investigation of "spirit photography" given by Mr Jay J. Hartman, hereby certify that we have closely examined and watched the manipulations of our own marked plates, through all the various workings, in and out of the dark-room, and have been unable to discover any sign of fraud or trickery on the part of Mr Jay J. Hartman. And we further certify that during the last sitting, when the result was obtained, Mr Jay J. Hartman did not handle the plate nor enter the dark-room at any time.

> " J. SLATTER, C. H. MURHMAN, V. CUTTER, J. P.
> WECKMAN, F. T. MORELAND, T. TEMPLE
> (all practical photographers); E. SAUN-
> DERS, WM. WARRINGTON, JOSEPH KINSEY,
> BENJAMIN E. HOPKINS, G. A. CARNSHAN,
> WM. SULLIVAN, JAMES P. GEPPERT,
> D. V. MORROW, M.D., E. HOPKINS,
> ROBERT LESLIE."

Dr B. F. Austin, B.A., editor of *Reason*, and director of the Austin Publishing Co., Rochester, New York, U.S.A., writing me recently, says :—

Spirit photography once proved, the continuity of life is demonstrated, and with spirit communication in its various forms is rendered so inherently probable that we may regard the case for spiritualism as proven.

Let us grant at once that there are many ways of producing "faked spirit photographs." Dr William Lockwood, an authority on photography, for years lecturer to the American Association of Photographers, an able author, physicist, and philosophical teacher, while pointing out many ways in which the "fake" photographs can be produced, is a strong witness to the fact of genuine spirit photography.

Some years ago I had, from his own lips, the story of the conversion to spiritualism of Mr Ruthven Macdonald, of Toronto, Canada, a famous baritone soloist, who, while a Methodist, accepted an engagement to sing at the Lily Dale Assembly of Spiritualists. While there—believing, as he had been taught, that all mediumship was essentially fraudulent—he thought he would visit a few mediums as pastime, and, among others, selected a spirit photographer, who was of course a complete stranger to him. When the first photograph was developed, the photographer asked

him to sit again, as the picture was unsatisfactory.
Mr Macdonald asked to be shown the negative, but
the photographer demurred, and wished to destroy it.

FIG. 32.—Test photograph obtained by Mr A. K. Venning,
who not only took every precaution as to camera, plate,
holder, lens, etc., but at the last moment placed his hat
in position shown. The lady sitting with him is now
passed over. The " extra " above her, which is identified,
is the portrait of a late member of the British House
of Commons, and related to a distinguished family, the
members of which made their name in India. (Name
can be had, if desired, on application to the author.)

Mr Macdonald insisted, and on seeing it beheld to his
amazement the form of his spirit mother standing
behind him in the picture and holding up a hand with

two clearly recognisable thumbs. This struck the photographer as "uncanny." Mr Macdonald, however, on seeing it exclaimed: "Destroy that! Why, that is my mother! She had two thumbs on one hand."

Mr Macdonald got many remarkably clear photographs of spirit friends. I saw the photograph of his mother. The face and form were clearly defined, and the hand with two thumbs made an impression on me—as Mr Macdonald told the story—which I shall never forget. Mr Macdonald received in this way, and through other forms of mediumship, so much overwhelming evidence that he became a convert to spiritualism and an ardent advocate of its teachings.

I am obliged to Dr Austin for calling my attention to the case of Judge Levi Mock. He says: "You can depend thoroughly on the accuracy of the statements made. I know the Judge well. He was president of the Chesterfield Camp at one time. You can safely quote him."

Leaving out all references to the Judge's eminent position, and his well-qualified training for the weighing of evidence, and his family and State connections, which appeared in *Reason*, October 1908, I summarise his important testimony in favour of spirit photography :—

Four years ago (1904) Frank Foster, of Grand Rapids, Mich., was at Chesterfield Camp meeting, posing as a spirit photographer, charging two dollars for producing the pictures. I first sat for my picture, and then went to the camera, and he placed his fingers on the same and I placed my fingers on his hand. He was in a quiver till a shock came, and he said,

" That is sufficient." Within a few days he gave me the developed pictures. I recognised none of them. I went to Mrs Herbine's cottage, taking the pictures along. None of the persons whose pictures I had were related to me.

While Mrs Herbine is a slate-writer, in her sittings independent voices converse with the sitter; and on that occasion my father, who had been in the summerland several years, told me to go back and have another picture, and that I should get pictures that I should recognise. Believing him, I went to Foster and had another picture. I at once recognised four of the spirit pictures. I immediately wrote out five questions, asking the names of the persons represented, locating each in the group, and went to Mrs Herbine's cottage. We sat down to a small stand. I took a double slate and placed it under my foot, and reached in my pocket and got one of the questions and placed it under one of my hands on the stand, I not knowing what question I had, and she not having seen any of the questions or pictures. The first question I drew out of my pocket was as follows: " Dr Coulter (the medium's control), what is the name of this dog on the picture in my pocket?" His answer was thus: " Blood."

I recognised the picture of " Blood " as my favourite foxhound (who is in dog heaven, or some other place), and called him " Blood " because he would never cease running till he caught the fox.

I took out the questions one by one, and the pictures, as I knew, were named. The picture first above the dog is my aunt Polly Reitnour; just over my head my sister Rachael; the one above to the left, Colby Luther (our famous lecturer); and that to the left is named Williams—Dr Coulter said that he was not related to me, and I do not recognise him. When I came home many of my neighbours recognised " Blood " and my sister.

What I have stated is literally true. I have no reason to state an untruth.   LEVI MOCK.

BLUFFTON, INDIANA.

I very much regret that the American reproduction of the photograph does not come out very clearly. We see in the Judge's statement that not only was he advised to go back and get another sitting, when he would get pictures which he would recognise, but other processes in evidence showing Intelligence in the Invisible somewhere operating and demonstrated in the results obtained through different mediums and by differing processes; the psychics being strangers to the Judge.

From the foregoing statement of the Judge it will be noted that Mr Frank Foster's methods differ from those of most mediums. In this case the operator takes the sitter's portrait in the ordinary way and then uses the camera itself as a dark chamber, and obtains the "extras" on the plate at the time when the shock is experienced by both sitter and medium. For this we find an explanation in psychography.

From reliable information I learn that Mr Frank Foster, of Grand Rapids, Michigan, is the oldest medium photographer now living. He has been taking "spirit pictures" for nearly forty years, in different parts of the States, and is still at work obtaining thousands of "extras," and his identifiable pictures are the best testimony as to the genuineness of his mediumship. The method usually adopted by this medium and his son, Mr Bennie Foster, is to make one exposure on sitter in the light, and then darken the room and make another exposure to get the psychic "extras" on the plate. I presume that in taking photographs at a camp meeting, where his operating room would be a tent, darkening would be impossible; hence the method described by Judge Mock.

Mrs Jane M. Samson, of Pasadena (who at one time lived in Boston, and was, with her husband, a member of the Rev. Minot J. Savage's congregation there) had a sitting with Mr Wyllie. Of this lady Dr H. A. Reid (in "Case Eight," reported in *Unseen Faces Photographed*) says :—

She is an intelligent and reputable lady, and attended sittings for psychical research at which Prof. James, Rev. Minot Savage, Rev. A. A. Miner, D.D., and others were critical investigators. In April 1900 she sat to Mr Wyllie in Los Angeles. He knew nothing of her former residence, relationship, or experiences, and this plate was produced.

I do not reproduce it here, but mention that the "extras" thereon in addition to herself were the faces of her deceased husband, who died in Boston, the wife of a brother of the sitter, and the face of her husband's father. Now, Mrs Samson has a brother, a practical photographer, Mr C. B. Scott, carrying on business at 340 Fulton Street, Brooklyn, N.Y. She wrote him about this photograph. He recognised the faces on it, and I give his reply (dated 6th May 1900), as throwing a light, and a favourable one, on the procedure of Mr Frank Foster :—

We have considerable to do with spirit photographs. Mr Foster, a spirit photographer and medium, has been bringing and sending photographs to us to be enamelled.   He has no studio, but goes from one place to another, and he sends us work from different cities. All his have from two to five spirit faces, and we have always been watching, as he sent prints from different cities, to see if we could detect the same faces, but we have never been able to do so.   When he sends them from Philadelphia they are covered with Indian and Quaker faces.   I don't think the spirits have much to do with the matter, but there is something about it that is hard to detect.

This is another out of several instances where a practical photographer does not believe in the spirit theory put forward for these psychic pictures; knowing not of any method of "faking" by which they can be produced, but admitting that they come, and that there is something about spirit photography hard to detect.

THE PHOTOGRAPH OF A CHINAMAN

I relate as nearly as possible the story of fig. 33, as given me by Mr Wyllie one evening in November 1909.   I have been fortunate enough to receive the original photograph, and have the story confirmed by my esteemed correspondent, Mr A. K. Venning, of 613 South Flower Street, Los Angeles, Cal., U.S.A. Mr Wyllie's account is accepted for the simple reason that he gave evidence, when in our house, of being a genuine medium for this phase of phenomena.   He said :—

I had been giving tests to some gentlemen in Los
Angeles in connection with the Psychic Research
Society. Some were convinced of the fact of psychic
photography, and others were not. It was suggested

Fig. 33.--The photograph of a Chinaman, with "extras,"
which was taken by Mr Wyllie, as requested by some
members of the Pasadena Psychical Research Society,
of which Dr H. A. Reid was the President.

by one member it would be a good thing if I could
obtain "extras" on the plate of someone wholly
ignorant of both the subject and of spiritualism.
Then it could not be said that their knowledge or
attitude had anything to do with the results. It was
not easy to get someone with the qualifications desired.

When one day "Charlie," a Chinese laundryman, called for my clothes, it struck me to ask him: "Charlie, like to have your picture taken?" "No," he replied. "No likee that." He knew that I was a photographer, but had a dislike, I think, to photography, as most Chinese have. I tried to persuade him after he had called two or three times. I showed him that there could be no harm in it, and I would take a "glass" (as negatives are called) for nothing, and print him some nice pictures of himself. Charlie wanted to go home and change his clothes, but I knew it would not do to let him slip, and got him to sit. He was very much scared. I made his mind easy and asked him to come in a few days, and I would give him the pictures. When I developed the negative there were two "extras" on it—a Chinese boy and some Chinese writing. When Charlie came round I showed him the print, and he said: "That my boy; where you catchee him?" I asked him if it was not one of his cousins in the city. He said, "No, that my boy. He not here; where you catchee him?" I asked him where his boy was, and he said, "That my boy. He's in China. Not seen him for three years."

Charlie would not believe that I had not by some magic got his "boy here." Charlie then brought other Chinamen—friends of his own—to see the picture, and they all recognised the youngster. Charlie did not know that his son was dead. As far as he knew, he was alive and well.

As to the Chinese writing, Mr Venning informs me that it has been shown to several Chinamen, and each one has refused to give a translation. Charlie's explanation is a curious one. He said the meaning of the letters was: "A fall; a crooked path; and a big house."

It appears that he left China in trouble, that was

the *fall*; he had lived a bad life, that was the *crooked way*; he was now a "Clistian man," and he had no doubt that the big house meant that he would be prosperous yet, and return to his father's *big house* at home. Such is the story as told by Mr Wyllie. I do not know whether the "extras" were correctly read or not, symbolical or not; but as for Charlie, he appeared to be in the crooked way still, as he fell into the hands of the police and had to leave the city. I give the picture if only for the story.

On the next page (fig. 34) I produce the photograph of a Negress, as it furnishes a suggestive answer to the question, "Are spirit photographs the photographs of spirits?"

Judge Edmonds says: "Spiritualists reason that these photographs are the actual pictures of disembodied spirits, but they do not know. I am not prepared to express a definite opinion."

The above is an extract from the evidence given by the learned Judge at the trial of Mumler. The Judge knew of a certainty that these psychic "extras" were genuinely obtained, and gave evidence to that effect, but he reserved his judgment when it came to claiming that the photographs were those of disembodied spirits.

Mr A. K. Venning, who possesses a life-experience of spirit photographs, in his letter to me, dated 16th December 1909, says:—

These portraits are probably taken not from the individual spirit, but *from a thought-form-picture, or something of that sort.*

This may be as difficult to grasp as the fact of spirit photography.   The evidence in favour of what are called " thought-forms " is too strong to be lightly cast aside.

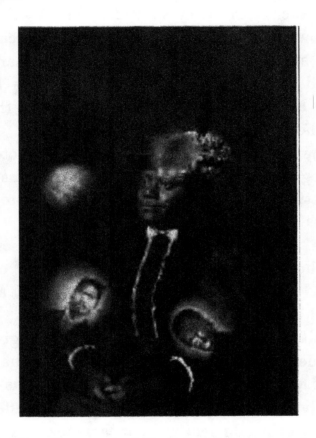

FIG. 34.—Photograph of Negress, and a number of spirit pictures of friends.   This is a Wyllie photograph which Mr A. K. Venning of San Francisco sent me.

Dr Alfred Russel Wallace is of opinion that the photographs are those of " forms " made up and presented to the camera, and not the photographs of actual spirits.

Mr Blackwell, whose belief in spirit photography is undoubted, is convinced, however, that the photographs are those of spirits.   He fell foul of me for employing the term "psychic extras" for spirit photographs. Yet this experienced investigator, in that letter, makes the admission :—

Some spirit people seem to find it very difficult to remember how they looked in earth-life, and refresh their memory by referring to a photograph or portrait. This they sometimes transfer so exactly that undeserved suspicion is cast upon the unfortunate medium.

Further, I have had the privilege of photographing some partially materialised spirits in my own house. They were perfectly clear and visible to my visitors and myself.   *Yet, two of these forms are exactly like their last earthly photographs, except that they are now surrounded with spirit drapery.*   [The italics are Mr Blackwell's own.]   They (the spirits) have exerted their will-power to build up a new form, and have appeared in quite a different pose.

The deduction, to my mind, is that these are photographs of something equivalent to the thought-forms or the double of the living, or some material form— albeit invisible—*representing what the originals were like in earth-life.*

CALIFORNIA WELL TOOL AND MACHINE WORKS,
114–116 COLLEGE STREET,
LOS ANGELES, CAL., 17th *October* 1910.

JAMES COATES, Esq.,
     Glenbeg House, Ardbeg,
          Rothesay, Scotland.

DEAR SIR,—I have received both your letters, of July and September respectively.   Yes!   I am well acquainted with Mr Wyllie [1] and his work, and can vouch for his honesty in his mediumship. Whatever one gets through Mr Wyllie's photography is genuine. I

Fig. 35.—Photograph of a (gold-bearing) district in California, referred to in Mr Geo. Gartling's letter. I am not at liberty to give identifiable particulars. It is a psychic picture not of a spirit but of a terrestrial scene, to which are added symbols having a meaning only to the recipient. I am indebted to Mr A. K. Venning for the photograph, and to Mr Gartling for his emphatic testimony to the fact of psychic photography.

very much doubt that there is another person living who has tested his genuineness as thoroughly as I have;

[1] To-night's mail (11th April 1911) brings me the news, as I am checking this page, that Mr Wyllie passed to the higher life yesterday, in Hampstead.

and besides being a pure medium, Mr Wyllie is also well worthy the name Gentleman. He has my best wishes wherever he may be. I have got quite a good many messages and pictures through Mr Wyllie's photography, but none that I would want to go into public print at this time. The most important are written messages which no one except myself—not even Mr Wyllie—knows what they read like. These messages are an explanation of a principle which I am to work out and not to divulge at this time. I have a few photographs which Mr Wyllie has made that are good enough to convince anyone who is not entirely obstinate, but conviction could not be brought about through publication. Anyone wishing to get proof of this would have to come here, and then I would have to take the party about 400 miles distance from here to effect the proof. I have gone there myself to test it, and I found it just exactly as it is described in the photograph, but it cost me fifty dollars to prove to myself that the photograph is correct. Then, I have also some faces of departed ones who have come on my photographs, whom I recognise, but such would be no conviction to others. But my real experience has proved to me that anyone who is sincere in wanting to know as to the truth of spirit phenomena will certainly be given that knowledge just as soon as ready for it, and as much of it as one is capable of absorbing.—I am, yours very truly,

GEORGE GARTLING.

The Gartlings, of Los Angeles, California, are known and respected as shrewd, level-headed men of business, the heads of a large concern there; and Mr George Gartling has everything to lose and nothing to gain by giving his testimony to the fact of spirit photography.

CHAPTER VIII

I AM indebted to the Rev. Charles Hall Cook, D.B., A.M., Ph.D. (Diocese of Colorado, U.S.A.), 1845 Grant Street, Denver, Col., for notes from his investigations. These were made in his capacity of member and representative of the American Society for Psychical Research. In these reports he deals not only with his experiences in psychic photography, but in other phases of psycho-physics, such as apports, materialisations, psychography, direct writing, etc. I, however, only quote a few notes on psychic photography, giving prominence to the Flora Loudon case, wherein the testimony of Dr Cook gets unanticipated corroboration. The whole affords evidence of the operation of Intelligences outwith that of the medium, Wyllie, and the doctor, as well as the doctor's scientific procedure to get at the facts.

Photographs have been obtained through Wyllie, Martin, and a boy named Charles Bartel, sixteen years of age, who only used a Kodak. The reports were made on psychic photography, and sent to the A.S.P.R., but have not been published. The late Dr Hodgson had then such a mental bias against psycho-physical phenomena that the facts recorded did not appear in the *Journal*. Not only so, but no steps were taken to officially investigate the truth of the statements made.

FIG. 36.—Photograph of Mr Ed. Wyllie, medium-photographer, and the psychic portrait of his mother (identified). The enlargement which Mr Wyllie had of this was lost, with all his belongings, in the great San Francisco earthquake. The above reached me from an esteemed correspondent in the States. Mr Wyllie was unaware there was a copy in existence.

There is nothing new in this; similar treatment was measured out to Dr H. A. Reid by the secretary of the S.P.R., London. The doctor furnished careful reports, with evidence corroborating his mode of procedure and the psychic results obtained with Wyllie. But beyond a few quibbles, and a courteous acknowledgment by the secretary of the reports, nothing was done.

Dr Cook freely gave of his valuable time and of his means in travelling and investigation. To all Dr Cook's conditions, as member and representative of the A.S.P.R. Mr Wyllie readily consented to submit. Notwithstanding the careful procedure adopted and the evidences submitted, the A.S.P.R. acknowledged but *suppressed the reports*.

From Dr Cook's notes, taken from his unpublished reports, I summarise a few cases, with photographs :—

In the summer of 1901 I conducted a series of twelve experiments in psychic photography with Mr Edward Wyllie, 507½ South Spring Street, Los Angeles, Cal., U.S.A. Mr Wyllie granted me the use of his gallery, dark-room, camera, and all accessories, and unhesitatingly complied with all conditions I prescribed—all this gratis on the part of Mr Wyllie. The photographic 4 × 5 plates I myself provided, being a box purchased from a regular dealer for the trade. This box of plates was always kept either in my coat pocket or inaccessible except to myself. The developing was done at different galleries, except in three instances, when Mr Wyllie assisted by my request, but efficient precaution was taken to prevent the possibility of exchanging plates.

Before every trial, I made a thorough examination of Mr Wyllie's camera, lens, plate-holder, background, and all accessories. I made no arrangement or engagement with Mr Wyllie at any time for a succeeding experiment; in fact, I did not know whether I should make another.

Nine of the twelve experiments were successful, *i.e.*

invisible faces, forms, and other phenomenal effects appeared upon the plates besides the sitter. [The prints referred to were sent me for inspection.—J. C.]

EXPERIMENTS 1 AND 2

In the first two successful experiments, June 25 and 26, Mr J. H. Disler, a capable investigator and experienced photographer, assisted me. Mr Disler and I made a most critical and thorough examination of Mr Wyllie's camera, lens, plate-holder, background, and all accessories. Mr Wyllie at no time came in contact with them, but stood at one side as a spectator, in the custody of special witnesses. On one plate there was the appearance of a "bright spot," or "spot of light," resembling a cube-shaped diamond, near the elbow of my right arm, emitting rays of light in lateral directions. On the other plate there was a phantasmal face, blurred and splotched, on the upper portion of my vest, with the forehead partly hidden under my collar.

EXPERIMENT 3

In the third experiment, June 27, Mr Wyllie acted as photographer, on my request, and did only what I asked him to do. While the conditions of this experiment were, by reason of my most careful observation and direct knowledge of them, as satisfactory—even more so—as those of the preceding ones, yet the result of the experiment and the developments of evidential facts that followed later on have proved it to be superior to all other experiments that I have made.

After Mr Wyllie made an exposure upon me, we retired to the dark-room, and I watched the developing process, and saw coming out on the plate an object or face before the face of the sitter became visible. It became more clearly defined as the developing process was nearing completion.

12

Returning to the gallery room, as Mr Wyllie held the negative up before the window, I saw on it a face that was very distinct, even more so than my own. Comparing it with that of the preceding experiment, we saw that it was the same face that had appeared

Lily — flower of spiritualism.
Lily of the Valley

FIG. 37.—Photograph of Dr Cook, and psychic portrait of Flora Loudon, with symbols.

upon the plate the day before. It covered my left shoulder, extended upon my breast, and was larger and much more distinct than the first attempt, with additional accompaniments, flowing and wavy hair, encircled with a halo or luminous radiance, star-shaped flower or lily in the hair, just above the forehead, and symbolic representations of a cross and heart below the face.

RECOGNITION

Aside from the conditions under which these experiments 1, 2, and 3 were made, I quote from my original notes, which were written out in full on the third day after the experiment, *i.e.* June 30, 1900, and attested under the seal of legal authority. This affidavit was also inserted in an extended report on psychic photography afterwards made to the Society for Psychical Research. It is as follows:—

"This face I recognised as that of the young lady or girl whom I first met in the month of September of the year 1866, as a student of Antioch College at Yellow Springs, Ohio. We were classmates at that institution, and passed two years of student life together Her home was at Higginsport, on the banks of the Ohio, twenty miles above my old home. She passed into the other life about four years after the short period of our student life together, that is, in 1873. The name is Flora Loudon."

TESTIMONY 1

STATE OF CALIFORNIA,
COUNTY OF LOS ANGELES.

WILLIAM LOUDON, being first duly sworn, deposes:

Being in Los Angeles, Cal., about the 7th of May 1905, as an idle visitor, I chanced to see a posted handbill announcing that Dr Cook would deliver a lecture that evening on " Psychical Research "

I had never up till that time known Dr Cook, but, attracted by the nature of the subject announced, I went to hear the lecture.

During the course of his lecture, the doctor exhibited a number of stereopticon views of pictures, purporting to be photographs of human forms that were at the time they were caught by the photographic plate entirely invisible to the eye.

Among these pictures **was** one which I distinctly recognised as that of Flora Loudon, who died more than thirty years ago.   Her death occurred shortly after her return from Washington, D.C., where she had been with her grandfather, General Loudon, to witness the ceremonies of the inauguration of General Grant as President of the United States.

She was my niece, and during all her life I was in her company very often, and knew her intimately, and hence am able to aver, from my own personal knowledge, that aforesaid photograph bears a most striking resemblance to the original, as I knew her near the time of her decease.

So far as I know, there was never taken during the life of Flora Loudon a photograph of her, with such symbols as are seen on said photograph, shown me by Dr Cook.   WILLIAM LOUDON.

Subscribed and sworn to ⎫ EDWARD   G.   KUSTER, before me, this 29th day ⎬ Notary Public in and for of May 1905.   ⎭ Los Angeles Co., Cal.
(Seal.)

TESTIMONY 2

On the same day (May 29th) that Mr Loudon made the affidavit, I met his wife, who, examining the psychic photograph, said: "Yes, it looks like Flora." Mr Loudon explained that Mrs Loudon was his second wife, and had had but slight opportunity to know his niece.   But Mrs Loudon's recognition was from a different point of view from that of her husband.   She said: "It resembles very much a picture I once saw of her."   Several days after this (July 3rd), referring to a picture of Flora she had seen many years ago, Mrs Loudon said: "I took occasion to examine and study the face carefully, as I thought it resembled a daughter of mine."   Several days later (July 23rd), describing her remembrance of the picture she had seen many years ago, Mrs Loudon said : "The picture I referred to was taken of Flora when—I think she was about sixteen at the time—her hair was down on the forehead and the face, a front view—just like the one you have. I think it was in the possession of her (Flora's) grandmother at Georgetown, Ohio."

TESTIMONY 3

Flora's Photograph

In reply to a letter to surviving members of the Loudon family at Georgetown, Ohio, they sent me a photograph of Flora Loudon (the only one obtainable). It had " May 1872 " on the back of it. This photograph was taken of her at the age of twenty-two, six years after I knew her in 1866–7 as a classmate at Antioch College. Although the lapse of six years at that period of life in a woman usually works a great change, and although the position of the sitter in the photograph is different from that of the psychic one —the former being a side view and the latter a front view—comparing the two faces, Mr Loudon repeatedly affirmed that the psychic photograph was " an excellent likeness of Flora."

TESTIMONY OF THE SYMBOLS

The symbols in the psychic photograph are pronounced in size and distinctness. These are, star-shaped flower or lily in the hair, just above the forehead, cross and heart below the face. Mrs Loudon observed that the flowers in Flora's hair were five in number, had five points, and were of the same form or shape as the flower in the psychic photograph. There are in Flora's photograph five small or miniature flowers in her hair, above the left ear, and near the top of her head; they have five points, and are of a star shape or form like a lily. The large flower in the

hair of the psychic photograph, just above the forehead, has five points, resembling a star or a lily, and is of the same shape or form as the miniature flowers in Flora's photograph.

Also there is in Flora's photograph, among the ornaments on her person, a small or miniature cross, fastened to the centre portion of her breast. This cross serves both as an ornament and a pin holder, to which are attached her watch-chain and another chain holding a ring. Examining them under a magnifying glass, there is plainly to be seen a strong resemblance between the cross on her breast and the cross in the psychic photograph—indeed a striking resemblance. The cross on her breast is Roman in design, and so too is the cross in the psychic photograph. They are alike in design and in the same position.

Comparing the symbols and ornaments of both photographs, the only difference is their size. The cross on her breast is a miniature compared with the cross in the psychic photograph, just as the flowers or lilies in her hair are miniatures compared with the large-shaped flower or lily in the psychic photograph. [Whatever other purpose the symbols signified, it is evident from the foregoing they proved a subtle mode of identification.—J. C.]

Soul-Life

The symbols of a star-lily, heart, and cross were perfectly appropriate to Flora Loudon. They confirmed even more impressively than anything else my recognition of the psychic photograph as being the likeness of my classmate and friend of bygone years. Associated with her daily in the class-room and in the various social relations of student life, I came to know her inner life quite well. I knew Flora was an intensely aspiring soul, noble, pure, childlike, untainted by worldly ambition. Her ideal of attainment was high; she sought most earnestly to realise it; she

strove for this with the utmost application of all her powers.

A star, in the likeness of a lily, just above the forehead, is certainly a fitting symbol of such aspiration. Flora was heartily in sympathy with humanitarian and altruistic principles, not because she was a student at a Unitarian College, where such principles were favoured, but because it was her nature to live the principle of love, to place emphasis upon the law of progress, the law of universal love. We know that the symbol of a heart appropriately expresses such sentiments. But in the psychic picture it represents the real, true life of the soul, the dominating principle of a transfigured soul in that other world.

After a year of absence, Flora returned to student life at Antioch. But it soon became manifest that a change had taken place. She did not resume the regular course preparatory for college, but pursued only a few selected studies. She appeared isolated and solitary. It seemed that circumstances over which she had no control had thwarted the realisation of high aims, and suffering and sacrifice were factors of her inner life. At the end of the year she left college. The symbol of a cross, as we know it, is the most fitting symbol to express such sentiments.

Rev. CHARLES HALL COOK, D.B., A.M., Ph.D. (Diocese of Colorado, U.S.A.), Member of the American Society for Psychical Research, New York; American School of Metaphysics, New York; English Society for Psychical Research, London (American Branch, 1900–1907).

Three and a half years after the foregoing investigations, Dr Cook visited San Diego, Cal., U.S.A. (in January 1905), and learned that Mr Wyllie was putting up at the Albion Hotel. The doctor deter-

hair of the psychic photograph, just above the forehead, has five points, resembling a star or a lily, and is of the same shape or form as the miniature flowers in Flora's photograph.

Also there is in Flora's photograph, among the ornaments on her person, a small or miniature cross, fastened to the centre portion of her breast. This cross serves both as an ornament and a pin holder, to which are attached her watch-chain and another chain holding a ring. Examining them under a magnifying glass, there is plainly to be seen a strong resemblance between the cross on her breast and the cross in the psychic photograph—indeed a striking resemblance. The cross on her breast is Roman in design, and so too is the cross in the psychic photograph. They are alike in design and in the same position.

Comparing the symbols and ornaments of both photographs, the only difference is their size. The cross on her breast is a miniature compared with the cross in the psychic photograph, just as the flowers or lilies in her hair are miniatures compared with the large-shaped flower or lily in the psychic photograph. [Whatever other purpose the symbols signified, it is evident from the foregoing they proved a subtle mode of identification.—J. C.]

Soul-Life

The symbols of a star-lily, heart, and cross were perfectly appropriate to Flora Loudon. They confirmed even more impressively than anything else my recognition of the psychic photograph as being the likeness of my classmate and friend of bygone years. Associated with her daily in the class-room and in the various social relations of student life, I came to know her inner life quite well. I knew Flora was an intensely aspiring soul, noble, pure, childlike, untainted by worldly ambition. Her ideal of attainment was high; she sought most earnestly to realise it; she

strove for this with the utmost application of all her powers.

A star, in the likeness of a lily, just above the forehead, is certainly a fitting symbol of such aspiration. Flora was heartily in sympathy with humanitarian and altruistic principles, not because she was a student at a Unitarian College, where such principles were favoured, but because it was her nature to live the principle of love, to place emphasis upon the law of progress, the law of universal love. We know that the symbol of a heart appropriately expresses such sentiments. But in the psychic picture it represents the real, true life of the soul, the dominating principle of a transfigured soul in that other world.

After a year of absence, Flora returned to student life at Antioch. But it soon became manifest that a change had taken place. She did not resume the regular course preparatory for college, but pursued only a few selected studies. She appeared isolated and solitary. It seemed that circumstances over which she had no control had thwarted the realisation of high aims, and suffering and sacrifice were factors of her inner life. At the end of the year she left college. The symbol of a cross, as we know it, is the most fitting symbol to express such sentiments.

> Rev. CHARLES HALL COOK, D.B., A.M., Ph.D. (Diocese of Colorado, U.S.A.), Member of the American Society for Psychical Research, New York; American School of Metaphysics, New York; English Society for Psychical Research, London (American Branch, 1900–1907).

Three and a half years after the foregoing investigations, Dr Cook visited San Diego, Cal., U.S.A. (in January 1905), and learned that Mr Wyllie was putting up at the Albion Hotel. The doctor deter-

hair of the psychic photograph, just above the forehead, has five points, resembling a star or a lily, and is of the same shape or form as the miniature flowers in Flora's photograph.

Also there is in Flora's photograph, among the ornaments on her person, a small or miniature cross, fastened to the centre portion of her breast. This cross serves both as an ornament and a pin holder, to which are attached her watch-chain and another chain holding a ring. Examining them under a magnifying glass, there is plainly to be seen a strong resemblance between the cross on her breast and the cross in the psychic photograph—indeed a striking resemblance. The cross on her breast is Roman in design, and so too is the cross in the psychic photograph. They are alike in design and in the same position.

Comparing the symbols and ornaments of both photographs, the only difference is their size. The cross on her breast is a miniature compared with the cross in the psychic photograph, just as the flowers or lilies in her hair are miniatures compared with the large-shaped flower or lily in the psychic photograph. [Whatever other purpose the symbols signified, it is evident from the foregoing they proved a subtle mode of identification.—J. C.]

SOUL-LIFE

The symbols of a star-lily, heart, and cross were perfectly appropriate to Flora Loudon. They confirmed even more impressively than anything else my recognition of the psychic photograph as being the likeness of my classmate and friend of bygone years. Associated with her daily in the class-room and in the various social relations of student life, I came to know her inner life quite well. I knew Flora was an intensely aspiring soul, noble, pure, childlike, untainted by worldly ambition. Her ideal of attainment was high; she sought most earnestly to realise it; she

strove for this with the utmost application of all her powers.

A star, in the likeness of a lily, just above the forehead, is certainly a fitting symbol of such aspiration. Flora was heartily in sympathy with humanitarian and altruistic principles, not because she was a student at a Unitarian College, where such principles were favoured, but because it was her nature to live the principle of love, to place emphasis upon the law of progress, the law of universal love. We know that the symbol of a heart appropriately expresses such sentiments. But in the psychic picture it represents the real, true life of the soul, the dominating principle of a transfigured soul in that other world.

After a year of absence, Flora returned to student life at Antioch. But it soon became manifest that a change had taken place. She did not resume the regular course preparatory for college, but pursued only a few selected studies. She appeared isolated and solitary. It seemed that circumstances over which she had no control had thwarted the realisation of high aims, and suffering and sacrifice were factors of her inner life. At the end of the year she left college. The symbol of a cross, as we know it, is the most fitting symbol to express such sentiments.

> Rev. CHARLES HALL COOK, D.B., A.M., Ph.D. (Diocese of Colorado, U.S.A.), Member of the American Society for Psychical Research, New York; American School of Metaphysics, New York; English Society for Psychical Research, London (American Branch, 1900–1907).

Three and a half years after the foregoing investigations, Dr Cook visited San Diego, Cal., U.S.A. (in January 1905), and learned that Mr Wyllie was putting up at the Albion Hotel. The doctor deter-

hair of the psychic photograph, just above the forehead, has five points, resembling a star or a lily, and is of the same shape or form as the miniature flowers in Flora's photograph.

Also there is in Flora's photograph, among the ornaments on her person, a small or miniature cross, fastened to the centre portion of her breast. This cross serves both as an ornament and a pin holder, to which are attached her watch-chain and another chain holding a ring. Examining them under a magnifying glass, there is plainly to be seen a strong resemblance between the cross on her breast and the cross in the psychic photograph—indeed a striking resemblance. The cross on her breast is Roman in design, and so too is the cross in the psychic photograph. They are alike in design and in the same position.

Comparing the symbols and ornaments of both photographs, the only difference is their size. The cross on her breast is a miniature compared with the cross in the psychic photograph, just as the flowers or lilies in her hair are miniatures compared with the large-shaped flower or lily in the psychic photograph. [Whatever other purpose the symbols signified, it is evident from the foregoing they proved a subtle mode of identification.—J. C.]

SOUL-LIFE

The symbols of a star-lily, heart, and cross were perfectly appropriate to Flora Loudon. They confirmed even more impressively than anything else my recognition of the psychic photograph as being the likeness of my classmate and friend of bygone years. Associated with her daily in the class-room and in the various social relations of student life, I came to know her inner life quite well. I knew Flora was an intensely aspiring soul, noble, pure, childlike, untainted by worldly ambition. Her ideal of attainment was high; she sought most earnestly to realise it; she

strove for this with the utmost application of all her powers.

A star, in the likeness of a lily, just above the forehead, is certainly a fitting symbol of such aspiration. Flora was heartily in sympathy with humanitarian and altruistic principles, not because she was a student at a Unitarian College, where such principles were favoured, but because it was her nature to live the principle of love, to place emphasis upon the law of progress, the law of universal love. We know that the symbol of a heart appropriately expresses such sentiments. But in the psychic picture it represents the real, true life of the soul, the dominating principle of a transfigured soul in that other world.

After a year of absence, Flora returned to student life at Antioch. But it soon became manifest that a change had taken place. She did not resume the regular course preparatory for college, but pursued only a few selected studies. She appeared isolated and solitary. It seemed that circumstances over which she had no control had thwarted the realisation of high aims, and suffering and sacrifice were factors of her inner life. At the end of the year she left college. The symbol of a cross, as we know it, is the most fitting symbol to express such sentiments.

Rev. CHARLES HALL COOK, D.B., A.M., Ph.D. (Diocese of Colorado, U.S.A.), Member of the American Society for Psychical Research, New York; American School of Metaphysics, New York; English Society for Psychical Research, London (American Branch, 1900–1907).

Three and a half years after the foregoing investigations, Dr Cook visited San Diego, Cal., U.S.A. (in January 1905), and learned that Mr Wyllie was putting up at the Albion Hotel. The doctor deter-

hair of the psychic photograph, just above the forehead, has five points, resembling a star or a lily, and is of the same shape or form as the miniature flowers in Flora's photograph.

Also there is in Flora's photograph, among the ornaments on her person, a small or miniature cross, fastened to the centre portion of her breast. This cross serves both as an ornament and a pin holder, to which are attached her watch-chain and another chain holding a ring. Examining them under a magnifying glass, there is plainly to be seen a strong resemblance between the cross on her breast and the cross in the psychic photograph—indeed a striking resemblance. The cross on her breast is Roman in design, and so too is the cross in the psychic photograph. They are alike in design and in the same position.

Comparing the symbols and ornaments of both photographs, the only difference is their size. The cross on her breast is a miniature compared with the cross in the psychic photograph, just as the flowers or lilies in her hair are miniatures compared with the large-shaped flower or lily in the psychic photograph. [Whatever other purpose the symbols signified, it is evident from the foregoing they proved a subtle mode of identification.—J. C.]

SOUL-LIFE

The symbols of a star-lily, heart, and cross were perfectly appropriate to Flora Loudon. They confirmed even more impressively than anything else my recognition of the psychic photograph as being the likeness of my classmate and friend of bygone years. Associated with her daily in the class-room and in the various social relations of student life, I came to know her inner life quite well. I knew Flora was an intensely aspiring soul, noble, pure, childlike, untainted by worldly ambition. Her ideal of attainment was high; she sought most earnestly to realise it; she

strove for this with the utmost application of all her powers.

A star, in the likeness of a lily, just above the forehead, is certainly a fitting symbol of such aspiration. Flora was heartily in sympathy with humanitarian and altruistic principles, not because she was a student at a Unitarian College, where such principles were favoured, but because it was her nature to live the principle of love, to place emphasis upon the law of progress, the law of universal love. We know that the symbol of a heart appropriately expresses such sentiments. But in the psychic picture it represents the real, true life of the soul, the dominating principle of a transfigured soul in that other world.

After a year of absence, Flora returned to student life at Antioch. But it soon became manifest that a change had taken place. She did not resume the regular course preparatory for college, but pursued only a few selected studies. She appeared isolated and solitary. It seemed that circumstances over which she had no control had thwarted the realisation of high aims, and suffering and sacrifice were factors of her inner life. At the end of the year she left college. The symbol of a cross, as we know it, is the most fitting symbol to express such sentiments.

> Rev. CHARLES HALL COOK, D.B., A.M., Ph.D. (Diocese of Colorado, U.S.A.), Member of the American Society for Psychical Research, New York; American School of Metaphysics, New York; English Society for Psychical Research, London (American Branch, 1900–1907).

Three and a half years after the foregoing investigations, Dr Cook visited San Diego, Cal., U.S.A. (in January 1905), and learned that Mr Wyllie was putting up at the Albion Hotel. The doctor deter-

hair of the psychic photograph, just above the forehead, has five points, resembling a star or a lily, and is of the same shape or form as the miniature flowers in Flora's photograph.

Also there is in Flora's photograph, among the ornaments on her person, a small or miniature cross, fastened to the centre portion of her breast. This cross serves both as an ornament and a pin holder, to which are attached her watch-chain and another chain holding a ring. Examining them under a magnifying glass, there is plainly to be seen a strong resemblance between the cross on her breast and the cross in the psychic photograph—indeed a striking resemblance. The cross on her breast is Roman in design, and so too is the cross in the psychic photograph. They are alike in design and in the same position.

Comparing the symbols and ornaments of both photographs, the only difference is their size. The cross on her breast is a miniature compared with the cross in the psychic photograph, just as the flowers or lilies in her hair are miniatures compared with the large-shaped flower or lily in the psychic photograph. [Whatever other purpose the symbols signified, it is evident from the foregoing they proved a subtle mode of identification.—J. C.]

SOUL-LIFE

The symbols of a star-lily, heart, and cross were perfectly appropriate to Flora Loudon. They confirmed even more impressively than anything else my recognition of the psychic photograph as being the likeness of my classmate and friend of bygone years. Associated with her daily in the class-room and in the various social relations of student life, I came to know her inner life quite well. I knew Flora was an intensely aspiring soul, noble, pure, childlike, untainted by worldly ambition. Her ideal of attainment was high; she sought most earnestly to realise it; she

strove for this with the utmost application of all her powers.

A star, in the likeness of a lily, just above the forehead, is certainly a fitting symbol of such aspiration. Flora was heartily in sympathy with humanitarian and altruistic principles, not because she was a student at a Unitarian College, where such principles were favoured, but because it was her nature to live the principle of love, to place emphasis upon the law of progress, the law of universal love. We know that the symbol of a heart appropriately expresses such sentiments. But in the psychic picture it represents the real, true life of the soul, the dominating principle of a transfigured soul in that other world.

After a year of absence, Flora returned to student life at Antioch. But it soon became manifest that a change had taken place. She did not resume the regular course preparatory for college, but pursued only a few selected studies. She appeared isolated and solitary. It seemed that circumstances over which she had no control had thwarted the realisation of high aims, and suffering and sacrifice were factors of her inner life. At the end of the year she left college. The symbol of a cross, as we know it, is the most fitting symbol to express such sentiments.

Rev. CHARLES HALL COOK, D.B., A.M., Ph.D. (Diocese of Colorado, U.S.A.), Member of the American Society for Psychical Research, New York; American School of Metaphysics, New York; English Society for Psychical Research, London (American Branch, 1900–1907).

Three and a half years after the foregoing investigations, Dr Cook visited San Diego, Cal., U.S.A. (in January 1905), and learned that Mr Wyllie was putting up at the Albion Hotel. The doctor deter-

mined to have a new series of experiments. For this purpose he purchased a new camera, with a supply of 4 × 5 Stanley plates and all necessary accessories, from Patterson's Photographic Supply House. With these, and his travelling-wrap, which he used as a background, he commenced his second course of investigations. As a measure of precaution, he loaded his carriers in his dark-room at the Willard Hotel, and, after exposure, took them with his camera back, and there developed the plates exposed. Giving the account of one of these experiments—too long to produce here—Dr Cook found, on developing the plate :—

There was plainly visible upon the lower part of my breast a man's face, with moustache, whiskers, and other interesting features. I did not recognise the face, though it seemed that I had seen it somewhere.

The facts to be noted in connection with this experiment are : (1) A definite result was obtained without using the medium's camera, and without contact on his part other than his personal presence ; (2) I used my own camera and was my own photographer, whilst Mr Wyllie and the lady assistant were merely witnesses, the former of the experiment (photographing in the Albion), and the latter of the result [that of the developing in dark-room at Mr Patterson's gallery.—J. C.].

In a note on this experiment, Dr Cook says :—

About a month later, in conversation with an expert photographer, at Los Angeles, I described in detail the conditions of this experiment, and then asked him if there could have been an invisible picture or image on Mr Wyllie's hand, transferred to the plate at the time he " magnetised " it.   He said it was impossible without the action of light, and if the photographer had a phosphorescent or "radium" picture in his hand, the light or luminosity of it would easily be discoverable in the dark-room.   Also, if it were possible for light to have any effect afterwards by an exposure through the camera, the impress of the invisible picture or image on the photographer's hand would not only have to be that of contact, but especially that of a very strong pressure upon the plate ; and even then the result, he said, if any, would probably be very indistinct or much blurred.

In Dr Cook's investigations with Mr Alex. Martin, a photographer in Denver City, he noticed the frequency with which groups of children and baby faces appeared on his plates.   Here the factor of identification did not enter, but another important one did, viz. the faces came under test conditions.   Why ?   Wherefore ? *Cui bono ?*—are questions not readily answered.   Mr Martin has been successful in obtaining identifiable " extras."   But, as the baby faces are so charming— not psychic figures behaving badly—I reproduce two photographs out of those sent, each obtained under different conditions.

Mr Martin is an old man now, but still carries on business.   His studio is at 2953 Zuric Street, Denver City, Colorado, where he has resided nearly forty years.   He is a man of upright character, retiring dis. position, and is esteemed in the community.   He is not supposed to give sittings for psychic photography now. Much to his regret, " spirit pictures " still intrude on his plates, and "spoil" them from a business standpoint.

For Dr Cook, as representative of the A.S.P.R., he took photographs under the doctor's own conditions.

From Dr Cook's hitherto unpublished reports I summarise the following :—

THE INVISIBLE PHOTOGRAPHED AT A MATERIALISATION

I was present, 15th April 1903, by invitation, at a materialisation in Lincoln Hall, Denver, Colorado. The phenomena were extremely interesting. Occupying a seat nearest to the cabinet, within about twelve feet of the platform and about five feet from the camera, I saw distinctly a white form appear.

Mr Alex. Martin, photographer at 1639 Platte Street, made (under flashlight) two exposures upon the white form that stood in front of the cabinet.

There were *no* flowers or decorations in front of the cabinet or anywhere about it, or on the platform. In the rear of the cabinet there was only the plain wall of the hall, with one picture hanging on it, and just above the cabinet the motto, " Welcome."

Upon developing the two plates exposed on this occasion there were other phenomenal effects than the white form which I saw appear from the cabinet and stand upon the platform. On one plate there was to the right a column of children's and baby faces, extending from the platform to the top of the cabinet. In front of the white form there were masses of flowers, and to the left the bust and face of a female on the platform.

On the other plate there was an oval cloud of baby faces enveloping the bust of the white form and totally obliterating its face, numbering not less than twenty faces.   (See fig. 39, p. 190.)

Without giving full details from Dr Cook's report,

it is sufficient to say the doctor's confidence in Mr Martin is of the most emphatic character. What he says about materialisations and photography I can accept—not so much because of this particular instance,

Children in Column

FIG. 38.—Flashlight photograph of materialised form, and also of invisible faces, and a head and bust.

as from the testimony of Sir William Crookes, other eminent investigators, and my own actual experiences. As confirming the possibility of photographing the invisible at materialisation séances, I give the evidence of Professor Willy Reichel. Apart from his eminent

standing, he has been and is associated in France—
if not in Europe—with the brightest scientific men
of the age, who do not stultify psycho-physical
phenomena with the shallow flippancy of egotistical
conjurers, but bring to their investigation calm reserve
and the keen watchfulness of the cultured intellect.
Professor Reichel is one whose observations demand
respect.   He had been investigating in California the
phenomena of materialisation with Mr Miller.   The
number, variety, and the nature of these were so
extraordinary that he says :—

On 29th October, and again on 2nd November 1905,
I sent for a San Francisco photographer, Mr Edward
Wyllie, to see what impression would be made on a
photographic plate by the beings who appeared.   Some
remarkable pictures were taken by flashlight.   *Besides
the fully materialised forms there were shown on the
photographs several spirits who could not be seen by
the physical eyes.   In one of the latter figures I
instantly recognised an uncle of mine whom I had
made acquainted with spiritualism about twelve
years previously through the assistance of another
medium.*   [The italics are mine—J. C.]

I may add that among the spirit forms which
materialised, one was that of Mme. Reichel's sister,
which the Professor recognised, and which helped to
enlarge his views of these phenomena.   Mr Wyllie on
several other occasions, although not stated in this
book, took photographs equally interesting to those
mentioned, for Professor and Mme. Reichel.

Whatever may be thought of the foregoing statements concerning materialisations, testimony of this

nature cannot be lightly thrown aside. Here we have evidence of the presence of intelligent persons—albeit invisible—at materialisations, and the fact of identification.

Dr Cook, following up his experiences, on 15th April 1903 decided to have a series of test experiments with Mr Alex. Martin. The doctor called upon Mr Martin and explained his object, and Mr Martin not only granted him the privilege, but gave him his services without remuneration. Not only were the conditions severe in their simplicity, but certain Intelligences had promised through the hand of an automatist to assist and give their "pictures."

The plates used and bought by the doctor were never out of his possession, save when he himself put them in the carrier. After exposure, these were taken away by him to his residence, 1906 Pearl Street, and developed by him. So that Martin had nothing to do except to take off the cap of the camera, time and make the exposures. From beginning to end Dr Cook had control of all the photographic procedure. In two experiments out of eleven, in addition to the camera, lens, carrier, and all accessories being carefully examined, all the rugs from the floor and the back screens were removed, so that there was nothing left in the room save the camera, and a wooden chair to sit on. The white wall of the room was used as the background. The weather being warm, Mr Martin was in his shirt-sleeves. There were no mirrors or trick appliances either in the room or about the old man, and under these conditions invisible forms and faces were obtained upon the plates.

Concerning this concluding experiment of the

FIG. 39.—Photograph of group of children's faces which enveloped the face and bust of the lady so as to hide them from view, i.e. the visible is not, but the invisible is, photographed.

twelve, which took place on 14th May 1903, Dr Cook says :—

On my way to Mr Martin's, I called upon Miss Elizabeth Maud Weatherhead, the automatist to whom I referred, thinking that her presence might help in my experiments. I explained to her that I was going to try for a " spirit " photograph at Mr Martin's, and wanted her to be the sitter. She said she would take the next car to the gallery. Before Miss W. arrived, I examined carefully the interior of Mr Martin's camera, lens, and plate-holder, removed the rugs from the floor, and the screens behind the sitter's chair, and there was only the white plastered wall as background, which I also carefully inspected.

On Miss W.'s arrival, at my request, Mr Martin removed the plate-holder from the camera, and we went into the dark closet together. I then took a plate from the box I carried in my side coat-pocket, and at my request Mr Martin drew back the slide, and we together, he holding the plate at one end and I at the other, placed it in the holder, fastened it, and closed the holder. With one hand resting on the plate-holder, I opened the door. At my request, Mr Martin, with the other, took hold of it, and we went into the gallery. Miss W. took the sitter's chair (whilst Mr Martin had placed the plate-holder on a chair near the camera). We focussed the camera upon Miss W. Mr Martin adjusted the holder in it, uncapped the lens, and timed an exposure. Removing the holder from the camera, we went into the dark closet. I took the plate and put it into an empty box that I carried in my coat-pocket. This plate I took to my residence and locked it up till I had time and opportunity for developing it. This was done shortly afterwards by an amateur photographer and myself, in the rooms of the former. The experiment was a success, for on the upper half of the photograph there was a cloud of baby faces, numbering more than thirty, over and about the head of Miss Weatherhead.

Psychic Photography in South Africa

The photographer, Mr Bland, referred to in these papers, has been testified to by several correspondents. Of these, Mr A. Brittlebank's testimony is the most important.   He is not only a photographer of forty years' experience, but has had ample opportunities to investigate.   He sent me a parcel of photographs. In reply to a request for details, Mr Brittlebank, writing from the Salisbury Hotel, Johannesburg, 19th June 1910, says :—

As regards the photographs, I am not able to recognise any.   I can only *imagine* that on the photo where Mr Horne and I are together, the female is the spirit form of my sister, to whom I was attached years ago.   The greater part of the photographs were taken under conditions which would satisfy any practical photographer as to the genuineness of the spirit forms.

The photographer, Mr Bland, was, at the time, carrying on business at Dorrnfontein, a suburb of Johannesburg.   In my opinion he had excellent psychic powers, but, as seen from the pose of his sitters, he was not an artistic photographer.   He was a very nervous man, and terribly afraid of being accused of fraud.   The opinion which I formed of him was, and is, that he " would not if he could, and could not if he would," impose on anyone.   So far as my experience goes, Mr Bland is a perfectly honourable man.   I vouch for all photographs when I am the sitter.   .

In No. 1, where the subjects are a gentleman sitting and a lady standing, the form of the gentleman is almost obliterated by the " extra's " aura, while in the left-hand corner is a full-sized figure of a lady draped in white, and surrounded by flowers.   The " extras " are differently focussed and out of proportion to the material subjects photographed.

No. 2. The subject is a lady, and the psychic
"extra" is the faintly defined face of a female surrounded by auric light.

No. 3. Photograph of lady in which there appears

Fig. 40.—Photograph No. 7 of Mr Brittlebank's
parcel; and psychic "extra" of Kaffir Umfaan
or servant boy of the sitter, taken under test
conditions.

the three-quarter length figure of a female, classically
clad, and sorrowful in expression.

No. 4. This photograph was taken in total darkness.
There is no subject. The psychic form is not unlike
a Greek peasant. The dress, style, and pose suggest

13

that. The scientific value of this picture arises from the undoubted fact of its being taken by its own light. Exposure eight minutes.

No. 5. The subjects are Mr Brittlebank and a friend. The psychic "extra" is that of a little girl standing behind a chair, on which the friend rests his hands.

No. 6. Same lady sitter as in No. 1, and two psychic forms (features ill defined) clad in white flowing robes. Of scientific but no identifiable value.

No. 7. Sitter a friend of Mr Brittlebank's, with psychic face of Kaffir boy well defined on background.

No. 8. Same lady subject as in No. 1, with psychic "extra" of old gentleman possessing intelligent features and graceful, flowing white beard.

No. 9. Photograph of Mr Brittlebank and Mr Horne, and the identified psychic portrait of Mr Brittlebank's sister. However valuable, the photograph is somewhat faded and does not lend itself to reproduction.

No. 10. Photograph of Mr and Mrs Horne, and the graceful face and bust of a young lady. Bust partly illuminated.

No. 11 is that of Mr and Mrs Horne, and the clearly definable face of an elderly person with whiskers.

The last two pictures were taken under test conditions by Mr Horne, who purchased the plates used from Mr Davis, photographer, who loaded Mr

Bland's slides.   When the portraits were taken, Mr Horne took the slides and contents back to Mr Davis' for development.   Mr Bland, the psychic photo-

FIG. 41.—The Horne photograph No. 10, and unknown lady, taken under test conditions by Mr Bland, psychic photographer.

grapher, had no opportunity of doing other than make the exposure.

The photographs of No. 7 (that of the Kaffir boy) and No. 10 (of the young lady) are given, not on account of recognition, but because of scientific value.

In addition to the photographs sent me by Mr Brittlebank, I received photograph of Mr O. W.

Menzel (of the Union of South Africa Department of Agriculture, Pretoria), who writes, dated 13th December 1910 :—

I have no objection to the publishing of my name in connection with spirit photo, which I maintain has a *great* resemblance to my father.   I am not a convinced spiritualist.

This testimony is valuable as testifying to the fact of psychic photography by one not warped in his judgment by a bias towards spiritualism.

On examination of the batch of photographs, I find the same old problems to solve as in most psychic photographs taken in the United States and in Britain, viz. that of focussing and light.   These problems are not solved until we find the key in psychography.

CHAPTER IX

THREE PSYCHIC PHOTOGRAPHS AND A SPIRIT MESSAGE

BEFORE Mr Edward Wyllie was induced to come to this country, Mr A. K. Venning, well known to the readers of the spiritualistic press, sent a letter to *The Two Worlds* (1st January 1909), to the effect that some simple plan be carried out to test Mr Wyllie's abilities. He suggested that "half a dozen of those interested send locks of hair for Mr Wyllie to photograph." He had no doubt they would receive proof. A nominal fee of two shillings was to be sent with the article. The editor was invited to arrange. There was no arrangement, and instead of six, probably forty applied. All got something, and some obtained identifiable portraits of departed friends. I could give some of these, but confine myself to those in which I have a special interest.

Among those who complied were two ladies, viz. Mrs A. S. Hunter, widow of Dr Archibald Hunter, Bridge of Allan; and Madame A. L. Pogosky, London. As we are concerned in the statements made by these ladies, I wish to emphasise my convictions as to their intelligence, sincerity, and probity. Mrs Hunter has been resident in Bridge of Allan, Scotland, for forty years, where her late husband practised as hygienic physician of the well-known hydropathic establishment, which he built, and which has been carried on for over half a century.

Madame Pogosky has resided in London for twenty-six years, where she directs a philanthropic undertaking, the Russian Peasant Industries. This lady and Mrs Hunter have long been friends, and both are interested in kindred subjects.

I now reproduce the photographs and the results of the experiments.

Mrs Hunter received the photo (fig. 42) early in February 1909. Taking a casual glance at it, and disappointed at not obtaining, as she had hoped, her husband's likeness, she posted the card to her friend, who sent it back with the card she had received. On Madame Pogosky's card there was Dr Hunter's face, and another not recognised. Before closing this account I will deal with this unknown "extra."

Mrs Hunter immediately acquainted Mr Wyllie of the strange fact that her husband's portrait came on Madame Pogosky's card. In Mr Wyllie's reply, dated Los Angeles, 17th March 1909, he says: "It is certainly hard to understand, but these have happened many times."

Mrs Hunter's photograph was returned to her, but she being seriously ill, it was put aside and overlooked. I had written to her about Mr Wyllie and the arrangements for his coming to Great Britain. In her reply,

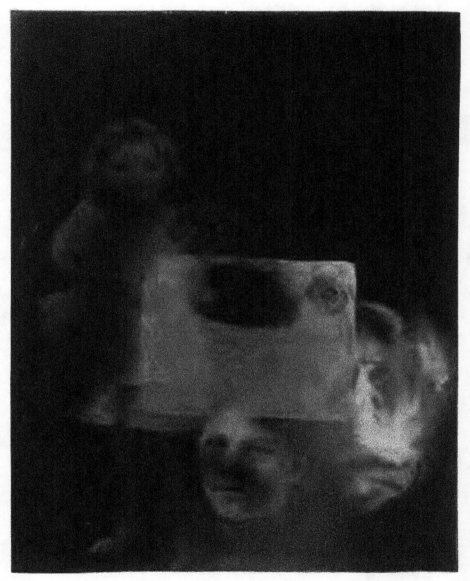

Fig. 42.—Photograph of letter and lock of hair sent by Mrs A. S. Hunter, and three "extras," done by Mr Edward Wyllie.

which I summarise, dated 2nd August 1909, she said :—

I think I told you my Russian friend held the photos

which she and I promised you.   My long and severe illness this spring seems to have played tricks with my memory, for I have found the card, which I must have got back from Madame Pogosky—-after she had shown it (with her own, which had my husband's face in it) to Mr Stead.   I must have laid it away and forgotten I had it.

But strange to say, I seemed to remember that I did *not* recognise any of the faces on my card—only Dr Hunter on Madame Pogosky's.   Yet, yesterday, when I got sight of it, I was at once amazed to find three faces, all quite clear and familiar.   One, an old schoolfellow who passed away a few years ago, and whom I saw the day after she passed—here—as if lying in bed and face muffled up.   On inquiry, my sister told me that was how she lay in her last illness. The other two are relatives of mine.   The youngest was named after me.   There were two girls and a boy. One of these sisters passed away before, and the other after him.   This child is very like the photos of several sisters of hers that we have in the house. The other is older, and more like what she would be now.   All three came to me several times through the mediumship of Miss Macreadie, of London.

To this is added the remarkable statement :—

I am certain that this photo has *become* more definite and clear and legible than when it arrived months ago.

Granting that there is no mistake in identification, and that the "extras" bear a striking family likeness to those portraits in her possession, and confirm communications received prior to being taken, this would be fair evidence from the spiritualistic standpoint.   As to the photograph becoming clearer, although this is the reverse of usual experience, I have taken the trouble to search all available records, and find that there have been similar cases.

Before recording what Madame Pogosky says, it is to be noted that Mrs Hunter's identification was promptly given me in two letters some time before her illness took place. The evidence of identity is substantiated by portraits of the doctor in the Bridge of Allan. I knew Dr Hunter well. He frequently visited me in Glasgow. I think it is a very good likeness of him. Mrs Coates knew him too, as the doctor was a friend of her father, the late Mr David Anderson, of Glasgow, and says it is much older, and not so virile as when she saw him last. I have shown the photograph to others, and all say it is a good likeness. One who knew him intimately, but declines publicity, says: "It is very like him as he looked towards the end."

From Madame Pogosky's letter I take the following :—

41 OLD BOND STREET, LONDON,
3rd May 1910.

DEAR MR COATES,—I read your note on Mrs Hunter's experience. Now I send you mine. The spirit photo enclosed was done at the same time as Mrs Hunter's, in Los Angeles, by Mr Wyllie. You can see my own handwriting on the envelope, and behind it Dr Hunter's face. Why Dr Hunter appeared on mine and not on his wife's photo puzzled us not a little. I expected my own brother, and never thought to get Dr Hunter, as he never saw me while on earth plane.

Psychic experiences cannot be taken in this fragmentary way, because they have a much deeper

FIG. 43.—Photograph of lock of hair sent by Madame L. Pogosky, on which appears the face of Dr Hunter, and a lady's face.

meaning and significance, and form not a separate happening, but are *part* of our life, and it seems to

me can be understood only in accordance with this
life. . . .

When the photo arrived from Los Angeles I asked
my unseen correspondent why he sent it to me
instead of Mrs Hunter's. he laconically said 'You
needed it more.' Now, this ... ...
was at the beginning of my psychic spiritual
evolution—from a state of traditional religious faith
to one of truth, or glimpses of it. There had been
awakened in myself a consciousness of spiritual and
life eternal. Only those who have passed through
painful processes in rebuilding every soul ... new
being to the new truth know how their ... are
are beset with doubts. Now when you have realised
this, you will understand why the doctor said 'You
needed this more.' Mrs Hunter is a spiritualist of
twenty years' standing, perhaps longer. She required
no proofs. Now, that is the explanation ... If Mrs
Hunter thought her photo got ... I am inclined
to think mine got hazier. I hope you will get a good
reproduction of it.—Yours sincerely,

                                    A. L. POGOSKY.

Madame Pogosky at first used to get messages from
the doctor through Ouija. Then she developed
impressional or telepathic writing, and many short
but clearly individualised letters were sent through
her hands to Mrs Hunter. who knew their import
when Madame Pogosky did not. Latterly this lady
developed both clairaudient and clairvoyant faculties.
and was able to see and converse with her friends,
including the doctor, and this photograph. most
prized, to her was the crowning evidence. Just one
point here. The lady is a stranger to me—not
unknown, however—but her remark that the doctor's

reply was a laconic one is to me very convincing. He had a quiet, direct, and often humorous way of speaking. It was just his style.

This is the first case on record where the invisible has been only clairvoyantly perceived, and whose photograph has been recognised on that basis. In this interesting case Madame Pogosky never saw Dr Hunter in the body. Photography demonstrates that that which is clairvoyantly perceived has often an objective, although invisible, existence. What the psychical researchers call "a veridical hallucination" is demonstrated by photography. Here again we are on the borderland of thought photography, dealt with in *Seeing the Invisible*.

The hitherto unrecognised face (fig. 43) of a lady proved to be that of the late Mrs John Auld. As soon as we saw this face, I at once notified Madame Pogosky that we identified it. In her letter, dated 6th May, from 41 Old Bond Street, London, W., she says :—

I am glad that you and Mrs Coates recognised Dr Hunter, and even the other face. I have given this experience as a proof in my article to the *Russian Theosophical Messenger*, as in Russia there are also so many who have no real faith, and look for tests.

I mention the foregoing to show that it was not an afterthought on our part, the recognition. I now give the testimony of the gentleman to whom this unidentified face (by others) proved of most interest.

Mr Auld first saw this likeness on Friday, 20th May 1910. He had been abroad for the winter. Had he been home sooner, I could not have shown him the photographs, which I had only received with Madame Pogosky's letter of the 3rd May, in which we learned that Dr Hunter's and Mrs Auld's portraits had been taken by Mr Wyllie in Los Angeles, long before his arrival in this country.

In giving Mr Auld's statement, I desire to say that I have known this gentleman, who is a neighbour, for about sixteen years. He is a practical man, one of the heads of an important firm of engineers, whose inventions are employed by all leading engineers. His caution, discrimination, and integrity I never have had reason to doubt. He has little to gain and much to lose by publicity in this matter. I now summarise his remarks on seeing the photograph :—

It is the portrait of my wife. I am surprised to get it in this way. It is better than the one on my breast [alluding to a psychic picture taken in Rothesay, dealt with elsewhere]. It is clearer. It is a better test than if I obtained it in your house. It is her face. Lest I should be misled by general resemblance, I recognise every feature in detail. It is a remarkable test. But it is not what I expected. I thought if I obtained her spirit photograph she would be more like what I thought she would be from the happy messages which I received through Mrs Coates. But instead of the likeness which I conceived would be given me, *this face represents her as she was in her last illness*, and is a very striking likeness indeed.

As the remark, " It is a better test than if taken in

your house," is somewhat cryptic, I may explain that
when Mr Wyllie's mediumship was talked over in
Rothesay, some ten months before Mr Wyllie's arrival
in Scotland, Mrs John Auld was asked, when controlling Mrs Coates, if she could not get a photograph
given us through Mr Wyllie's mediumship. She said,
" I will try, John "; and we laughingly replied : "If
you succeed, it will be a good test." Shortly before
Mr Auld left Rothesay, when the subject was again
discussed, Mrs Auld informed him that he " would get
a great surprise," and he did; for I received this
photograph just seventeen days before his return.

When Mrs Coates and I saw the unrecognised (?)
photo, it was indeed a surprising bit of evidence.
We knew the face at once, having seen the same
face on Mr Auld's breast, in a photograph taken of
that gentleman by Mr Wyllie in Glenbeg House in
October 1909.

No one who has given any attention to spirit
photography but realises that identifiable portraits
are the *crux* on which the value of evidence turns, as
far as spiritualists are concerned. All the rest—
testing — is so much research, scientific or otherwise,
into the possibilities of photography. Here we have
an identified photograph of a lady, taken by a
stranger six thousand miles away, wholly ignorant of
either Mr Auld or ourselves. I had not written this
medium till the 17th of March 1909, nearly two
months after this picture was obtained, and of its
existence none in Rothesay were aware till it was

sent from London in May, nearly fourteen months afterwards.   Truly truth is stranger than fiction.

Whether coincidence or design, the fact remains that Mrs Auld's first photograph was obtained in Los Angeles.   Mrs Coates's grandmother was obtained there also, and neither Mr Auld nor Mrs Coates was aware of the fact for months afterwards, and both obtained confirmatory psycho-portraits of these departed ones in Glenbeg House, as shown elsewhere.

A Spirit on Spirit Photography

On Sunday evening, 22nd May 1910, at a little private sitting held in our house, Mr Auld spoke about the two portraits which he had received of his good lady, the one which came on his breast, and the other and better—or at least clearer—portrait which was obtained in Los Angeles.

Mrs Coates, being controlled by Mr Auld's wife, said in reply to Mr Auld's questions:—

I wish to dispel sadness from your mind, John, about myself, owing to the photograph which you have received.   Even now I feel sad in coming back, when I think about my last illness.   There were complications to make me doubly sad at that time. I did not feel prepared to go.   I had in mental vision over and over again portrayed the many happy days we would have together.   The change came so soon and so severely, I cannot honestly say that I was either willing or ready to go.   No wonder that I was sad.   I did not look upon life then as I do now. Everything then seemed so cross-purposed.   I had not the opportunity to develop my own powers, or to do you justice. I always felt something behind telling me that I would not be a long liver. I had the impression that there was something wrong. When having this photograph—unknown to myself—I was overcome with the memories of the past. The few short years and the many troubles rolled over my mind again. I tried to get over it, *but the deed was done*. My face had on it the impression of my last illness.

I certainly went to Los Angeles as you suggested, and tried to influence the photographer; but when I was photographed, I wish to tell you that I was not aware of it at the time. You cannot understand this. You know as much about photography as we do. *What you have got, John, is not me as I am, but what I was, and what you remembered me to be in those last days.* I cannot explain it otherwise. When we think what we were like upon the earth, the ether condenses around us and encloses us like an envelope. We are within those ether-like substances which are drawn to us, and our thoughts of what we were like and what we would be better known by, produce not only the clothing, but the fashioning of our forms and features. It is here the spirit chemists step in. They fashion according to their ability that ether substance quicker than thought, and produce our earth features so that they may be recognised.

Our thoughts produce our garments, the cut and colouring of the same, and the chemists, using their own magnetic power over the etherealised matter, mould it so, and give to it an appearance such as we were in earth-life. It is made to look like what we were, and instantly after we are photographed, this etherealised or materialised figure or face is disintegrated. Many faces are presented and photographed of which we have no idea until that fact is made known to us; many forms are photographed of which the originals are not aware; but when I was photo-

Chemists, thoughts, &

graphed and coming into contact with the medium at Los Angeles, that etherealised matter was attracted or clung to me, taking on the features fashioned by my thoughts, which were, by some sudden impulse or mysterious law, those of my last illness on earth. There is a creative power of thought which is used by all, although little understood, and this power is used by us more fully and determinately than I can explain. We are employing it freely here and using it continuously in producing phenomena on earth. We are limited by many things, and principally by the scepticism, indifference, and want of sympathy of those on earth. We are clothed in beautiful garments of many colours, and our garments correspond to our spiritual and mental conditions. Our homes are fashioned by our thoughts out of grosser ethers, and many other things out of the finer ethers. But the substance drawn to us (on the earth plane) when we are photographed is grosser still than anything we have in the spirit world. It is this material which is used for spirit pictures. If you were less anxious to get a spirit photograph — for anxiety is a great hindrance, too, John—you would be more successful, for then you would furnish better conditions both for us and the spirit chemists to utilise the thought-forces and this etherealised matter therewith to produce our pictures. It is when you and we are in passive states that the subconscious thought - forces are liberated; and when the physical mediums on earth realise too that mental passivity is as necessary as moral and physical states of health, then on your side we will have better material to work with. We have to economise; hence symbols are given to convey important lessons, and faces instead of full forms. *And all that which is given is within your own atmosphere of thought and being.* Maybe when the spirit chemists on our side, and the mediums on your side, and the sitters on both sides, are more united and in sympathy it may be possible to give you pictures of ourselves as we are, but till then you must be content to get what you can, namely, the work of spirit acting on your subconscious planes of thought and on material substances, although that in its refined and etherealised condition may be considered by you to be spirit substance. I know that all this is difficult for you to understand, but my photographs given you should help you to appreciate that in this matter we are governed by laws, and that which is given are earth pictures, and not of ourselves in the life of spirit.

Mr Auld, to whom this message was given, consented to its publication, and the two photographs, one of which is presented here, with Dr Hunter's psychic picture.

Although somewhat out of chronological order, I give another case where articles photographed produced an " extra," but the photograph was taken in our house. It is of interest to note that the first identifiable psychic portrait which was obtained through Wyllie's mediumship in Great Britain came in this fashion.

Mr Oscar E. Drummond called at Rothesay shortly after Mr Wyllie's arrival, and asked me if I thought the medium could obtain the portrait of his father, if he (Mr Drummond) gave Mr Wyllie some articles to photograph. I said it might be worth a trial. He gave me a letter from his mother (in India), a photograph of his father (deceased), and another of his mother. These I placed in a large envelope and gave it to Mr Wyllie. That gentleman pinned the envelope on the back screen and photographed it. Upon the

plate being developed, there appeared on it, besides
the envelope, a man's face.   Both the negative and
the print were shown (29th September 1909) to Mr
Drummond, who declared: " It is the head and face of

FIG. 44.—Photograph of envelope and contents, with
psychic picture of William Adolphus Drummond,
done by Mr Wyllie in Rothesay.

grandfather; . . . when I return to Glasgow, I will
make an affidavit in support of my statement."
In due course I received his attestation, from which
I take the following extract:—
I wish to testify to the following extraordinary
facts:—I called on Mr Coates, Rothesay, where I had

several sittings with Mr Edward Wyllie, medium-photographer. The first sitting was from a package containing a letter from my mother, a photo of my father (deceased), and a photo of my mother (now living). The above were placed in an envelope by Mr Coates, and marked by Mr Wyllie, No. 3, and then pinned on the screen. When the plate was developed, there appeared on it what Mr Coates called a "psychic extra." Upon examination of the print, I found—and here certify my conscientious belief that the same is—the portrait of my grandfather, the late William Adolphus Drummond, who died in India in 1866. I knew him from a photograph which was in our house, and from descriptions from my uncles, and found a resemblance to my eldest uncle, who was his living image. The psychic picture is exceedingly like him, with this difference: grandfather had a beard in the photo, and my uncle in life was clean-shaven. As a family likeness the spirit portrait is remarkable. . . .

OSCAR ERIC DRUMMOND.

KEIG VILLA,
BISHOPBRIGGS, GLASGOW.

Sworn attestation before, and signed by, John Macdonald, J.P. for the County of the City of Glasgow, 20th October 1909.[1]

Mr Drummond had several sittings subsequently with Mr Wyllie in Rothesay and in Glasgow, and obtained several psychic pictures, interesting enough, but, from the point of identification, blanks.

Each testimony given in this chapter has been that of sane, clear-headed, and sincere persons, and if not corroborated by other evidence, the combined effect is substantial, as the testimonies interlink. In these

[1] Reproduced from *The Two Worlds*, Manchester, in which it was originally published.—J. C.

cases I know that evidence could be given in substantiation, but is withheld because of the fear of being associated with what might be illegitimate—spirits or spiritualism. I could fill a large work with photographs and the most telling evidence if I would only suppress the names and addresses of those most concerned and the witnesses. I have given the foregoing cases, and thank the writers—who through modesty shun publicity, but in the interests of truth have given me the facts recorded.

If some of the good people who had articles photographed by Mr Wyllie in Glenbeg House, and who obtained identifiable portraits of departed friends, had consented to permit these to be reproduced, and allowed the details, with their names, to be published, I could —because the photographs would make better blocks —have given some striking cases. The foregoing shows Mr Wyllie's methods and what we suppose he did with the locks of hair sent him to Los Angeles. That a lock of hair or other article should form a *nexus* between the owner of it and (the photograph of) a departed requires some thinking out. But those who have read my book, *Seeing the Invisible*, will find a possible clue to the solution.

CHAPTER X

THE story of the Los Angeles photograph is very interesting, especially as that photograph has been the means of causing considerable discussion of a nature which I little anticipated when the facts, as I knew them, were first related by me.

I sent a letter to Mr Wyllie, with two small locks of hair—one of Mrs Coates's and the other of mine. With the exception of our signatures, the letter and the address on the envelope were typewritten. The letter was dated and posted at Rothesay on 17th March 1909.

I did not get a reply as I expected, and on waiting two months, I wrote again reminding Mr Wyllie of the letter and its contents. His, of later date, informed me that he had sent on " pictures," and that he was surprised that I had not received them. Although negotiations were entered into which subsequently brought Mr Wyllie over to Scotland, nothing further was heard by me of the experiment till he arrived; when unpacking, on 24th September 1909, in our house, his trunk, which held his camera, with other things, he came across a print of the photograph which he took in Los Angeles. He seemingly was unaware that it was there, and it must have been put there by a friend who did his packing.

FIG. 45.—The photograph of envelope and contents, sent 17th March 1909 to Los Angeles, with psychic "extras" of an old man, old lady, and letter with initials "E. D. G.," done by Mr Wyllie in June or July of that year.

Of the date of taking this last picture for me Mr Wyllie has no remembrance; but he thinks he took it in July 1909.

The print discloses the envelope, the date and the address of the letter, also my name and address printed in the top left-hand corner.   In addition to the envelope and letter which form the subject of the photograph, there appear as " extras " three (psychically produced) pictures.   These are two clearly defined heads, a man's and a woman's, and what looks like a letter with the initials " E. D. G." written on it.   As soon as Mrs Coates examined this card, she at once recognised the portrait of the woman as that of her maternal grandmother, Mrs Tweedale, who resided in Rothesay many years before passing over.   I did not know the old lady, but her photograph, owing to the death of her son-in-law (my father-in-law), came into our possession about three years previously.   Whatever has been said about the man's face, that of the old lady has been fully identified.   A critical examination of the psychic portrait and the photograph in our possession clearly demonstrates two things: first, that of identification; and second, that the psychic extra is neither a copy of the latter, nor of a corresponding period.

With reference to the identification of Mrs Coates's maternal grandmother, I will mention, in addition to Mrs Coates's opinion, the following :—

Mr J. J. Morse, editor of *The Two Worlds*, Manchester, who had the opportunity, on 29th September 1909, of examining both the enlarged photograph of the old lady, in Glenbeg House, with that of the *original* Los Angeles print, cordially endorsed the foregoing statement in *The Two Worlds* of 22nd October 1909.

As to the two other psychic productions, viz. the man's head and the symbol, with the letters " E. D. G." thereon, the solution did not come so readily; but *I was impressed* to send a *copy* of the Los Angeles print to Mr E. W. Wallis, editor of *Light*, with a note.   He says :—

In *Light* of September 25th we announced that we had received a telegram from Mr Coates, dated September 22nd, that Mr Wyllie had arrived. Writing three days later, on September 25th, Mr Coates says :—

" I have now a photograph lying on my desk which somehow had been mislaid, and which turned up when Mr Wyllie was unpacking yesterday, and contains, with two other 'extras,' the undoubted likeness of Mrs Coates's grandmother.   You will remember that this came from photographing a lock of hair in Los Angeles, and the likeness is corroborated by a likeness which we have in the house.   Of the other 'extras' there is a profile of a man, older and not unlike myself—so I am told—but who it is I cannot truly say, although the face appears familiar. The other item seems to be a letter on which is written, largely, the letters 'E. D. G.'   The hand-writing is familiar to both of us, but what they mean and what this symbol is we cannot yet tell."

On receipt of the print of the photograph referred to above, the written initials reminded us of those of our esteemed correspondent, the late Mr E. D Girdle-stone, whose letters appeared in *Light* for many years, and although we had seen him but once, the face on the photograph seemed to resemble his.   Consequently, we communicated with Mrs Girdlestone, and in her reply that lady stated that in the autumn of last year she sent portraits of Mr Girdlestone and of herself to Los Angeles, Cal., U.S.A.—" in the hope

that Mr Wyllie would be able to let us have some of
his spirit photographs back.   He sent us a photograph
with the portraits of my husband and myself in the
centre and a lot of faces all over—but neither he nor
I could in the least recognise a single one."

With her letter Mrs Girdlestone kindly sent us a
print of the photograph of Mr Girdlestone that had
been sent to Mr Wyllie.   On comparing this with the
photograph received from Mr Coates, we found them
to be identical, save that the face had been reversed,
and in the Wyllie photograph the *left* side was
apparently shown   We say "apparently," because
the hair was exactly the same in both.

We then sent the Wyllie photograph to Mrs
Girdlestone, who, when returning it, wrote as
follows :—

"This photograph of my husband is *certainly a
reversed* copy of the one I sent to Mr Wyllie a year
ago.   My husband never parted his hair on the *right*
side of his face, as it appears here.   The signature
'E. D. G.' is *mine*, and not my husband's.   I signed
all letters dictated by him to me with his initials;
his handwriting is quite different.   If you compare
this photograph with the one I sent you, you will see
that it is a poor copy of a reversed one ; which is easily
done by printing from the *glass* side instead of the
film side of the negative.   I am a photographer of
considerable experience, although only an amateur,
and therefore know.   Printing from the glass side
gives a blurred print."

The importance of the facts stated by Mrs Girdlestone is indicated in the following comment written
by a spiritualist, who, like ourselves, would have been
greatly pleased to have a completely convincing
photograph.   He writes :—

" A photograph showing (apparently) the *left* side of
a head and *not* showing the parting that *ought to be
there* cannot be a real photograph of a spirit form,

and it is *in every probability and according to all normal physical laws* a print from the reverse side of a negative showing the *right* side of the head. To take such a photograph normally would be *impossible.* It can only be done by the reversal of a photograph previously taken."

As regards the initials " E. D. G.," which Mrs Girdlestone says are in her handwriting, Mr Coates says: " The initials to be imitated would have to be actually forged at least eight times as large as the original letters, to appear as they do in card all out of proportion with the letter sheet with which they appear to have connection."

With reference to the portrait of Mrs Coates's grandmother (on the same plate), Mr Coates says:—

" It has been identified by one of our local magistrates, who knew her when he was a youth, and remembers her perfectly ; and it is also sustained by a local photographer—a thorough sceptic as far as psychic photography is concerned, although that is no qualification—who compared the photos, the one in the house and the 'psychic extra,' and it is his opinion that while the identification is complete there are several differences, viz. the photograph in the house is a finished, touched-up photograph of later date, and the psychic portrait of earlier date, as Mrs Coates remembers her, and is not touched up in any way. He cannot account for it, or for those done in the house."

So far for the Los Angeles photograph and the reception of the matter by *Light.*

From the foregoing it will be seen that Mr Wyllie is—by suggestion—charged with fraudulent practices. The charge amounts to this, that Wyllie, for a paltry sum of four shillings, puts himself to a great amount of labour (which no ordinary photographer could possibly do for the money) and produces a photograph which would require at least the following operations :—

(a) To take a photograph of the head of Mr Girdlestone.

(b) To take a reduced photograph of the reversed side of a print of (a).

(c) To carefully and exactly forge the initials "E. D. G." on a blank sheet of paper.

(d) To fold the paper and take a photograph of it.

(e) To pin up my letter and contents, as seen in the Los Angeles photograph, with the forgeries on the back screen—or in some other manner —and while photographing them get the so well attested, genuine psychic photograph of the late Mrs Tweedale.

Both the lady and the spiritualist may be competent amateur photographers, but the assumption of fraud makes one thing clear, that they are not experts in spirit photography. They do not seem to know anything of the history of the subject, nor do they appear to have heard of the *reproductions, duplications,* and other efforts made by the Intelligences in the Invisible to make their power and presence known to us. The fact of the recognised and fully identified spirit portrait of Mrs Tweedale is overlooked by these amateur experts, in their haste to charge Mr Wyllie with dishonest practices.

A careful examination of even the *copy* of the Los Angeles photograph and of the Girdlestone head reveals the fact that, although it is that of the reversed side of the head, and a very much reduced one at that, *it is neither a poor nor a blurred print.* such as printing from the glass side of a negative would give. Dismissing this, we have the two facts so common in spirit photography, two *reproductions,* viz. of a head and of the initials " E. D. G.," and it is admitted at once that the pictures of material things at present, or having been, in existence are not and cannot be photographs of spirits. That is, if psychic photographs of departed persons, of themselves, as they appeared in bodily form while on earth, can be called photographs of spirits. Letting that pass for review elsewhere, it is agreed that these two "extras" are not and cannot be called spirit photos. Does this mean that they have been dishonestly made? By no means. Even on the other charge, I have submitted both this and similar photographs to non-spiritualistic, practical photographers, and asked them if they would produce me a similar photograph, and they admitted that they could not.

There is another item left out of the calculations of those in haste to condemn rather than investigate, and that is as follows :—

Mrs Coates obtained a second picture of her grandmother (fig. 46) on 17th October 1909. This portrait is not only larger but clearer than the first received in the Los Angeles photograph. When Mr Wyllie was packing up his old and favourite camera and all his accessories, prior to leaving for Glasgow on the day mentioned, Mrs Coates was suddenly impressed to ask for a sitting. She did not like to do this, as we knew that Mr Wyllie was busy packing. When Mrs Coates went into the room everything was packed

Fig. 46.—Photograph of Mrs Coates, and the psychic picture of her grandmother, taken by Mr Ed. Wyllie, in Glenbeg House, Rothesay.

up save a Kodak camera and some 7 × 5-inch plates, supplied by Mr Wm. Meldrum, M.P.S., chemist, Victoria Street, Rothesay, of which four were put aside in carriers, for three visitors who were coming before he left. Mr Wyllie said he had a plate to spare and he would use that. My back screen was wheeled into the room, the Kodak mounted and adjusted, and the one plate exposed on Mrs Coates. When developed there was an " extra " on it. That " extra " was this other fresh portrait of Mrs Tweedale, larger, fuller, and in a different position than in the much discussed and, as we have seen, much condemned Los Angeles photograph. It is well to note the fact that Mr Wyllie's special camera and accessories were packed away; his favourite black back screen and the negatives of pictures taken in Glenbeg House, of which prints were taken, *were in my possession*; that he did not even have the negative of the Los Angeles photograph, that being left behind in America; and yet this psychic picture of a relative came in response to Mrs Coates's obedience to the sudden impression received by her to sit again. I merely state the facts, and truly think they are corroborative of the genuineness of the other photograph under review.

I sent all letters received from Mr Wallis, with marked copies of *Light*, to Mr Wyllie, and obtained the following :—

30 CORUNNA ST., GLASGOW, W.
Saturday, 23rd *October* 1909.

DEAR MR COATES,—I gave the (Glasgow Test) Committee another sitting this afternoon. As to the Girdlestone affair, I can only say that if it is him (which must be, as his widow says so), she certainly thinks I placed it there. So Mr. G. has passed out ? (I never heard he had.) It may be a *reproduction*. I do not know, for, as you know, I have had many of them.—Yes. I got the photos, as Mrs G. says, but do not remember it. I cannot really say whether this is a reproduction or not. I told you of many which I had had.—Yours faithfully,   EDWARD WYLLIE.

In a subsequent note, returning the prints which Mr Wallis was good enough to send me, Mr Wyllie says :—

Sorry I omitted to post these in my last. If you look at *the first photo you got you will see the head is perfectly sharp* instead of being out of focus.

This is quite true, not only in the copy sent to Mr Wallis, but in the first photograph the head is sharp and well defined. Mr Wyllie did relate to me some instances not only of reproductions which came under peculiar circumstances, but of other cases in which the *doubles* of living persons were also photographed. While I do not say I know of either the one or the other in his case, his statements have been vouched for by investigators. Not doubting the same, however, for anyone acquainted with the history of this subject is quite familiar with these puzzles. I might also add that whether these " psychic extras," faces, heads or symbols, are faint, blurred, clearly defined or unrecognised, mere copies of prints, reproductions, duplications, differently lighted to the subject, in or out of focus, or most perfectly defined pictures of either the living or the dead—so-called—has absolutely nothing to do with the greater problem of genuineness. All the foregoing have been obtained under rigid test conditions, when there could be no question of the genuineness.

I sent Mr Blackwell, among others, a copy of the Los Angeles photograph. I knew he was engaged in writing up his experiences in spirit photography, and called his attention to the discussion in *Light*, and to special articles in *The Two Worlds*. He went into the matter and sent a letter to *Light*, 27th November 1909, treating ably the whole from the standpoint of actual experience. It was not only an explanation, but a testimony to Mr Edward Wyllie's *bona-fides* as a medium photographer.

In a private letter dated 25th November 1909, Mr Blackwell wrote me as follows:—

I went to *Light* office to see Mr Wallis and the photograph complained of. So far from being a poor copy of a reversed one, it shows a painstaking endeavour on the part of the spirit to give satisfactory evidence. You will see my defence of Mr Wyllie in this week, but I wish I had known about that splendid further bit of evidence of Mrs Coates's grandmother coming again and claiming to be taken. I brought into my letter several other matters I was reserving, but as there has been a great deal of prejudice and suspicion, I thought it would be useful to bring them forward now.

Mr A. K. Venning, writing from 613 Flower Street, Los Angeles, Cal., U.S.A., sent the following to *Light*, and it appeared in its issue of 25th December 1909:—

With reference to Mrs Girdlestone's statement in your article on experiences with Mr Wyllie (*Light*, November 6th) that a reversed print from the glass side of a negative gives a blurred picture, may I say that among the photographs taken for me by this medium years ago, there are three examples of reversed

15

portraits; that is to say, portraits of spirit friends who came at one sitting, and came in reversed position at another, but they are all equally distinct. These reversed pictures are so frequent among this medium's photographs that they seem to be purposely given for some object. Is it not reasonable to suppose that the reversing is done on the spirit side—these portraits probably being taken not from the individual spirit *but from a thought-form-picture, or something of that sort.* Many of the facts of physical mediumship go to prove that the operators on the other side constantly make use of material objects in the medium's surroundings as aids in producing phenomena.

I do not know enough about photography to dogmatise, but throw this out as a hint to those better able to judge. At the same time it seems to me that those who fancy that these reversed pictures are evidence of tricky mediumship have not thought out the subject.

Take this case of Mrs Girdlestone's. First, the photograph of Mr Girdlestone sent to Los Angeles would have had to be photographed, then a print made from the negative from the glass side, this again photographed on to the plate after, presumably, being worked up and clearly defined in some manner. All this work and waste of time the supposed medium undertakes at considerable loss to himself, all for the sake of what? To play the fool and impose on the public for a joke!

Is not all this very absurd, impracticable, hyper-critical, and far-fetched? No one could carry on such a tricky business for a couple of weeks without being caught and exposed.—Yours, etc.,   A. K. VENNING.

Mr Venning's letter and photographs enclosed confirm the experiments already recorded by Mr Traill Taylor. Suppose we admit that the conclusions of our sceptical friends are correct, then it must be conceded that Wyllie is not only an impostor, but an idiot as well to waste all this time and energy in producing this Los Angeles photograph—a conclusion at which any practical photographer would laugh.

Acting from a thorough study of my subject, on the view which I was led to accept, " that while it is not judicious to conclude that all these spirit (produced) photographs are the photographs of spirits, it is a greater folly still to accept fraud as the first and only hypothesis to account for the appearance of these ' extras' beside the subject on the plate," I thought it best to wait, and see what further light might yet be obtained on the vexed subject of the head of E. D. Girdlestone, which appears in the Los Angeles photograph.

In February 1910 I wrote to the Ven. Archdeacon T. Colley, Rector of Stockton, Rugby. On the 12th of that month I received a very interesting reply, with copies of the spirit photographs of his father and mother. In reply, I sent the Venerable gentleman, among other things, a few copies of spirit photographs, including the Los Angeles photograph. His acknowledgment contained elements of surprise—namely, that he himself, under totally different conditions, obtained a head of identical character. I now append the portion of his letter which refers to the matter:—

STOCKTON RECTORY, RUGBY,
Feb. 15, 1910.

DEAR MR COATES,—Thank you very much for spirit photographs, with letter. . . . Most of my plates, pictures and writing, have *never* been exposed in camera: therefore I term them psychographs and not photographs, since *phos*, as we understand it, does not play any part in the matter.

I want you to give me, *as soon as possible*, ALL the information about the face above the envelope—Girdlestone. For I have the same face, which came as a psychographic production at my Leamington Hall parlour, with friends, with a Welsh county J.P. on a visit. I also have heard of his coming for another friend in London—just in the same way as my long-ago friend, Mr Thomas Everitt, came for my friend Glendinning, in spirit *photograph*, even in the *very same pose and look* that he afterwards came to me in, in my own *psychograph* cluster of about sixteen other faces, including the faces of my father and mother again, as in the spirit *photograph* of which you have the photo engraving.

We are in very deep waters aground, however, as yet as to these *replicas*.

Please tell me all you can of the face of Mr Girdlestone, and the letter, and whose hair was in the envelope; when and where it was taken, and if through camera, and all you know of him—for one of my closest friends at Oxford was a Girdlestone. I should like to know all about the matter, on which for the world—in this particular case—perhaps next to my father and mother, bring the most conclusive evidence that will arrest public attention.—Believe me, faithfully yours,   T. COLLEY.

In reply to this letter, I sent in brief the information contained in the foregoing pages. I, however, did not know at the time the following facts, viz. :—

That Mr E. D. Girdlestone had passed away at Sutton Coldfield in February 1909. My letter was sent to Los Angeles on 17th March 1909; the print which I received was done in June or July of that year. It was not a photograph taken in Glenbeg House—as assumed by Mr Venning—but given to me by Mr Wyllie on the day when he unpacked his trunk, which arrived 23rd September 1909. A copy of this photo was made in Glenbeg House. It was forwarded to Mr Wallis as soon as I could thereafter. There is a coincidence here which I was not aware of till now. I could not have informed Mr Wyllie when he asked about Mr Girdlestone. It is clear, then, *that the psychic picture of this gentleman was taken subsequent to his death.*

Subsequent correspondence with the Ven. Archdeacon Colley brought to light the following facts revealed by Mr W. T. Stead, in his pamphlet, *How I know the Dead Return*, pp. 14–17. Although the name of the titled lady is suppressed, and the name of the medium too, through whom another psychic photograph of the Rev. E. D. Girdlestone was obtained, I condense the long and interesting statement made there by Mr Stead, and it amounts to this: —

A society lady well known in literary and scientific circles lost an esteemed friend. She went to London, having been advised to go to Mr Williams, an old medium, for materialisations. At a circle held in the latter's house, she suddenly heard herself called by a familiar name, and was informed that she was wearing a watch in her breast which once belonged to the owner of that voice. There was much more, but as it has nothing to do with photography, I refrain from further reference, except to say that this lady's heart

was greatly comforted. By direction, she went to a
septuagenarian photographer (the late Mr Boursnell,
London), being careful not to announce her name.
Poor old Boursnell thought she was a duchess, he
afterwards told Mr Stead. The old man described a
spirit invisible in her surroundings, but who came in
with her. The lady inquired if a spirit photograph
could be obtained. Mr B. could not tell; he would
try. To her intense surprise, the photo-plate showed
the beloved features of this friend, whom she never
hoped to see this side of the grave.

Upon learning from Archdeacon Colley that this
special photograph was no other than that of E. D. G.,
I wrote Mr Stead for a copy and particulars. This
he could not give, as the lady had ordered the negative
to be broken, and had forbidden the mention of her
name and further publicity. But this being not an
unusual experience, that not only are the evidences of
these genuine psychic photographs suppressed, but the
names of the mediums (through whom the genuine
evidence has come) are suppressed too, I was not
surprised.

On 25th June 1910 I received a long account from
Archdeacon Colley, from which I take the following :—

Stockton Rectory, Rugby,
June 24, 1910.

Dear Sir,—. . . In Warwickshire we have a mystery
surpassing even the case related by Mr Stead, and a
fitting conclusion to the facts which you have presented of the Los Angeles photograph—a mystery
touching all human knowledge, yet beyond us to
fathom, pertaining as it does to happenings in Warwickshire about the same time occult events were

taking place at Los Angeles on the Pacific, so many thousand miles west of Leamington.

The Rev. E. D. Girdlestone, known in earth-life to the writer of these perplexing facts, from his residence in the Brighter and Better Beyond, had his spirit face impressed on a photo- late in a camera of one there to whom he had acted as Army tutor years ago, while the elder brother of E. D. G., the Rev. A. G. Girdlestone, who had predeceased his brother by two months, was, in 1868, my tutor at Oxford, when I was reading for Holy Orders. Last year, viz. July 9, 1909, the same face of E. D. G. came on a photo-plate (no camera used) held in the hands of eight members of a devotional circle of psychical researchers, held in my residence, at Leamington.

The lady of whom Mr Stead speaks, and others, recognise the face which, on or about the same period— under wholly different circumstances and in distinct hemispheres—came on the plates, as the face of the Rev. E. D. Girdlestone, of whose departure from this life Sir Oliver Lodge so regretfully wrote in *Light*, March 6, 1909. The Warwickshire worthy, with impressive, scholarly look, was last seen in the repose of death at Sutton Coldfield, March 1. His concurrent return, therefore, to show himself at Leamington and Los Angeles gives us furiously to think of all the perplexities involved and of the facts so puzzling.

But as the sacred Scriptures say, "It is the glory of God to conceal a matter, and the honour of kings to search it out." The kingly-minded will patiently try to do so in these and many other instances recorded of occurrences parallel touching psychology and spirit photography.—Truly yours,   T. COLLEY.

I had several other letters from the venerable gentleman confirmatory of the above, as well as nine cases for this book.

I now close this chapter of interesting testimony

with what I esteem good evidence of spirit direction in these phenomena :—

1st. We were influenced to interest ourselves in spirit photography.

2nd. Led to write to Mr Wyllie, and ultimately to get him over to this country from Los Angeles, Cal., U.S.A.

3rd. On photograph received there were two " extras " in addition to visible articles photographed. These were the portraits of the late E. D. G. and Mrs Coates's long-departed relative.

4th. It has been ascertained that the rev. gentleman departed this life 1st March 1909. We wrote to Wyllie on the 17th of the same month. There had been delays. This particular photograph was taken somewhere in the early days of July, in Los Angeles.

5th. In the Stead account, noticed, E. D. G. appeared to clairvoyants, spoke, was seen and felt at a materialising séance in London ; was again seen and photographed by Boursnell.   As Mr Stead says :—

There was no doubt as to the resemblance.   It was he and no one else than he, yet he had not been in the spirit world a week when he returned and was photographed in the way I have described.

6th. On 9th July in the same year, the Rev. E. D. Girdlestone was psychographed in Leamington, about the same period, if not on the same day on which he was photographed in Los Angeles.

7th. The photographs and the psychographs have appealed to and been recognised by the titled lady referred to by Mr Stead, and by Archdeacon Colley, whose statements are emphatic and circumstantial.

8th. While none of these circumstances were known to me, I was influenced, almost on the receipt of the Los Angeles photograph, to write to the editor of *Light*, and later on to Archdeacon Colley, when the matters discussed in this story came to light. The design or coincidence—call it what you please—was most remarkable.

9th. E. D. G. appears several times, and is photographed in three different places—Los Angeles, Cal., Leamington, Eng., London, Eng.—by persons miles apart and wholly unknown to each other, and by different means.

10th. Mrs Coates's grandmother, whose picture is given on the Los Angeles photograph, is taken again in Rothesay when Mrs Coates obeyed the impulse or impression to be photographed.

From the foregoing and other considerations, I conclude that the evidence is remarkable. I also assume that the unseen Intelligences—some of them our friends and relatives—*have some higher aim* in all these efforts, than merely to console or gratify those to whom these phenomena come.

CHAPTER XI

I THOUGHT I could not do better than produce photograph (fig. 47) as an introduction to my personal experience with Mr Wyllie. The negative mentioned was found in a house where Mr Wyllie had been, and the hasty deduction is, that the medium-photographer employed *it* and similar plates to put "spirits" on his patrons' photographs. This is Mr Jensen's charge. The next charge was one by a Dr Woillard, who said he paid Mr Wyllie to be taught how to take "spirit pictures." This gentleman declared he had discovered the trick, viz. that Mr Wyllie put the "spirits" on the plates by "magnetising," *i.e.* holding in the hollow of his arched hand a photo prepared with luminous paint *over plates in dark-room* prior to exposure. He had found two such miniatures prepared with Indian ink and luminous paint, and—Wyllie confessed that was how the thing was done.

Mr P. A. Jensen had a notoriety to sustain as a modern witch-finder. According to his own statements about his friendship (?) for Mr Wyllie, and his general tactics, he must have possessed all the *virtues* of the detective sleuth-hound of the dime novel. He appears not only ignorant of the most elementary facts in photography, but of psychic photography. Apparently he has never heard of a case where the subject

Fig. 47.—Photograph from the negative upon which a Mr P. A. Jensen founded his charges against Mr Wyllie's *bona-fides* in *The Progressive Thinker.*

stood alongside of the back screen, instead of sitting before the camera.

In the case reported in *Borderland* (pp. 269, 270, vol. iv.) by Mr J. Wade Cunningham, 327 South Spring Street, Los Angeles, Cal., Mr Wyllie obtained the psychic picture of a beautiful lady, and that of a living but invisible dog—a very remarkable but by no means an isolated case where the subject did not sit before the camera.

There are well-authenticated cases where the living subject could not be photographed. This has occurred with hypnotised subjects. Indeed, I have recently had the facts presented to me by Mr Bailey, of Birmingham, where he failed to photograph Dr Hooper when the latter was in a semi-trance state. The testimony in this case was most conclusive. Sir William Crookes, F.R.S., was greatly interested in the facts, which were presented to him by my esteemed correspondent, the Ven. Archdeacon Colley.

This Mr P. A. Jensen has not been able to produce a single case where the foregoing negative has been used to produce by double printing "spirits" on the photograph of any living person. His repeated charges have been widely read in the States and in Great Britain, but they remain until to-day unsubstantiated.

The merest tyro in photography knows that Dr Woillard's statements are not true. But there are many persons, including "experts," who will readily believe piffle of this kind.

Having been kindly tutored by the press and correspondents as to what to expect from Mr Wyllie before he arrived, I took heed to my ways, and experimented accordingly to discover the truth for the truth's sake.

Mr Wyllie arrived—with two cameras, a few printing frames, and other accessories, but *no portrait negatives*, except one of his brother taken in Newark, N.J., before leaving the U.S.A. on 22nd September 1909 —and on the 25th of that month took his first photographs in our house. His " gallery " was our drawing-room ; the plates used and the back screen were mine —the dark-room being our bathroom, fitted up for the purpose. Two plates out of a new box were exposed as follows. Mrs Coates was the first subject. On development there was nothing on the negative save herself. Jennie Mathewson, our maid, was the next experimented on, the second plate being exposed on her. Upon development, there appeared as " extras " the clearly defined face of a woman at her left side, and a very young infant, dressed, lying across her lap. This was the first psychic picture obtained by Mr Wyllie after his arrival in Rothesay, and in this country. I do not produce the photograph, owing to the indecision of her relatives about the female portrait. As to the baby, Jennie's mother lost a similar little one, but identification is not possible. This was the beginning of a successful series. I do not propose to give the details of all the photographs taken. Many of the best psychic photographs were not definitely identified ; *many were*, but, owing to the dread of publicity, the subjects declined to permit the use of their names and addresses. The following selection will suffice.

The photograph (fig. 48) on the next page was taken on 1st October 1909. The plate came out of a new

264

box was marked X before, and developed by me after exposure. Mr Wyllie simply took the cap off the lens. At a séance held the previous evening, Mr Wyllie, who sometimes appeared to be clairvoyant, described

FIG. 48.—Photograph of the author, with psychic "extra," said to be that of the late Mr John Adamson, of Messrs Adamson & Son, expert naval and portrait photographers, Rothesay.

a man who was present (invisible to us), making special note of his peculiar cap or headdress. In the negative I noted the peculiarity, but it was not till I saw the print that the likeness to the late Mr John Adamson was detected by Mrs Coates and myself.

Many of those I have shown it to said it was Mr Adamson. Mr Whiteford, photographer, who was for many years in his employment, told me he was not sure, but it certainly was very like him. Mr Robertson, of Glasgow, said : " That's Adamson, and a splendid likeness too." Further than knowing and doing business with Mr Adamson, I had no special interest in him. Why I obtained this " extra " I do not know, except that the bulk of the " furniture " used by Mr Wyllie was originally Mr Adamson's. I do not positively insist that this is his portrait, but I do that this photograph was taken under perfectly satisfactory conditions which would satisfy anyone—except *an expert*.

The photograph, fig. 49, was taken by Mr Wyllie on 3rd October 1909. Mrs Coates, on seeing the print a few days afterwards, immediately identified it as that of her aunt Bella, viz. Miss Isabella Tweedale.

The photograph, fig. 50 (p. 241), was obtained on 4th October 1909, and the face is a duplication of the one on the Los Angeles photograph of Madame Pogosky, mentioned in a previous chapter. The rose and bud are specially significant to us. At a sitting held in our house three years previously to Mr Wyllie's arrival, Mrs Coates, under the control of "White Rose," Mr Auld's daughter—who passed over shortly after birth — promised, among other things, that we would have a photographer in Rothesay in three years from then, and she would give her father a photograph of herself. Mr Auld asked her, how would he know her ? She said she would come with roses, as a symbol of her spirit name. The matter was overlooked till we saw this print. There was, however, no portrait of Rosie, but with

FIG. 49.—Photograph of Mrs Coates, and the psychic portrait of her aunt, the late Miss Isabella Tweedale.

her mother came this large rose and bud, symbolical of mother and child.

This photograph was obtained on the same day as Mr Auld sat for the photograph on which the roses came. Now, it happened on the same evening, when Mr Auld got the promise about the roses, that Mrs Coates, in trance, under the control of her daughter

FIG. 50.—Photograph of Mr John Auld, and the psychic portrait
of the late Mrs Auld, with roses.

Agnes, said: "I am coming too." Mr Auld said:
"How can your mother know you, having passed

16

FIG. 51.—Photograph of Mrs Coates and her daughter Agnes,
with lilies.

over in childhood?" She said: "Oh yes, she will
know me. I will come with white lilies, symbolical of

my spirit name, White Lily." The photograph given presents her, we are told, as she would have been at the age of thirty-eight. Whether so or not, no one can tell. I relate the matter as it occurred.

I consider it worthy of note that Mr Auld, Mrs Coates, and I had forgotten all about the promise of a spirit photographer coming to Rothesay, and the promise of the departed ones to be photographed through his mediumship, till we saw the prints. Then, suddenly impressed, we realised that here was the fulfilment of the promises in a most remarkable manner. Mrs Coates, on seeing the photographs, said: " Our spirit friends are far more in earnest than we are ; they endeavour to keep their promises, and that under great difficulties, when we carelessly forget they ever made them, till the fact of fulfilment brings conviction home."

The foregoing certainly does suggest the work of Intelligences in the Invisible.

Mr John Auld's Certificate

HAZELCLIFFE, ROTHESAY.

On Sunday evening, the 7th May 1911, I read the two foregoing brief descriptions, and certify that the same are correctly stated. JOHN AULD.

The Testimony of Mr J. J. Morse

Mr Wyllie knew nothing of Mr Morse's visit until he arrived at Glenbeg House (29th September 1909). As the time had been taken up with interview and dinner, and as the day was dull and unsuitable, the taking of the photograph was an afterthought.

There was only one plate exposed, and this was developed by the writer after Mr Morse had left.

From the editor's full account in *The Two Worlds*, 29th October 1909, I take the following :—

On the previous Sunday we filled an engagement

FIG. 52.—The photograph of Mr J. J. Morse, editor of *The Two Worlds*, and psychic picture of Miss Florence Morse's guide, "my friend."

with the Glasgow Association of Spiritualists, and being in Scotland, availed ourselves of the opportunity of visiting Mr Coates at his residence in Rothesay for the purpose of obtaining a personal interview with Mr Wyllie, who was then the guest of Mr and Mrs Coates. We found Mr Wyllie to be a modest and retiring gentleman, quite devoid of any sort of assumption. He replied to all our questions with the utmost frankness, and manifested an evident sincerity in all he said, either in response to our questions or when making any voluntary remark. In brief, he impressed us, after a two hours' chat, as he has all who have met him, as a straightforward man. We examined his camera. . . . The sitting took place in Mr Coates' drawing-room, and he, Mr Wyllie, and ourselves were the only visible persons present.

The cap of the lens was removed and replaced in the ordinary way, and the sitting ended. The "slide" was then taken into the bathroom, which was the improvised dark-room. We were impressed with a desire to examine the "slide," which we did, and all it contained was the plate. There was absolutely nothing else, no trick appliance, extra plate, or anything else. We awaited the receipt of a print, which reached us after our return to Manchester. On inspecting the print, we found our portrait was there, and on the left-hand side of the print was the psychic extra—a marvellously clear and well-defined face of a man. The face was unknown to us. We knew of no spirit friend whose description would in any way fit the face before us, when suddenly the impression came: "Take it home, it will be recognised." We did so, and submitted it to Miss Morse, who remarked: "Yes, I know it; it is 'My Friend,' and it is exactly as I have seen him many times."

I may explain that "My Friend" is one of Miss Morse's guides, who has been intimately associated with her for a number of years. She wished to make assurance doubly sure, and said: "You are going to London next week; take the picture with you, and show it to Mr Vango. He has seen him clairvoyantly at various times. Do not say anything to him, but see if he recognises it." We did as suggested, when Mr Vango at once repeated almost the same remark

The...
de...
..."Yes, I know the face."
...: "Yes, I have it; it is Florrie's
...likeness too." We do not know
...spirit, who simply describes himself
..."Your Friend."
...reasons we consider this a far better
...of evidence of Mr Wyllie's *bona-fides* than if the
picture had been someone whom we personally knew.
Mind and thought transference are out of court, for,
apart from our not desiring anyone in particular, the
portrait is of someone of whom we absolutely knew
nothing as to appearance. The interested party, Miss
Morse, was 250 miles away at least, and did not know
on what day we intended visiting Mr Wyllie, so no
"waves" could have reached Rothesay from her.
The above is a simple narrative of the facts in the
case, and the picture can be seen at this office.

Mrs Coates's daughter, Mrs Hector, having heard
that Mr Wyllie was with us, paid on the 8th October
1909 a flying visit to Rothesay, and decided suddenly
to sit for a photograph. It was taken in the usual
way—one plate (mine), and a single exposure. When
it was developed by me there was an "extra" of a
little girl on it in addition to the subject. Upon
examining the print, they had reason to conclude it
was the psychic picture of Mrs Coates's eldest daughter
(Mrs Hector's sister Agnes), who had passed away at
an early age. The points of identification are satisfactory to us. We possess a crayon portrait of the
departed, also a photograph of her sister, Mrs H., taken
when a child. From the first comes the identification,
and the second shows a remarkable family likeness.
The psychic has the little bead rings on her fingers

which her mother (my wife) made for her as a child, and on her arm a little snake bracelet which her aunt Mary used to place on her when on a visit.

About twelve months after this picture was taken, a niece of Mrs Coates and a daughter of Aunt Mary paid a visit from South Africa to Rothesay. She was shown a number of spirit photographs, including this and the better one taken with Mrs Shaw in Glasgow. This lady said: "How funny! mamma has an old bracelet just the same as that "—little knowing that the old bracelet and the one on the child's arm were identical.

In the next chapter I give the photograph of Mrs Shaw and Agnes, as the latter comes out much clearer than on Mrs H.'s card. On another day Mrs Coates and Mr Auld sat together for a photograph. Mr Auld had been hoping to get a clear photograph of his wife. Mr Wyllie proceeded as usual. A little later in the day Mrs Hector thought she would have a sitting. Mr Wyllie went into the dark-room, but did not trouble to light the red lamp, picked up what he thought was a fresh plate, put it into his single slide, and exposed it on Mrs H. Upon developing, two facts were discovered: 1st, it was a double exposure, viz. the plate previously used on Mrs Coates and Mr Auld; 2nd, there were two "extras" thereon, viz. a relative of Mr Auld's, whom we all recognised, and the other was recognised by the said niece and Mrs Coates as being exceedingly like a Miss Armour. This double exposure by inadvertence is the only one in our experience.   The psychic "extras" were defined enough for recognition, but not for production in these pages.   Subsequently to this, Mrs H. sat to Mr Wyllie in Glasgow, and obtained a beautifully defined portrait of the late Miss Armour, which was somewhat spoiled in the prior double-exposure accident.

I have discussed the subject of spirit photography with Mr Robert Whiteford, sole partner in the firm of Messrs John Adamson & Son, expert marine and portrait photographers, Rothesay, whose firm has carried on business in Rothesay for over half a century. This gentleman is not only a practical photographer himself, but he stands high in the community as a man of character and responsibility, whose word may be fully depended on.   Mr Whiteford, like many practical and professional photographers, *was* wholly sceptical about psychic photography, specimens of which, on being shown to him, elicited critical and not always flattering remarks.

On 8th October 1909 Mr Whiteford came to Glenbeg House and had a sitting under Mr Wyllie's own conditions.   Mr Whiteford, however, selected the day and hour, as well as his position before the camera. He watched keenly all that was done, but otherwise took no active part in the procedure.   The plate— only one was used—was taken from a box purchased by me from Mr William Meldrum, M.P.S., chemist, Victoria Street, Rothesay.   This plate was developed —with all others taken on 8th October — in my presence, and there was on it, besides the sitter,

Mr Whiteford, the psychic picture of a child about fifteen months old. The negative was taken into Mr Whiteford's and examined by that gentleman, and a print of it taken by him. It appears Mr Whiteford

FIG. 53.—Photograph of Mr Whiteford, and psychic picture of little boy (unknown).

had a little boy, whose photograph was never taken, who passed away at this age. He says it has the Whiteford features, but he does not recognise it as his child.

The next sitting this gentleman had with Mr Wyllie was on the next day, 9th October, and was held under

Mr Whiteford's own conditions.   The plates used were taken from a fresh box of 5×7 inches, supplied by Mr William Meldrum, M.P.S., it being the only box of this particular size sold by him during the season.   For this, as the former, Mr Whiteford chose the day, moment, and position of the sitters, of whom I was one.   I will note in passing that on two occasions Mr Whiteford did not turn up, owing to the climatic conditions being unfavourable for even ordinary photography.

ATTESTED REPORT OF MR ROBERT WHITEFORD

JOHN ADAMSON & SON, PHOTOGRAPHERS.
STUDIO : 23 ARGYLE STREET,
ROTHESAY, 22nd October 1909.

I, Robert Whiteford, photographer, Rothesay, solemnly and sincerely declare I entered upon this investigation on the understanding that I should have a free hand to make my own conditions, and this was agreed to by Professor Coates and Mr Wyllie. Although I had inspected Mr Wyllie's old camera and lens, with which he had taken my photograph the previous day, for convenience, I declined to take its single dark slide with me.   I then inspected another and more modern ordinary outdoor camera—by Kodak, Limited—which Mr Wyllie had, and which he used for outdoor work.   I took away a double dark slide belonging to the latter and filled it with two plates from a box—supplied by Mr Meldrum—which was opened by me in my own studio.   I marked the plates with my initials and the date, viz. " R.W., 9/10/09," just prior to leaving for Glenbeg House.   When there I again examined the Kodak camera thoroughly, and neither in it nor in or about the lens was there anything out of the way.

Mr Wyllie and I entered into the dark-room, where he asked me, "Is the light satisfactory?" I said, "No." He then desired me to turn up the light to suit myself. This I did, at the same time opening the slide and showing him the plates. Closing one shutter and leaving the other open, I held the dark slide with one of the plates uppermost for Mr Wyllie to magnetise, but the dark slide with the plates was never out of my hands or sight. Mr Wyllie proceeded to do what he called "magnetising the plate." I then closed the shutter and went into the operating room, where I was joined by Professor Coates. I again examined the camera and lens, and posed Mr Wyllie and focussed him, and set the shutter of the camera ready for exposure, and made everything ready for taking the subject.

Mr Wyllie then rose, and I took his place as subject, and Mr Wyllie exposed the plate for about sixteen seconds. I then rose and closed the slide, took it out of the camera, and posed Professor Coates. When finished, I took away the dark slide to our studio in Rothesay. Upon developing the plates, I found to my astonishment what is called "a psychic extra" on my own plate—apparently that of an old woman. On that of Mr Coates there was nothing save himself as subject.

I entered into this matter with an open mind, with neither knowledge of the subject, as claimed by some, nor with the slightest faith in it. In fact, as to the so-called spirit photographs which I have seen, I have put them down as "faked" pictures or double exposures, except some of Mr Wyllie's, for which I could not account. The test picture taken of me is *not* and *could not be* a double exposure.

I went into this test as a photographer, with my eyes open, and thoroughly on the alert to detect fraud. *I found none.* Mr Wyllie never refused to submit to any test conditions which my knowledge of photography could put him to.   Nothing would have given me greater pleasure had I detected fraud of any description than to expose it.   I claim this photograph of myself to be *a genuine psychic photograph.*

With regard to the other photograph, taken the

FIG. 54.—Photograph of Mr Whiteford, and the psychic
picture of an old woman (unknown).

previous day in Glenbeg House, on which there appears a child holding with its little hand the lapel of my coat, although I did not see the plate fitted into the dark slide, or that plate afterwards till developed and dry, I will state that there was only one exposure made while I was in the operating room.   I subsequently examined the negative and made a print from it.   I now conclude, based on this examination, and on the experiment of the test photographs. that this too is *a genuine psychic photograph*.

It may be asked: "Why did you not make further tests?" My reply is: "I am a practical photographer. and the test made, producing the result mentioned. is as fully evidential as if I had made a dozen similar tests."

I wish now to state emphatically that I am favourably impressed with Mr Wyllie himself. and with his mode of working, he having granted me all I asked for. Based on twenty-four years' practical experience as a photographer, I assert. whatever the result. that I could not detect, either in himself or in his work. any signs of fraud or double dealing.

ROBT. WHITEFORD.

Sworn Attestation:—

Sworn at Rothesay in the County of Bute this 22nd day of October Nineteen hundred and nine years, before me,

DONALD GRANT, Solicitor in Rothesay.
Notary Public.

Two facts not mentioned in the affidavit are: 1st. Mr Whiteford saw that there was nothing concealed in Mr Wyllie's hands; and 2nd, as the dark slide was a reversible one, he reversed it in carrying it from the dark-room to the camera, so that had it been possible to put a "contact" figure on it by magnetising (?), that would at once have been detected.

THE GENUINENESS OF MR WYLLIE'S MEDIUMSHIP ESTABLISHED

Report of Glasgow Association Test Committee [1]

The Glasgow Association of Spiritualists approached Mr Wyllie for a test sitting, stipulating that a camera,

[1] Taken from *The Two Worlds*, by permission.

plates, and slides other than those of Mr Wyllie should be used.

Mr Wyllie, recognising the purpose of this arrangement, readily acceded to the request. Two test sittings, however, were held, one in Rothesay on 9th October, and the other in Glasgow on 23rd October, and both, considering the stringent nature of the tests and conditions, and also taking into account the adverse atmospheric conditions and the natural nervous tension of the medium and sitters, were eminently successful and satisfactory.

Every precaution was taken that experience could suggest. The test committee consisted of expert photographers, chiefly directed by Mr H. H. Thomson, the Association's treasurer—a lecturer on photography of twenty-five years' experience, and a frequent prize-winner in open photo competitions. Other members were Mr Richard Thomson, vice-president; Mr John Sclator, financial secretary; Mr Roehead, and myself. Full reports were independently given by each member of the committee, and a synopsis made.

The camera used was Mr H. H. Thomson's half-plate teak-wood camera, fitted for the Mackenzie-Wishart patent slide, with envelopes for the same. The plates were purchased at the nearest chemist's twenty minutes before the sitting. Two of the committee entered the chemist's dark-room, and filled up eight plates in the slides.

At Rothesay the committee were introduced to Mr Wyllie by Mr James Coates in Glenbeg House, and the second sitting took place in Mr Wyllie's apartments in Glasgow.

The process adopted was simple. Each sitter entered the dark-room separately with the medium, and the sitter carried the slide, which never left his possession. The medium took hold of the opposite corners to the sitter, and held it there for a short time. Presently the medium asked the sitter to draw out the slide, and placed his left hand below the slide and his right hand *arched* over the open plate. After some minutes a series of raps or percussion sounds were heard below the wooden slide, and this signal being given, the sitter was requested to close

FIG. 55.—Photograph of Mr George P. Young, President of the Glasgow Association of Spiritualists, residing at Burnside Cottage, Colston, Bishopbriggs, Glasgow ; and symbolic cluster of lilies.

the slide and place it in the camera. Mr Wyllie's hands were examined frequently. No phosphorescent or other suspicious appearance was observed by any of the committee, who were specially instructed to use their keenest faculties of observation. Before development, the plates were examined minutely to detect any markings of the gelatinous surface.   None were discovered.

Each member of the committee went through this part of the test process.   All the exposures in the camera (with one exception, when he himself sat) were made by Mr H. H. Thomson.   Mr Wyllie merely held his hand above the camera and gave instructions as to the period of exposure.

After the plates were exposed they were immediately placed in the camera bag and taken away by the committee for development in a specially fitted-up room in Ebenezer Church, Glasgow.   All the committee were present and watched all the stages of development.   The following is the result:—

Rothesay Test Séance

First plate developed—Mr R. Thomson, sitter. Small face on right arm.

Second plate—Mr Roehead, sitter.   Small figure in centre of body.

Third plate—Mr H. H. Thomson, sitter.   Large face over sitter's; also one in centre of body, and a symbol.

Fourth and fifth plates—blank.

Glasgow Test Séance

First plate developed—Mr Young, sitter.   Bouquet of large lilies near region of heart, probably symbolical (see fig. 55).

Second plate—Mr R. Thomson, sitter.   Large face showing on left side and arm.

Third and fourth plates—Blank, or faint markings too indistinct to be mentioned as results.

These psychic " extras " obtained under such conditions of control sufficiently testify to the highly developed powers of Mr Wyllie as a psychic photographer.

The test committee unhesitatingly and unanimously testify to Mr Wyllie's marked and convincing mediumship, and publicly thank him for his uniform courtesy and honourable dealings.

Signed on behalf of the sub-committee,

GEO. P. YOUNG, President.
R. THOMSON, Vice-President.
H. H. THOMSON, Treasurer.

Miss M. M'Callum, residing in Gourock, hearing through the press that Mr Wyllie was taking photographs for subscribers in Glenbeg House, wrote for a sitting, and came on Saturday, 9th October, for that purpose. She was an entire stranger to both the photographer and the writer. Mr Wyllie had just been giving sittings under strict test conditions to a special committee sent for the purpose by the Glasgow Association of Spiritualists, but, hearing that this lady wanted a sitting, he agreed, but suggested, as she was dressed in white, that she had better have something dark on, as white often obscured a psychic face which otherwise might be an identifiable one. Miss M'Callum at once put on her dark waterproof coat, and Mr Wyllie made *one* exposure. I was present at the development of the plate, and there were two "extras" on it, a man's and a woman's head. The print was sent on to Miss M'Callum, and she was delighted to recognise in the female face that of a cousin. Concerning this photograph she said: "This is very good. The lady is my cousin, but I do not know who the man is yet."

Miss Payne, in answer to a request for her account of photograph received by her, gave me the following:—

KAMES BANK,
PORT BANNATYNE, 17*th February* 1910.

DEAR MR COATES,—In reply to your inquiries as to the photograph which I obtained the second time I sat in Glenbeg House, 17th October 1909, Mrs Coates and I went upstairs together. I sat down in front of the curtain, and Mrs Coates on a couch to my left.

FIG. 56.—The photograph of Miss Payne, and the psychic portrait of her cousin, by Wyllie, taken at Rothesay.

Mr Wyllie took me and said: "I think you have got something this time, for I saw a light near you." On the Friday evening following, at a séance held in your house, Mr Wyllie said "I hear the name of 'Addy.'" I had a cousin of that name. She was dead. I did not get the photograph before he left for

Glasgow. I received it afterwards by post. The face on it is that of my cousin, Adeline Jones. Addy and I were very fond of each other. We went to school together. When I last saw her, she was keeping house for her brother. She had very pretty fair hair, dressed and worn on the top of her head; she had blue eyes, and her mouth and chin were as they appear in this photo. She would be forty-five or thereabouts when she died. The resemblance to her is so marked, and her likeness to the family so strong, I am convinced that it is herself.

This spirit photograph—so unexpectedly received, for I was hoping that I should get someone else—has given me great pleasure. It is only recently I have learned that our loved ones are neither dead nor indifferent to the welfare of those left behind. I believe that she has given me this to comfort me, and I prize it very highly.—Yours faithfully,

MARIA PAYNE.

Miss Maria Payne resides in the district, is a member of St Ninian's (Parish) Church, and is one who, having taken an active interest in church and the Literary's Society's work for the last seventeen years, is well known and of good repute. By "accident" she was led to take an interest in spiritualism. In coming to get a photograph, she hoped to get a certain friend, failing whom, her mother. Miss Payne was much surprised to obtain the spirit portrait of one of whom she had not thought for many years, and not those whom she expected to come.

As to the "extras" of departed persons being obtained when, instead of a subject sitting, articles were placed before the camera, we had the case of Mr Oscar E. Drummond, to which we have already referred. There were two others. Mrs Hector had one of her children's hats, with some small articles of apparel in it, pinned to the back screen. With these were obtained another but different likeness of her sister Agnes; and the other of an aunt of her mother's, a Mrs Dalglish. Another of our regular visitors had a photograph of her late father and some other articles placed in an envelope. These were attached to the back screen and photographed. With these as the subject, there appeared on development of the plate a high, irregular head and face. No one could really tell till we saw the print. It proved to be the portion of a head and face in which half the forehead was not visible, but the nose, one eye, cheek, and side head came into view. When Miss A—— saw this, she said: "How funny! This is uncle James——." That evening two of Miss A——'s sisters arrived, and without hesitation said: "That is uncle James." I was present when the above identification was made; but I am sorry I cannot give either further particulars or the photograph, as "the fear of man" hinders publicity. There are one or two points to consider in relation to these. Mr Drummond thought of and expected to get the photograph of his father, but instead obtained that of his uncle Adolphus. Mrs Hector had no definite ideas, just wanted an experiment, and obtained persons of whom she had not consciously thought.

Miss A. certainly hoped to get a picture of her father, and instead obtained a curious, but thoroughly identifiable, portrait of an uncle. Many other similar results have been obtained, but not with me. In the next chapter I give the remarkable testimony of Mr Henry Standfast (Belize, British Honduras, Central America) as to his wife's photograph and others, which came in this way, and which should cause some furious thinking—complimentary or not, matters little.

Concluding my notes of personal experimentation with Mr Wyllie, I have had no "reversions" or "reproductions," except the "E. D. G." case mentioned.

Concerning what Archdeacon Colley calls "replicas," I have had several with Mr Wyllie — for instance, those of Mrs Coates's maternal grandmother, the one taken in Los Angeles and the other in Rothesay; the duplication of Mrs Auld, psychic photograph also obtained in Los Angeles and repeated in Rothesay; Mrs Coates's daughter Agnes, whose psychic portrait was first obtained when her sister was the subject in Rothesay, and on the second occasion, with Mrs Shaw, in Glasgow. In these there were differences; nevertheless they were practically duplications. Mr A. W. Orr, of Didsbury, reports the duplication of Mrs Orr. The foregoing are of identified psychic photos of departed persons. There were others not identified. Mr Auld obtained twice the face of one who claimed to be a relation. Another duplication was that of a man's face which appeared on one of Mr Auld's photographs, and again on the photograph of a visitor well known to us.

In a photograph of Miss M'Callum, of Gourock, with the identified portrait of a military chaplain, there is also an unidentified face, which that lady thought resembled a Boston professor. The features are duplicated on a photograph taken by Mr Wyllie in Middletown. It is of the type of face which repeats itself in the Wyllie photographs.

I have found other duplications. The psychic "extra" of a little boy (which I have reproduced), obtained in Mr Whiteford's experimentation, is duplicated on a plate with Mrs Wallis, of Middletown. I might mention other cases.

Why do these things happen? Mr Wyllie does not know. He possesses no control over the phenomenon. He thinks there are two explanations: 1st, that these "astral" forms or figures are made up within his surroundings, and are either produced when the conditions are not so favourable—weakness in himself, bad weather—or, 2nd, the repetition is due to the desire of the spirit intelligences for recognition, and these "extras" are given again and again till recognised.

There seems to me something in both these suggestions. In the latter case I have had proof, viz. unidentified psychic portraits have been repeated again and again till recognised.

My procedure with Mr Wyllie (while our guest, and acting as the representative of those ladies and gentlemen who subscribed to the Wyllie Fund, and also as special commissioner to *The Two Worlds* newspaper) was sympathetic, simple, and effective.

1st. Sympathetic. In making due allowance for a stranger among strange people, and our unfortunate weather, I allowed Mr Wyllie to have (apparently) his own way for a short time, except using my plates, back screen, and dark-room arrangements.

2nd. Simple. No plates were used without my knowledge, and only one exposure was made on each subject. Whenever I thought fit, I marked the plate—which in all cases was my own, purchased either from Mr Wm. Meldrum, chemist, or other reputable agent—and I was either present during the development or developed the plates myself.

3rd. Effective. While honouring and doing nothing to stultify mediumship, or forcing my presence on the visitors—the majority of whom I knew personally—when not present in the operating room, I learned from my visitors that only one exposure had been made. This eliminated at once double exposures and double printing from the category of operations. As I knew what was on each negative, I also knew what should be on each print. Practically all operations were done under my supervision. Mr Wyllie operated where I wished—in one room or another, with my back screen or his own, with my marked plates when desired, only making the exposure; submitting to the test experiments of Mr Robert Whiteford, as reported in that gentleman's affidavit, and to the tests required by the committee of experts sent down by the Glasgow Association of Spiritualists. The whole of these proceedings, forming a complete *prima facie*

CASE FOR SPIRIT PHOTOGRAPHY,

were submitted by me, with vouchers and ten psychic photographs, to Sir Oliver Lodge, but failed, beyond courteous acknowledgments, to bring about an investigation under circumstances so freely offered. No medium - photographer's psychic gift has been so thoroughly examined and powers tested as were those of Mr Wyllie in the short month during which he resided in our house.

About 60 per cent. of the photographs taken exhibited psychic "extras," and 25 per cent. of these were identified as those of departed persons. To all the subjects Mr Wyllie was a complete stranger, and of the origins of the psychic "extras" or portraits he could have no knowledge; and except in the cases where flowers—roses and lilies—were produced, there was a marked absence of symbolism in the photographs taken.

Owing to poor eyesight, Mr Wyllie frequently over-developed his negatives, and often did not see defects before sending prints out. Coming from a land of almost perpetual sunshine, he appeared to be unacquainted with bromide processes, but he was evidently a thoroughly practical photographer. He had no interest whatever in making a portrait of the subject, always sacrificed in psychic interests; and lastly, there was no touching-up. The sitter got what the exposure produced—nothing more and nothing less.

CHAPTER XII

Miss M'Callum, shortly after Mr Wyllie left here, had a sitting in his rooms, 9 Corunna Street, Glasgow, and was fortunate to obtain fig. 57 (next page). On this there are two psychic faces, one of which she again was able to recognise, the Rev. Mr Nicolson, late of Tighna-bruaich, a gentleman well known on the West Coast and in the Highlands. I wrote to Miss M'Callum asking her permission to get a copy of these photo-graphs from Mr Wyllie, and informed her of my intention to make use of the same. In her reply from Lorne Place, Gourock, dated 10th November 1909, she says :—

In the photograph taken at your house the spirit face is that of my cousin, who died a year ago in the south of England. As to the second picture, taken in Glasgow, the gentleman with the military cap is my brother's late master, Roderick Nicolson, of Tighnabruaich. He was a retired minister, and had been a chaplain in the army. His brother founded the Nicolson Institution in Stornoway, and the Rev. Roderick left his money to that too. My brother William was with Mr Nicolson for eight years, and nursed him on his deathbed. I did wonder how it was that this gentleman came, but it may interest you to know that I was wearing his gold albert, which was made up as a bracelet. He left a legacy to my

FIG. 57.—Photograph of Miss M. M'Callum, and the psychic portrait of the Rev. Mr Nicolson.

brother. It is just him. I hope you will find this of use to you.—Yours truly,   MAGGIE M'CALLUM.

I requested Miss M'Callum to write her brother for his testimony, which I would use if satisfactory, and she sent me the following somewhat laconic reply :—

LORNE PLACE,
TIGHNABRUAICH, *May 1st*, 1910.

MY DEAR MAGGIE,—I consider the photo an excellent likeness of my late master, Mr Roderick Nicolson, of Ravenswood, Tighnabruaich.—Your loving brother,
WILLIE.

Miss M'Callum wrote me on 3rd May 1910 to the effect that she had been able to recognise the other photos, and that she had another satisfactory photo taken by Mr Wyllie at Christmas.

The photograph on page 268 is an example of one of the puzzles of psychic photography. It is not a reproduction of a previous psychic portrait, although similar in attitude, in features and pose, but not either in focus or position, as when taken with her own sister at Rothesay some weeks before. Mrs Shaw is a stranger to us, but when Mr Wyllie discovered what he had obtained, he immediately sent the results to Mrs Coates; and Mrs Shaw gave her permission for the disposal of the negative, from which the above has been taken. Why we should get a better and clearer picture with a stranger than with the mother or sister as sitters, is a question not easily answered. Particulars concerning identification are given in previous chapter.

I wrote to Mrs Grant about the photograph, fig. 59, on the 6th September 1910, and that lady, accompanied by her daughter, Miss Jean Grant, called upon me on the 10th of the same month. In reply to questions, I learned that Mrs Grant felt strongly impressed to go to Mr Wyllie and sit for a photograph. She called at his rooms in the month of November 1909.   While

FIG. 58.—Photograph by Ed. Wyllie of Mrs Shaw, and the psychic
picture of Mrs Coates's daughter, Agnes Tweedale Simpson.

going up the stairs, she had a second impression
through feeling a hand patting her cheek.   Mr Wyllie,

owing to the foggy weather, at first declined to take her, but rather than disappoint her did so. She was very pleased, because she felt that she would get someone, and said so to Mr Wyllie.

FIG. 59.—Photograph by Wyllie of Mrs Charlotte Grant, with the psychic portrait of her boy, Alexander Grant.

"But," she said, "I was not thinking of Alex: I was hoping and expecting to get the photograph of another person. When I got the proof I was both delighted and surprised to get the picture of my son Alex. I never had a photograph taken of him in life."

The above statements were corroborated by Miss Jean Grant.

Miss Ross — residing in West Princes Street, Glasgow—an old friend of Mrs Grant (who knew little Alex well, and was with him in his last hours in life), called to see the Grants a few days after they obtained this photograph. Mrs Grant, knowing her friend was not a spiritualist, merely mentioned to her that she had had her photograph taken, and let her see it without comment. When Miss Ross saw it she exclaimed: "Oh! that is little Alex with his smiling face. How did you get that?" Mrs Grant said: "He is dead, you know."

Miss Ross said that she knew that, but was anxious to know how Mrs Grant got it. Mrs Grant explained as best she could. Miss Ross could not understand, but expressed delight at the marvel.

I sent the above to Mrs Grant for confirmation, and received the following:—

30 DERBY STREET, GLASGOW,
23rd September 1910.

DEAR SIR,—Please find enclosed with signatures. I forgot to mention to you on the 10th inst., that when little Alex took the illness from which he died, he was very fevered, so I cut his hair to try and cool him. I did not cut it very evenly. When I received his spirit photo from Mr Wyllie, his hair was just as I had cut it before he died.—Yours truly,

CHARLOTTE GRANT.

CERTIFICATE

We have read the foregoing account and beg to testify that it is correct.

We also add that Alexander Grant was three years

and seven months old when he died, and that this photograph of him was taken twenty-six years after his death.

Signed by—

CHARLOTTE GRANT, 30 Derby Street, Glasgow.
MARGARET ROSS, 151 W. Princes Street, Glasgow.
JEAN GRANT, 30 Derby Street, Glasgow.
ISOBELLE M. GRANT, 30 Derby Street, Glasgow.

The testimony in this case is most conclusive. A stranger to Glasgow and this family produces the photograph of a boy who passed away many years ago. The identity and the evidence are as complete as the laws of both ordinary and expert evidence demand.

THE STORY OF MAGGIE'S PSYCHIC PORTRAIT

While I have to suppress the names of both the sitter and the originals of the psychically produced " extras," the evidence will be sufficiently strong to permit the case being recorded as " identified."

I am indebted to Deacon Convener John Duncan, of Edinburgh, for the photograph. To this gentleman Mr Wyllie left all his Edinburgh negatives, save one, that of his own mother's psychic picture, which he obtained when a relative of his sat. When we examined the prints taken from the negatives mentioned, Mrs Coates and I immediately recognised the psychic portrait of Maggie. We told the story to the Convener, at which he was astonished. He wondered what the lady on whose photograph this

had some sound links. The history may be briefly summed up in a story of a woman's imprudence and a man's selfishness. The young woman was in our

FIG. 60.—The photograph of Miss B——, Edinburgh, and the psychic "extras" of Margaret M—— and child, taken by Mr Edward Wyllie.

service many years ago, and had to leave owing to her condition. She went to relatives in ——shire, and for eighteen months thereafter she corresponded with Mrs Coates. We knew the reputed father too, and the child is very like him. Maggie was a foolish girl, but not a bad one. Whether dead or living we do not know, as the correspondence had ceased suddenly, but the following, which took place many years after she left us, suggests she is on the other side :—

One evening (Friday, 8th October 1909)—a short time before Mr Wyllie had so successfully passed the tests described elsewhere—we had our usual weekly sitting, at which Mr Wyllie and several others were present. That evening Mr Wyllie described a spirit of a man wearing a peculiar cap or fez on his head, and who was looking at me. Next day this man's face, as described, came on a plate of which I was the subject. At the same sitting, Miss Kate M—— described a tall, dark-haired woman, who said, "Do not despise me, Mrs Coates." The latter said, "I do not despise anyone. Who are you?" "Don't look down on me; I am your old servant, Maggie." Mrs Coates remembered, and so did I, but neither Miss Kate M—— nor the rest knew what was meant in that plea. Certainly we both had forgotten this young woman, but Miss M—— never knew her. The incident was a very good bit of psychic evidence. I append the names of those present that night in corroboration of this incident, of which the psychic photographs were unexpected and remarkable sequels.

We were present on the evening of the 8th October 1909, when Miss Kate M —— described a tall, dark spirit, and heard the message which Miss M—— said she heard clairaudiently, and bear testimony to the fact that the said description and message were immediately recognised by Mr and Mrs Coates.

JOHN AULD, Hazelcliffe, Rothesay.

MARIA PAYNE, Kames Bank, Port Bannatyne.

FLORA STEWART, Stratford House, Port Bannatyne.

AGNES M——,

INA M——,   } Ladies residing in Rothesay.

KATHERINE M——,

JAMES COATES, Glenbeg House, Rothesay.

JESSIE COATES,   „   „   „

ROTHESAY, 7th October 1910.

I can offer no explanation.   Mr Wyllie was certainly our guest, and present at that sitting.   He did not know and could not have obtained a photograph of her, as none existed.   The portrait of this woman must have been produced by some psychic process of which we are ignorant.   Humanly speaking, it is not a case of mistaken identity.   The points of interest are as follows:—

1. We had a female domestic, whom we both knew intimately.

2. She left under such circumstances as to doubly impress her features on our memory.

3. She had passed out of our thoughts till either herself (or some Intelligence in the Invisible) influenced a lady—a recent acquaintance—to describe her and give us a very striking and thought-provoking message.

4. Several thoughtful and intelligent persons were present on that occasion, and noted that we recognised the spirit described and the message.

5. Some months afterwards a lady in Edinburgh—

a stranger to us—sits for a photograph to a stranger to her. She obtains two extras on her photograph. They are not recognised.

6. Another stranger, Convener John Duncan, of Edinburgh, visited us (April 1910), and having shown us a number of prints, we recognise Maggie's photograph, *the only photograph in the whole collection which has been recognised.*

In all this we have evidence of the work of intelligent operators in the Invisible who are able, through a suitable medium, to produce psychic pictures.

Cui bono? And to what purpose? These questions I cannot fully answer, but I do suggest, as to "what good?" that we have a hint here that *the record* of what we are and have been exists in the Akasa or thought-atmosphere of the psychic world wherein we partly exist now and where we will see ourselves as we really are ultimately. And the purpose is probably to show us that neither by change of name nor place, neither in the body nor out of it, can we escape from our real selves; that we begin our progress in the discarnate state where we left off while in the body, no better or no worse. If poor Maggie has been the means of driving these thoughts home, we should welcome her visit and prize her spirit photograph.

The foregoing was sent to John Duncan, Esq., who brought us the prints and the psychic picture of Maggie, with the request: "If the statements are correct, I will be glad to have your certificate to that effect." I append it:—

6th October 1910.

I, John Duncan, residing at Dunearn, Granton Road, Edinburgh, do hereby certify that the story of "Maggie's" psychic portrait, as related by Mr James Coates in his work, entitled *Photographing the Invisible*, is correct in every detail. I have known the young lady who sat for her photo with Mr Wyllie for a number of years. The negative was in my possession, and the prints Mr Coates refers to taken from it. I was also present at the sitting in Mr Coates's house when Miss Kate M—— at once recognised the photograph as being that of the young woman she had described to Mrs Coates at a previous sitting. I may also say that the young lady in Edinburgh who sat with Mr Wyllie is a spiritualist, but knew nothing of the young woman or child, and she has never been in Rothesay.   JOHN DUNCAN,
                    Convener of Trades, Edinburgh.

I have always maintained that the Intelligences at work in the Invisible have a higher object in the production of psychic photographs than the mere comfort and gratification of the sitter. This is a case in point. The sitter was not personally concerned, but the lesson for all is most obvious. The photographer and the subject are instruments in the production of the picture, but wholly ignorant of the purport—a story of true human interest, with a moral.

THE EVIDENCE OF MR A. W. ORR

Mr A. W. Orr, writing from 15 Moorland Road, Didsbury, Manchester, 18th April 1910, says:—

I enclose you a copy of the photograph on which appears the likeness of my wife, and also a copy of another later photo on which I hoped to get another likeness of her, but in this I was disappointed. I enclose statement as to the identification of the " extra " as being the likeness of my wife, signed by people who knew her well and used to see her frequently

FIG. 61.—Photograph of Mr A. W. Orr, and the psychic portrait of his wife.   Done by Mr Edward Wyllie.

during the many years of our life here, face to face, if I may so express myself.   No similar photograph was taken of her in life.

Miss Lee used frequently to be in our house for days together, and Lucy Turner was my wife's maid. Mr Shaw, a neighbour and friend, living opposite to us, knew us both intimately.

CERTIFICATE OF IDENTIFICATION

I consider the psychic "extra" on the photograph
of Mr A. W. Orr, taken by Mr E. Wyllie, to be a good
likeness of the late Mrs Orr.

(Mr) W. SHAW, Grove Lane, Didsbury.
(Miss) L. M. TURNER, now of 113 Fairfield
      Road, Buxton.
(Miss) A. LEE, now of 113 Fairfield Road,
      Buxton.

Regarding the second photograph, which I think is
of sufficient importance to reproduce, Mr Orr, writing
on the following day, 19th April, says:—

I know neither face which appears, but one afternoon I showed it to a friend, who said he thought it
was his uncle's likeness, his mother's brother, of whom
he had only a faint recollection, as he (the uncle) had
gone abroad when my friend was a child. He showed
the print to his father, who declared that it was a very
good likeness of the uncle, after whom he was named.
Shortly afterwards, without comment, I showed the
print to another person, who said: "Isn't there a
likeness to Mr R. (my friend) in the man's face?"
There is a resemblance between the "extra" and my
friend, as often seen in family likenesses, and I give
the foregoing not so much as evidence as being very
suggestive.—Yours truly,   A. W. ORR.

In interesting confirmation of the fact of Mrs Orr's
psychic portrait, Mr Orr wrote me from Mendip
Cottage, Coombe Warren, Kingston-on-Thames, on
26th April 1910:—

I may mention that the day before I left Manchester,
the photographer who (a great sceptic himself) is
printing from Mr Wyllie's negatives showed me a

print of an " extra " *only* which had come on a negative taken a few days previously by Mr Wyllie, and asked if I could recognise the face. I at once said that it was extremely like my wife. He said that he was so much struck with the likeness that he had made a copy of the print to show me it. This "extra" is a better and clearer likeness of my wife than that which appears on my photograph. I suppose that she and the spirits who direct these matters happened to see that through this particular gentleman they could probably build up a mask substantial enough to appear on the plate, and they took the opportunity accordingly. No doubt many spirit people are around while Mr Wyllie is taking photographs, and those who are able—finding the conditions suitable—press forward and produce the "extras," quite or very largely indifferent to the question of who the sitter may be, trusting to luck, so to speak, to being recognised by somebody at some time or other.

A Photograph of " The Double "

As to the face of the little girl on the second photograph, when Mrs Coates and I saw it we at once commented on the amazing likeness of the "extra" to that of a child of a friend of ours. We could not be mistaken about the face, as the little one had a strongly individualised physiognomy. Although wondering if the child had passed over, we did not like to write to the parents. Hoping that we should hear from them or have a visit in due course, we did not write. Our friends called on 9th September 1910. Among other photographs we showed them this. Both were extremely surprised when they saw the face of their own child on the photograph of an entire stranger—in fact, to see it at all.   I need not dwell on their conjectures, but summarise the result in their certificates :—

I have examined the photo thoroughly, and am con-

Fig. 62.—Second photograph of Mr A. W. Orr, with two psychic "extras," taken by Ed. Wyllie in Manchester, in March 1910.   The face of little girl is that of a living person.

vinced that the face of the child is that of my daughter.   JAMES S. PATERSON,
                    Glenkiln, Belmont Drive, Giffnock.

I have also examined the photograph, and am convinced that the face of the child thereon is that of my daughter Mattie.   MARTHA PATERSON.

Both certificates were written in our presence, in Glenbeg House, Rothesay, on the 9th September 1910.   JAMES and JESSIE COATES.

Now for the facts, which I have been able to verify. The psychic photographs were taken in Manchester, 22nd March 1910. Neither Mr Orr nor Mr Wyllie ever saw the child. Little Mattie is very much alive. The photograph cannot be that of a departed, and if anything it is a picture of her " double."

Mr Orr says :—

I am obliged for your letter of the 27th (September 1910), and the photographs which accompanied it, which are extremely interesting. . . . I am glad that the little girl's face on my photograph has been recognised. As the photograph was taken in the afternoon, I believe she would be wide awake and " all alive " as to her state of consciousness; so that the question, How came her face on my photograph ? is a mystery of an extra degree of mysteriousness. The face is so clear that its recognition can hardly be erroneous. It is a face having a good deal of individuality.

I am content to state the facts. As to explanation, life is too short for that.

A word as to the testimony of Mr A. W. Orr. I find that he is a man of standing in the community of Didsbury, where he has resided for twenty-nine years. He became interested in spiritualism in 1894 for a similar reason to that given by Dr Alfred Russel Wallace, F.R.S., O.M., viz., "The facts were too many for me." He was many years President of the Manchester Psychic Research Society. He is held in high repute in Manchester and district as a man of probity and strong scientific tendencies.   He has been and is now one of the directors of *The Two Worlds* Publishing Company.   As a man of integrity, his testimony and opinions merit consideration in these cases, as they would have due weight in a court of law.

Mrs Ashworth, 17 Kent Street, Milkstone Road, Rochdale, at my request sent me three photographs. In two of these Mrs Ashworth is the subject, and the "extras" are the psychic portraits of her own sister— a very clear and convincing likeness, and well attested. The second photograph (fig. 63) gives as an "extra" the likeness of Miss Alice Whittaker.   In the third photograph, in which Mr Eli Holt Seanor, of 4 Franklin Street, Rochdale, is the subject, the "extra" is the psychic picture of his little brother, who was eight weeks old when he passed away.

When Mr Wyllie was at Rochdale, Mrs Ashworth— who is herself a psychic—sat twice for a photograph, viz. on 4th June 1910, when she obtained the likeness of her sister, and on 5th June, when she received that of Miss Alice Whittaker.   At the time of sitting she did not know what she had got on the plates, but went hoping to get the photograph of her father.   In this respect her hope did not materialise.   Of one thing, however, she is certain: that Mr Wyllie, the photographer, a perfect stranger in the community, and only there for a brief visit, could neither know nor get photographs of either her sister or the late Miss Alice Whittaker.

On the morning before getting her prints, Mrs Ashworth saw, in luminous letters, the name "Alice Whittaker." She did not know what this meant until she secured the photographs. I have only her

Fig. 63.—Photograph of Mrs Clara Ashworth, and the psychic portrait of Miss Alice Whittaker.

word for this, but I at once accept it. Mrs Ashworth is much respected in the world in which she lives, and many of her psychical experiences have been thoroughly substantiated.

I took some little trouble to get a few—out of many—to bear testimony to Mrs Ashworth's reputation, and to the identification of this psychic photo-graph.

We, the undersigned, knew the late Miss Whittaker well. Some of us actually worked with her when she was at Schofield's Mill, in Rochdale, where she lived the most of her life. Miss A. Whittaker was an active, energetic woman, well known in the town. She was found dead sitting in her chair, April 18th, 1910. The spirit photograph we all recognise as hers.

Mrs M. I. ASHWORTH, 26 Crawford Street, Rochdale.
JANE INGHAM, 32 Mere Lane, Rochdale.
NELLIE PARRY, 18 Talbot Street, Rochdale.
MARY ELLEN WHELDEN, 87 Durham Street, Rochdale.
Miss WILSON, Woodford Street, St Annes-on-the-Sea.

Frank Crossby, Miss E. Furness, Mrs E. E. Lord, and Mrs Parry worked with her in the same mill. Mrs H. A. Wilkinson knew her all her life; Mrs Ingham and Mrs E. Holden for years traded with her in business; and Mr James Cooper, 141 Osborne Street, Rochdale, was a co-worker with her for several years in church and mission work.

I have omitted the address of some of these witnesses, but as all of them except Miss Wilson are at present residing in Rochdale, their opinions and signatures can be readily verified. The evidence to the fact of spirit photography cannot be easily gainsaid.

TESTIMONY TO MR WYLLIE'S MEDIUMSHIP FROM A NOTED LECTURER, MRS R. S. LILLIE, OF SAN FRANCISCO, CAL.

This lady was among those who occasionally denounced spirit photography and physical phenomena from the platform. Her influence was very great— under inspiration. She was a most effective and charming speaker. Mr J. J. Morse, editor of *The Two Worlds*, says: "Mrs Lillie was a truly good woman, and beloved literally from Maine to Texas, from New York to California. She will be much missed upon the Pacific coast, where she was for many years an honoured resident, and a tireless worker for our cause. She passed out on the 28th February 1911."

Her letter to Mr Wyllie has been in my possession since October 1909. It is as follows:—

> MONTECITO, CALIF.,
> *12th July* 1905.
>
> MR EDWARD WYLLIE.
>
> DEAR BROTHER CO-WORKER,—The proof of photo is at hand. Many years ago N. B. Starr, of Port Huron, Mich., who was controlled to paint spirit pictures, presented me with a life-size portrait of my guardian spirit, a beautiful female form. The picture hangs by me as I write. I have always valued it very highly. The form by my side in your sitting is a good likeness of that portrait; the face is very like it: the position is different. The painting is a bust, while yours is full length. The face in the folds of my garment I do not recognise, but I shall be greatly obliged if you will send me a finished copy of the picture. Am sorry I did not sit earlier. With many thanks, I am, sincerely and truly, yours,   R. S. LILLIE.

Our readers who have doubts about spirit-painted pictures are referred to the chapters devoted to that subject. In the above letter we have testimony, in good faith, given not only to the foregoing, but also to the fact of spirit photography—an unwilling concession compelled by the resemblance of the psychically produced picture to that of the psychic painting.

I am not concerned here with the honest belief in her guardian spirit, but with her testimony—in conjunction with that of others—to the reality of the phenomenon of spirit photography.

Concluding Testimony to Mr Wyllie's Psychic Ability

Some months ago I wrote to Mr Wyllie, informing him that I was engaged in writing a work on spirit photography. I was somewhat surprised he did not give me cases, or the names and addresses of those who had received " extras " which had been identified. I recognised the value of his objections, which rested mainly with the sitters, who generally refused to give particulars for publication. Some did not like their names given; others thought the matter too sacred for publicity. However, in due course I was informed that Mr Henry Standfast, of British Honduras, had sent an account to his old friend and correspondent, Mr J. J. Morse. It appeared in *The Two Worlds*, 21st April 1911, in the same number containing the account of Mr Edward Wyllie's transition.

The friends to whom Mr Standfast had shown the photograph knew his wife in life, and were astonished, and more so as the simple facts were put before them.

Mr J. J. Morse says :—

It is a remarkable testimony to the medial powers

of Mr Wyllie, the noted medium for spirit photography.   Mr Standfast, the writer, is well known to me as a thoroughly honourable man, and his plain, straightforward testimony can be accepted without reserve.   He has resided in Belize, British Honduras, for many years, holding a responsible position in the United Fruit Company there.

I very much regret, owing to the miscarriage of the negatives, I have not been able to produce the photographs.   Mr Wyllie posted them, but unfortunately Mr Standfast never received them.   The photographs were too precious to forward with the account given of them.

In his article in *The Two Worlds*, Mr Standfast says:—

I had read notices of Mr Wyllie's gifts, and not finding his address, I sent to Mr Morse a package containing a lock of hair and letters, one to Mr Wyllie and one to my wife, who had gone to the "other side" about two years before.   I furnished no information about age or cause of death, but asked Mr Wyllie to do the best he was able for me under the circumstances.

The letter to my wife contained words to this effect: "You know we have seen spirit photos before, at the time of the Gurneys' Studio lawsuit in New York some years ago.   Now, I want to express plainly that the extremely accurate likeness to the earthly person was a sort of disappointment to me, it looked so earthlike.   A photo sometimes takes you at your best, even idealising, as everyone knows; sometimes at your worst—and both are exact.   Now, I want you to give me one of yourself at your best, or as you are now, if that be a possible thing.   I do not dictate what I know nothing about, but just request this as definitely as I can, so my thought may be clear to you on the other side of the veil. I am not wishing for an anatomical duplicate of the fleshly face. I want a portrait of the being."

I received a photo depicting my letter addressed to my wife attached to a dark screen. Underneath the letter, in the right-hand corner, was a *painfully accurate* portrait of my wife as she was a few days before her death. She was tortured to death by cancer, which wasted the flesh off her body, and was seventy-two years of age. Above the letter, in the left-hand corner, is a portrait of her at about thirty or thirty-five years of age, except there is a sort of serenity of expression, and a deep, penetrating, or soul-searching look about the eyes, very difficult to describe.

The features are exact in all details. Noticeable is the way she had fixed up her hair. She would curl her hair in a particular manner, not in her everyday style, but curled all over her head and down the forehead. When finished, she would come and look at me straight in the eye, to see if I really admired it. (Being an artist, and she having good features, I preferred the classic style.) I used to laugh at her earnestness over decoration, and tell her she was beautiful in any style.

When I saw this photo I could not help smiling, and thought I could see the personal effort to please me, answer my request, and put me in mind of other times, and to show me that is how she is *now*. The actual and well-known features and the idealised expression are complete.

In the portrait showing the face at the latest period there is the shoulder on one side down to the breast, given with a dress she sometimes wore of a peculiar pattern which I could identify in the dark. It is pleated or folded or embossed or raised—I don't know the proper feminine name for such work ; but it is not printed, and not what any lady might happen to have, because it was arranged by herself for occasional wear. It would be a difficult matter for me to think of any particular thing I could ask for in the way of a so-called "test," more than what is given in these portraits of my wife.

I wrote again to Mr Wyllie, enclosing a lock of hair, and another letter to my wife, asking for a three-quarter view (for a particular reason). In due course I received another photo. The second letter was made fast to a dark sheet, and at the lower right-hand corner was a repetition of the first portrait, with some little change; but above the envelope to the right was a portrait of a little child who left us at an early age, showing as far down as the shoulder, unusually wide, a characteristic feature (over each spirit portrait there is a radiance).

Now, in regard to this latter, about this same period I had written to Miss Florence Morse, asking her if she would kindly try to get something for me from my wife. I enclosed a letter to my wife, part of which was written in shorthand, asking her to give me some news about that child in any way she could find possible. I may say it causes no particular strain on the imagination to feel that she sent me this portrait in reply. I have written in shorthand and various languages to spirits, and find it does not make any difference what language you use; they receive the *sense*, if it is clearly defined!

Such personal points as these are more satisfying and convincing to a plain mind like mine than years of lectures and stacks of hypotheses. I only know that anybody exists by their personal characteristics and the personal phenomena attending them, intellectual or physical, whether the other side of a wall, at the end of a telephone wire, or in what we call another world, but which is only another state of being. Nothing at all can be proved anywhere in the universe except by corroborative evidence. I have had a very gratifying experience, and want to make it as widespread as I can.

HENRY STANDFAST.

BELIZE, BRITISH HONDURAS,
CENTRAL AMERICA.

Please note that the photographer was a stranger residing at a distance of over 5000 miles from Belize, and the *nexus* was a lock of hair in each case. See Chapter XVII. on "Most Favourable Conditions."

TRANSITION OF MR EDWARD WYLLIE

Mr Wyllie passed to the higher life on 10th April 1911, in his sixty-third year.

Although barely a month with us in Rothesay during September and October 1909, it was long enough for us to appreciate his quiet heroism and his genuine medial gifts. From experimentation in our home, I gleaned a keen insight into his character, and our sympathies, unasked, went out to him. Coming from the summer land of California, although in moderately fair health when he arrived in Rothesay, he soon suffered severely from the cold weather and almost perpetual rain and fog which he experienced during his stay in Glasgow. There he had an attack from his old enemy, malarial fever, contracted many years ago; and in Edinburgh he was again attacked by influenza, and he went an invalid to Manchester, and never really recovered.

Mr Wyllie, after an eventful and most varied life,

and considerable prosperity till he became a medium, was at the zenith of his power as a psychic when he lost all save his life and his mediumship at the great San Francisco earthquake. Due to that and the exposure and hardships in the Public Park, his wife, Mrs Louie Wyllie, died six months afterwards, and he lost all trace of his son Willie after the disaster. Mr Wyllie, although he concealed the fact, it was evident never got over the mental shocks sustained.

I am inclined to think that we in Rothesay, and perhaps the friends in Glasgow, obtained whatever was best in his mediumship; but after the illnesses contracted in Glasgow and Edinburgh, I do not think he ever was the same. He concealed his ill-health to the last from his relatives, and wrote a pleasant letter to his sister a short time before his last attack. Throughout all his trouble he remained the quiet sufferer and the gentleman.

He had been a captain in the New Zealand A.C., and took an active part in the Maori campaign. He was of the Scotch family of Wyllies, who, as statesmen and soldiers, have been connected with India for over a hundred years. The late Lieutenant-Colonel Sir W. H. Curzon Wyllie, K.C.I.E., C.V.O., who was shot in London, was his cousin. Mr Wyllie was born in Calcutta in 1848, his father being the late Colonel Robert Wyllie, of Elderslie, North Devon, who was for many years Military Secretary to the Government of India.

With his departure the last of our gifted professional mediums for photography is gone.   Mrs Coates and I will ever cherish pleasant recollections of this gifted but misunderstood man.

TESTIMONY OF MR WALTER JONES, STOURBRIDGE

STOURBRIDGE, 19th April 1911.

DEAR MR COATES,—Your letter of the 17th duly to hand. Poor Wyllie passed over in harness, as he himself desired, and I believe it was infinitely better than a lingering, painful illness; so we will hope that all is for the best. I quite agree with you that he was honest, genuine, and too simple to be a fraud. In fact, he was a man without guile; I am thankful that I made his acquaintance, which came about as follows:—

My first meeting with Mr Wyllie was in a London hotel. I invited him to dine with one lady and two gentlemen friends who were, I believe, Agnostics. The four were strangers to each other. When we had nearly finished dinner, I remarked to them: "Our friend here is a psychic, and takes psychic or spirit photos; I don't know whether he is clairvoyant also." He replied: "I am not a good clairvoyant, although I see things occasionally; but I am not the only clairvoyant in the company." I looked at him, and he continued: "The lady opposite is also clairvoyant. Are you aware of it, madam?" "No," she replied. "Well, I see a young girl by your side, with long curls and bright blue eyes, looking at you intently, and I am sure you often see that girl." "Yes," she replied, "that is my sister Jessie, who died in my arms eighteen years ago, and I have seen her every day since." This was a greater surprise to her husband than to any other member of the party.—With kind regards, believe me, yours faithfully,   WALTER JONES.

In concluding my testimony to Mr Wyllie's character and mediumship, it is singular that at the close of this chapter I have also to record his passing into the Invisible. His departure has brought abundant evidence of his great gifts. But what I have given must suffice.

THE TESTIMONY OF MR WALKER

This gentleman (who resides at 3 Palace Road, Buxton) has been an investigator of spiritualism for twenty-five years. I cannot do better than give recent cases obtained at the Crewe Circle, under test conditions. I premise the account by stating that, although Mr Walker is a spiritualist, he is also an old photographer whose experience goes back to the beginning of the wet-plate days. To this I add that the mediums at this remarkable circle are non-professional, and by request I do not furnish their names and addresses.

Mr Walker says :—

On November 7th, 1910, I sat with the Crewe Circle, and was photographed by the camerist of the Circle. Two plates were exposed on me—time, 15 seconds each, the day being dull. On one plate, in addition to other ".extras," is the portrait of my friend Mr Alfred Smedley, late of Park Mount, Belper, so well known years ago in spiritualism. On the second plate Mr Smedley appears again, but on the opposite side of me, with another "extra," said to be that of the spirit responsible for the phenomena produced at this Circle. The background used was the grey side of an American cloth table-cover, and the plates were mine.

I purchased the plates, which no one handled after the maker packed them save myself. In the dark-room I cut open the box and, after carefully examining the dark slide, I inserted two plates. The remaining ten plates in the box were carried in my pocket.

FIG. 64.—The photograph of Mr W. Walker, with portrait of the late Mr Alfred Smedley, taken at the Crewe Circle, November 1910.

The camera, which I examined, was empty and the lens clean. I inserted the dark slide. After exposure, I took it, with plates, into the dark-room and developed the latter, with results which I have already sent to *The Two Worlds*. I now send you the photographs, which I have enlarged at your request, for *Photographing the Invisible*. The camerist withdrew the shutters and made the exposure, but neither he nor anyone else touched the plates.

Apart from the signed certificate obtained from all present as to the facts recorded, my confidence in Mr

FIG. 65.—Photograph of Mr Walker, and of the late
Mr Smedley, taken on second plate.

Walker's skill and honesty is unbounded, and his evidence is sufficient.

Mr Alfred Smedley and Mr W. Walker were life-long friends, and there can be no doubt as to identification.   But since receiving the foregoing account, I have obtained the following :—

DERBY ROAD, BELPER,
April 8th, 1911.

Certificate.

I have much pleasure in certifying that the spirit photographs taken with Mr Walker at Crewe in November last, are of my father, the ascended Alfred Smedley, and also that the portraits are identified by the undersigned, whose names are appended to this certificate.   LILIAN R. SMEDLEY.

THOMAS F. SMEDLEY, Derby Road, Belper.
GEO. WHEELDON, Joseph Street, Belper.
HY. WIGLEY, Bridge Street, Belper.

CHAPTER XIII

PORTRAITS PAINTED BY INVISIBLE ARTISTS

FOR years I have heard and read of the mediumship of the Bangs Sisters of Chicago. They are as well known at Chesterfield, Indiana; Lilydale, New York; etc., as at Chicago. Consequently they have been tested in the exercise of their mediumship in residences not their own. Although super-normally produced "spirit paintings and portraits" stand apart from psychic photography, I thought, as the agents for their production—intelligent operators in the Invisible —were identical, it might be possible that a little research would reveal a similarity in the laws underlying both the paintings and the photographs. It has. This will be seen in the agreement running through the statements made by various reputable persons in their letters. It must be borne in mind that the writers are unknown to each other. I have purposely selected as evidential the testimonies of reputable persons in centres as wide apart as the United States, Canada, India, and Great Britain. For obvious reasons, the greater number of the writers and the attestations are American.

The Bangs Sisters have been mediums since child-

had a home in Chesterfield & worked at Lilydale

hood, but it was not till the autumn of 1894 that they began to get spirit paintings. It was necessary to curtain the canvas, or place it in a dark chamber, and several sittings were required to finish one picture. Then locked boxes were used; but all these

Fig. 66.—A photograph of the Bangs Sisters, *i.e.* Miss Lizzie S. Bangs and Miss E. Bangs, referred to in these pages.

processes, where the canvases were out of the sight and control, so to speak, of the visitors, suggested the possibilities of fraudulent procedure, and of charges made to that effect. Latterly the pictures have been obtained in broad daylight, and are finished in one sitting, lasting about twenty to forty minutes.

The room is shaded sufficiently to cause all the light

from the window to pass through the canvas, thus enabling the sitter to witness the development and detect the least change in the shadows.

No two sittings are exactly alike. Usually in the development of a portrait the outer edges of the canvas become shadowed, showing different delicately coloured lines, until the full outline of the head and shoulders is seen. When the likeness is sufficiently distinct to be recognised, the hair, drapery, and other decorations appear. In many cases, after the entire portrait is finished, the eyes gradually open, giving a lifelike appearance to the whole face.

The above statement (by Miss May Bangs, in letter, 17th September 1910) is supported by the letters and statements produced.

In spirit photography, as many of the processes do not lend themselves to the observation of the sitters, this rare phenomenon of portraits painted by Invisibles is enhanced by the fact that all the work can be followed, from the purchase of the canvases to the " precipitation " of the finished portrait.

There are two styles of work. For the more delicate and spiritual and symbolical pictures, the spirit artists furnish their own colouring matter; but for the usual portraiture, coloured French pastels are placed in front of the canvas, and these are used by the spirit artists—by a process called "precipitation." The effects are harmonious, and the refined blending is truer to nature than if similar portraits were produced by material portrait painters.

I now give a few concrete cases from their mediumship :—

This gentleman went to the Chesterfield Camp in 1905, and obtained the picture of his own father, who had died fourteen years previously. I summarise the statement furnished in *The Light of Truth*, 9th September 1905 :—

It was made in the daytime in an ordinary room that was not darkened. The frame containing the canvas set on a stand before the window. Mrs Charles Payne and Mrs John Weesner, who do not believe in spiritualism, were with me, and we sat within five feet of the picture The two Bangs Sisters, the mediums through whom the likeness was produced, sat on either side of the table and supported the frame, each with one hand. No brushes, paint, crayon, or other substance of any kind was used as far as we could tell, and it was light enough to have seen a pin on the table. The sisters had never seen or heard of my father, nor a photograph or likeness of him. *All they asked was that I fix his features in my mind.* [Italics mine.— J. C.] The picture was not made in spots or a little at a time. At first it was a faint shadow, then a wave appeared to sweep across the canvas, and the likeness became plainer. It was a good deal like a sunrise—got brighter until it was perfectly plain and every feature visible. Until the picture was completed, the eyes were closed, and then they opened all at once, like a person awakening. It did not take more than a half-hour, and is the best picture of my father we ever had. I do not pretend to say how it was done, simply that the picture was produced before our eyes without the mediums having ever seen a photograph or other copy.

This picture of the late Mr John Payne is now hanging in the Citizens' Bank, and the owner of the portrait is a level-headed business man, and one of the most substantial in Spiceland, Indiana.

THE TESTIMONY OF VICE-ADMIRAL W. USBORNE MOORE, 8 Western Parade, Southsea, Hants

I know of no one in Great Britain in whose powers of observation I could place greater reliance than those of Admiral Moore. This distinguished naval officer occupied several important positions, and served the Government of his country in command of warships specially fitted out for scientific research—which need not be detailed here—all of which redounded to his credit, and received his country's thanks.

In writing to me, of date 18th July 1910, the Admiral expresses the utmost confidence in these remarkable mediums:—

Since I returned from America [he says] a conjurer, Mr W. Marriott, has endeavoured to prove to me that the pictures precipitated in the presence of the Bangs Sisters are fraudulent. The result of our many conferences has been to confirm me in my original belief. I have six pictures here which I should have much pleasure in showing you, if you are ever down here.

In his second favour, dated 21st July 1910, referring to his articles in *Light*, the gallant Admiral writes:—

The Bangs Sisters are quite genuine. There was a suspicion about them last August (1909), but all was satisfactorily cleared up.[1]

In looking up the files of *Light*, I have omitted references to his other experiences with these mediums, and have taken the Admiral's account, which I condense, of how he obtained the spirit portrait of his wife :—

The next day a portrait was precipitated on to a Steinbach canvas within two feet of me. The Bangs Sisters each held one side of the canvas, which was put up against the window, while I sat between them and watched the face and form gradually appear. A few minutes after they began to appear, the psychics (apparently under impression) lowered the canvas toward me until it touched my breast. Mary Bangs then got a message by Morse alphabet on the table: "Your wife is more accustomed to see me in the other aspect." Up went the canvas again, and I saw the profile and bust, but turned round in the opposite direction; instead of the face looking to the right, it was looking to the left. The portrait then proceeded apace, until all the details were filled in, and in twenty-five minutes it was practically finished. Beyond a little deepening of the colour, and touches here and there by the invisible artist, the picture is the same now as when we arose from the table. The precipitated portrait is very much like a photograph of

[1] I have made a special study of the trial in July 1909 of Mary Bangs for violating section 2 of an Ordinance passed by the city of Chicago, on the 16th day of December 1907, against the practice of mediumship, and obtaining money for so doing, etc. Although—and most conclusively—no fraudulent practices were proven, the lady was fined. Not only so, but subsequently the false evidence led against the lady was thoroughly exposed.—THE AUTHOR.

the person, taken thirty-five years ago (shortly before death), *that I had in my pocket during the sitting* [the italics are mine.—J. C.], but which the Bangs, of course, had never seen. The expression of the face, however, is far more ethereal and satisfied than in the photo.

These instances are but two out of many manifestations I witnessed at the Bangs Sisters' house.

I learn that in all precipitations the portrait appears on the side next the sitter. Admiral Moore, referring to one beautiful full-length portrait which he obtained, says:—

On this occasion the canvases arrived from the shop wet, and we had to wait half an hour for them to dry. The next day I went to the shop and complained. The woman who attended said: "The boy who brought your order said you wanted stretched canvases. When he came to take them away, we found he wanted the paper as well, so we put it on at once, and of course they left the shop wet." I relate this little incident for the benefit of those who vainly imagine that the phenomenon of precipitation may be due to normal causes.

As the gallant Admiral will soon publish his complete experiences with these and other mediums, the foregoing, which I take with his special permission, will suffice.

Following the important testimony of the Vice-Admiral, the attested evidence of several intelligent witnesses will be appropriate. Attention is called to three points:—

1st. The portrait was produced under test conditions; the canvas selected by committee.

2nd. A correct, identifiable portrait of a late associate was artistically finished in eight minutes.

3rd. No photograph taken in life of the late Alex. P. M'Kee was produced as a probable basis for the portrait.

The Bangs Sisters are themselves convinced that they get undoubted portraits of spirits. I give this case in illustration :—

CHESTERFIELD, INDIANA, 21st August 1909.

STATE OF INDIANA, MADISON COUNTY, S.S.

Tom O'Neill, President of the Indiana Association of Spiritualists; James Millspaugh, Vice President of said Association; Lydia Jessup, Secretary of said Association; Henry Bronnenberg, Treasurer of said Association; and Rebecca M'Kee, J. M. Walker, S. J. Louiso, and Lewis Johnson, Trustees of said Association, being duly sworn, upon their oath depose and say : That on the 20th day of August 1909 they were present at a séance held by the Bangs Sisters, under test conditions, for these affiants above to receive a portrait of some former member of said Association, deceased, which portrait is to become the property of said Association, to be hung in the auditorium; that these affiants witnessed the development of said portrait, which portrait they recognised as the portrait of Alex. P. M'Kee, a former member and Treasurer of the said Association; that said picture was developed upon a canvas, or stretcher on a frame, which stretcher and frame were selected by one of these affiants from an assortment of such articles, all similar in form and appearance, without any suggestion or indication from the said Bangs Sisters; that said portrait developed upon said canvas or stretcher in a period of eight minutes within the full view of all of these affiants, in daylight; and affiants further say that they are firmly convinced that said portrait was so developed by spirit powers solely, and that no human, earthly agency contributed to the development of said portrait. That said affiants recognise in said portrait the excellent likeness of the said Alex. P. M'Kee.

TOM O'NEILL, President; JAMES MILLSPAUGH, Vice-President; LYDIA JESSUP, Secretary; HENRY BRONNENBERG, Treasurer; REBECCA L M'KEE, J. M. WALKER, S. J. LOUISO, LEWIS JOHNSON, Trustees.

Subscribed and sworn to before me, this 21st day of August 1909.

(Seal.) WILLIAM ROWLAND, Notary Public.

(My commission expires March 15th, 1913.)

The following letter of experience is from Mrs Gertrude Breslan Hunt, a well-known student of economical and social questions, who has lectured all over the United States on child labour and other like evils. Both for the supreme interest of the letter and the prominent position of the writer, I give her letter in full:—

I take great pleasure in telling the story of my investigations into the phenomena of spiritualism, begun only three months ago, yet revealing so much! I was a sceptic until that time, regarding the few people I knew who believed in such things with pity, perhaps slightly mixed with contempt, for their abnormal credulity and imagination. I am therefore all the more anxious to make expiation for my former prejudice and dogmatism. After years of study and thought, I had given up the belief in a continued life after death; but last October, a dear friend, a loyal comrade, a brilliant but martyred friend of humanity, passed out under circumstances so terribly sad as to

20

supreme tragedy. I had looked
for months that same year, and
for myself, but now death seemed a
er. If a beautiful and noble life of
love toward humanity could be ended in
; broken heart, wrecked hopes, ignominy
heaped upon him, when the natural and
reward should be love, honour, health, long life,
"every good and perfect gift," I said to myself:
"If this be all, life is not worth living; I could only
die damning so terrible a universe. I dare not wait
to see my beloved husband and precious mother face
such awful exigencies." In this hour of anguish the
thought came of the claims of spiritualism, and now
I decided to "investigate." I went to the best
mediums, and there learned that I was wise. While
the body of our friend and comrade was being
cremated, I went to the Bangs Sisters and asked for
a letter. I wrote four questions addressed to my
friend, folded five blank sheets of paper around my
note, sealed all in an envelope, and placed it between
two slates, in broad daylight; put strong rubber
bands about the slates, and never took my eye off it
where it lay before me on a bare oak table, and under
my hand. After a time, Miss Bangs, who sat back in
her chair, not touching the slate, said I might open
the envelope. I saw the writing through the envelope
before I tore it open, for it was sealed and the seal
undisturbed. I kept up my investigations, and finally
decided, with the consent and co-operation of friends,
upon getting a spirit portrait of our comrade, especially
for a memorial meeting we proposed to hold for him.
To me, this transcends all other phenomena, for you
have something you can retain, carry away with you,
and show to friends, and relate the wonder of seeing
it produced.

I informed myself of the devices claimed to be employed in certain newspaper "exposures." I learned

that the only negative of the deceased was destroyed, and I held the only copy in this State. I examined floor, table, windows, and every part of the room, and selected a life-sized canvas from a lot of fifteen or twenty. It was placed in a window, and I sat facing the canvas. I did not remove my eyes from the canvas, and would stake everything I possess that no hand touched that canvas after I placed it in the bright light of the window, until the picture was finished. Three pairs of eyes showed on the canvas at once in different poses and places. The background appeared first, as though successive layers of dust had been thrown on, then in a few minutes the whole face appeared, with the colors of life. I criticised the pose, and asked for a full-face view. The whole face faded out and was rapidly sketched again. I was requested to take the picture out and set it on the floor in such a light as it would be likely to have when finally placed. I did so, and remarked that the hair was too light; and there, where it sat, I saw the shadows creep into the waves of hair and it darkened. I asked that more colour be put into the cheeks, and the canvas blushed to the tint it now bears. The sleeves of the robe were corrected, and in two hours the picture was complete; and a competent artist has stated that he could not finish such a picture in less than three days, working eight hours each.

The mediums did not know the name of the person, whether man or woman, had never seen or known Dr Burson, *never saw the photograph, and had no chance to copy it.* [The italics are mine.—J. C.] I am therefore forced to conclude that life continues after death and that we may receive messages, and that this portrait is a spirit portrait. I have had many other convincing evidences, some of them in other cities where no one could possibly know anything of me. Nothing has brought me so much happiness, except the hope of the Co-operative Commonwealth and the resulting abolition of poverty and incentive to crime, when I believe we shall all " feel the soul within us climb," and reach heights scarce dreamed of now, and probably evolve, so that each may communicate with those in the spirit world without the aid of any other medium.

NORWOOD PARK, ILL.

Here we find the spirit artists responding to the express wishes of the still embodied friend of the departed, and they comply with her wishes and also produce as a spirit portrait a picture which can be, and was, identified by a photograph taken in earth-life of the late Dr Burson. It does not make the spirit (produced) portrait any the less valuable, but more so, that Mrs Hunt possessed a clear mental vision of the departed, and its independent identification from the unseen but solitary print in that lady's possession strengthens the evidence. At this stage the question arises: Are these spirit portraits the portraits of spirits in discarnate state, or are they the portraits of something which exists—although invisible —on the psycho-metaphysical plane ?

Elsewhere I have given the statement of Judge Levi Mock, of Duffton, Indiana, concerning psychic photographs which he obtained of relatives, and of a dog, at Chesterfield Camp, through the mediumship of Mr Frank Foster. In this I give his experience, and that of a friend who obtained a portrait, at the same Camp, through the Bangs Sisters. Dr J. H. Annis, whose article to *The Light of Truth*, 16th September 1905, I condense, says :—

The Judge selected a canvas from a pile of fifty or more on which the picture was to be made. This was all the preparation necessary. One of the sisters sat on either side of an ordinary centre table, supporting the mounted canvas by one hand, while the bright sunlight shone in through the open window. Mr Ripley and Judge Mock sat directly in front of, and about four feet from, the canvas. In this position they watched the development of the picture. First the outline appeared, then disappeared. Then it came again, and continued to grow brighter, lifelike features filling in. The eyes were closed; but to their surprise, they suddenly opened, and gave an expression to the face that they felt that it ought to speak. Up to this time, neither of the Bangs Sisters had ever *seen the photo which Mr Ripley had concealed in his pocket. But, upon his bringing it out, a comparison showed an exact copy.* [The italics are mine.—J. C.] In earth-life the friend usually wore a Masonic pin, but from some cause he did not happen to have it on when he sat for the photo. Mr Ripley desired it on the painting, and so made a mental, not verbal, request for it, and immediately it appeared upon the lapel of the coat, just as he used to wear it. All this occupied about twenty minutes.

This is one of dozens of other cases I might relate, with the Bangs Sisters, that are just as good in their respective cases.

In the foregoing, we see that the invisible artists responded to the mental request, as well as producing a portrait of the deceased, a likeness similar to that contained in an unseen photograph.

BANGS SISTERS,
Chicago, Ill.

122 LANCASTER AVE.,
SYRACUSE, N.Y.

OUR DEAR FRIENDS (for such we must call you),—
The painting arrived safely, and to say that we are

both well pleased with it does not half express our sentiment.

Our little darling looked just as though he was ready to step down and out of the frame, he is so natural. We fully realise no earthly artist could

FIG. 67.—Photograph of the portrait obtained of a little boy who passed out of their material life two years previous to the precipitation of the portrait, and of whom they had absolutely no likeness, not even a Kodak.

possibly produce such wonderful work. One cannot see where the picture is started or finished, so perfect is the blending of the colours.

We notice the appearance of a certain little ring on the third finger of his left hand, the partial request of his mamma's. This marvellous work has been a great revelation to us; one year ago we would hardly have thought this manifestation possible, and we feel very grateful to you for your efforts in securing for us such a wonderfully satisfactory likeness.

May you have grand success in all the coming years of your life, that we trust the Over-Ruling Intelligence may prolong to a ripe old age, that others may have similar blessings that we are in possession of through your instrumentality.—Very sincerely your friends,

MR and MRS MILFORD BADGERO.

Particulars of the artistically finished portrait, fig. 68, reached me from good sources. It was on exhibition at Leach's Opera House, Wamego, Pollawatomie County, Kansas, during the whole month of April 1910, where it was fully recognised by many persons, intimate friends and many others who knew the late Mrs Leach. The matter was also fully reported, 28th April 1910, in the *Wamego Reporter*, in the town where Mr and Mrs Leach are so well known.

The facts of obtaining the picture are these Mr Louis B. Leach, desirous of obtaining the portrait of his wife, arranged to have a sitting with the Bangs Sisters. They were holding séances in a room on the fourth floor of 1200 Pasco, in Kansas City. Mr Leach called upon them at 3.40, on 30th March 1910. His wife, Mrs Ella Leamon-Leach, had passed into the spirit world little more than three years before, and her personal appearance was not known to the mediums. About seven minutes' time was employed in discussing as to the style of picture which would be most appreciated. The following took place. The

30 × 48 inches, was selected and placed on a frame before the window — which was four stories from the ground — in such a way that the light fell on the back of the framed canvas. The colours began to develop in about four minutes, particularly rose

Fig. 68.—Photograph of the spirit-painted portrait of the late Mrs Ella Leamon-Leach, produced in the presence of the Bangs Sisters.

red, quickly followed by darker colours and green. In thirty-five minutes the picture was practically developed in the presence of Mr Louis B. Leach and the Bangs Sisters. The former states :—

No pigments or colours were furnished. No human hand, agency, mechanism, or contrivance rendered any assistance to the spirit forces executing the work. In this picture there are trees, vines, and flowers, with a depth of scenery that is not often observed in portraiture. It is a striking likeness of my late wife. The dress she wears is to me a well-known study in Parisian art fashion. The hair and eyes are perfect; the expression is hers; and in this beautiful picture the colours of the trees, vines, and flowers are distinctly true. I pronounce it a good likeness and a gem of art.

Louis B. Leach.

Since obtaining the above, Mr Leach, writing on 30th April 1910, from Wamego State Bank, to the Bangs Sisters, says :—

I have engaged a photographer to take a negative of Ella's picture, and will send you a cabinet, as soon as they are ready. I am very glad to let you have the use of the picture, or help you in any way I can. Your success will do us all good. I hope your experiences will lead to prosperous issues. I believe they will. My admiration of your work is only equalled by my love of the cause of truth.

On my application to Mr Leach for a photograph of this painting, in his letter (4th December 1910) he regretted he had none available, having given the last away, and added :—

You may take it from me that I am in favour of the Bangs Sisters and their work, and nothing has happened to make me change my mind in regard to their genuineness.

This gentleman is a man of standing in Wamego, where he is President of the Wamego State Bank of Kansas, and he is also proprietor of Leach's Opera House. I have a long list of names, including Dr

C. H. Carson and various prominent citizens of Wamego and of Kansas City, to whom Mr Leach is well known. But I think the foregoing statements adequate.

As to fig. 69, although I withhold the names, I give the portrait for the simple reason that the Bangs Sisters obtained it in their first public demonstration for spirit paintings, held in the presence of a large number of people. It took place at the Chesterfield Camp on the evening of 30th August 1908. *The Nuncie Morning Star* says:—

Upon a table on the stage was placed a frame with an opening large enough to hold an ordinary-sized crayon portrait mat   Behind the aperture was placed a coal-oil lamp. . . . The mats remained in position in full view of the audience until the developed picture was completed.

A few moments after the mats were placed in position the canvas assumed a mottled cloudy appearance, and gradually the outline bust form of a person appeared in the centre of the canvas. Gradually the picture became more distinct and the features were distinguishable, then the colouring of the hair and the face developed, and lastly the eyes apparently opened, and the picture of a girl about twelve years of age was completed, and plainly distinguished by all the audience. The work required a period of about twenty minutes, and when the eyes opened the audience cheered the young women. The picture was handed about the audience for inspection. The Bangs Sisters are the only persons known to develop pictures in the manner described, and have produced portraits for many people in this city, among whom are Fred Macomber, who has a portrait of his mother; Mrs B. F. Timmons; Mrs Richard Hunt; C. M. Payne, of Newcastle; and J. W. Payne, of Spiceland, Ind.   The only explanation of their work given by the sisters is that spirit artists do the work.

The picture thus obtained proved to be the likeness of a daughter of a prominent Marion, Indiana family, who are not spiritualists in belief, and this was their first visit to Camp Chesterfield. *The mother*

FIG. 69. —Photogiaph of spirit-painting of the daughter of a prominent Marion family who are not spiritualists.

wore around her neck, hid from sight, a locket containing a photograph of her daughter almost duplicate in likeness of the picture obtained [the italics are mine.—J. C.], but different in pose and position. The psychics had not seen the locket picture or any *photo of the child.*

I am quite aware the foregoing is only an item of news

from the columns of a secular paper. Taken by itself it would not count for much. Although the names are not given of the family—who are not spiritualists—the names of those having similar experiences are, and these—especially the Paynes of Newcastle and of Spiceland, Ind.—are sufficiently well known for my readers in Indiana to respect their evidence.

I am aware that, since the foregoing exhibition of the Bangs Sisters, certain imitations have been produced in public and called "spirit paintings." I also know that Mr Wm. Marriott, of London, Eng., says that he can produce them. Since this book was written, Mr Careward Harrington, another expert, declares that he has a friend who can do so. Were it worth while, I might give more attention to these claims.

Have they produced pictures *under similar conditions* to those obtained by the Bangs Sisters? For this there is no evidence beyond the usual expert assertions.

Have they produced identifiable portraits of persons whom they never saw, and from photographs which they have never seen? No.

Have any of their productions presented evidence of intelligences *outwith* their own? The answer is in the negative.

CHAPTER XIV

PORTRAITS PAINTED BY INVISIBLE ARTISTS
—*continued*

MR G. SUBHA RAU, editor of the *West Coast Spectator*,
Calicut, India (and who is not a spiritualist), visited
America some two years before Vice-Admiral Usborne
Moore, and gives a detailed experience in the number
for March 1909 of *The Hindu Spiritual Magazine*.
I do not propose to give his account in full. When
he obtained the precipitated portrait of his wife, *he
had the photograph of that lady in his pocket*, which,
however, the mediums did not see. In his statement,
which I summarise, Mr Rau says:—

I had heard that the Bangs Sisters could produce
through spirit agency a portrait of any deceased
person. I had found it hard to believe such a claim,
and when I arranged to have a sitting for a portrait
of my deceased wife, I did so with no little incredulity.
The Bangs Sisters claim that they can get a deceased
person's portrait precipitated on canvas even when no
photographic or other likeness exists. In my case
there was a photograph, which I was carrying with
me. I took every care to see that neither of the
mediums nor any of their friends saw it. At this
sitting both sisters took part.

In the course of conversation, one or the other
would describe what she professed to see. *They saw*

apparently a life-size image of the photograph I had with me, and described it correctly in the details. [The italics are mine.—J. C.] For instance, they saw that I sat; that my wife stood behind, with her hand on my shoulder; that her face was round; that she wore a peculiar jewel on the nose; and her hair was parted; that a dog lay at my foot, and so on.

Incidentally, I may mention that they described visions of one who, from the description, could be my mother; a third, my friend with whom I had been trying to communicate, and so on. But to proceed, they asked me to pick out any two canvas stretchers that lay against the wall, adding that I might bring my own stretchers if I liked. I took out two which were very clean and set them on the table against the glass window. I sat opposite, and the two sisters on either side. Gradually I saw a cloudy appearance on the canvas; in a few moments it cleared into a bright face, the eyes formed themselves and opened rather suddenly, and I beheld what seemed a copy of my wife's face in the photograph. The figure on the canvas faded away once or twice, to reappear with clearer outline; and round the shoulder was formed a loose white robe. The whole seemed a remarkable enlargement of the face in the photograph. The photograph had been taken some three or four years before her death, and it was noteworthy that the merely accidental details that entered into it should now appear on the canvas. For instance, the nose ornament already referred to, she had not usually worn. Some ornaments were clumsily reproduced. One that she had always worn, but which was not distinctly visible in the photograph, was omitted on the canvas. I pointed out these blemishes, and as the result, when I saw the portrait next day, all the ornaments had disappeared. I was satisfied that the portrait had been precipitated by some super-normal agency. As soon as the portrait was finished, I touched a corner of the canvas with my finger, and a greyish substance came off. The portrait is still in my possession, and it looks as fresh as ever. I had omitted to say it was all done in twenty-five minutes.

The above remarkable testimony by a sceptic and an eye-witness must be of great weight. The fact of reproduction does not take away from the value of the undoubted psychic action.

Mr Rau is perfectly satisfied that the portrait was a case of precipitation; that the photograph in his pocket was the basis of the likeness, and not any mental picture which he had in his mind. He is also certain that the Bangs Sisters are genuine psychics, and the phenomenon obtained through them arose through occult causes; but he did not think either his wife, or the spirits from whom he desired to hear, had anything to do with the production of this portrait.

Mrs Lucy E. Adams, 356 East 60th Street, Chicago, Ill. (in her letter to me dated 2nd July 1910), says:—

I have had very little experience with spirit photography, but I have for my friend, Mr Ghose, editor of *The Hindu Spiritual Magazine*, obtained a precipitated picture of his son through the mediumship of the Bangs Sisters. Mr Shishir Kumar Ghose will be interested in your book on spirit photography, and so will I.

There was a desire expressed that I should investigate personally the powers of these ladies. I wrote the esteemed editor of the *Hindu Spiritual Magazine*, for he being a man of standing in Hindu society, and lately honoured by the Indian Government, I would highly esteem his testimony. I received the following letter from his son, Mr P. K. Ghose :—

"HINDU SPIRITUAL MAGAZINE" OFFICE,
CALCUTTA, *September* 29, 1910.

DEAR SIR, — Your favour, dated the 30th July. My revered father, Babu Shishir Kumar Ghose, has been lying seriously ill for the last two or three weeks; hence he could not reply directly to your letter. I am, however, enclosing you, by his direction, a full description as to how the picture was precipitated. If possible, we shall try to send you a photograph of the picture.—Yours very truly,

P. K. GHOSE, Manager.

(The photographs were duly received, 7th December 1910.)

I should much prefer to give the report in its lucid completeness, but lack of space compels me to summarise it. I may state in passing that it was owing to the successful personal experience of Mr G. Subha Rau that Mr Ghose was induced to try to get a portrait of his departed son. Mr Ghose could not proceed to Chicago, and had to depute the mission to a most trustworthy resident in that city, viz. Mrs Lucy E. Adams, an esteemed correspondent.

From the testimony of Babu Shishir Kumar Ghose, referred to in Mr Piyush Kanti Ghose's letter, I take the following :—

Having heard from a friend of his experiences with the Bang Sisters in Chicago, I determined to get, if possible, the portrait of my beloved son, Poyesh Kanti. I could not go in person, so I wrote to a very dear friend (distinguished for her exceeding piety and sound (judgment) who resided in Chicago. I asked her to visit the Bangs Sisters and get me a picture. Not believing in mediums, she objected, having no desire to help me to throw my money away. I insisted, however, and sent her a photograph of my son, so

FIG. 70.—The photograph of the precipitated painted portrait of Poyesh Kanti, the departed son of Babu Shishir Kumar Ghose, Calcutta, done by the Bangs Sisters.

that she should have decided and available means by which to identify the picture ; *but she was not on any account to permit the sisters to have a glimpse of the photo.* She finally consented. Taking her own canvas, and accompanied by an intimate friend, Mrs P.—who had no faith in spiritualists—she called on the Bangs Sisters. There was only one of the sisters present, by whom they were taken into a small room where there was one small window, which was open to the street. Before it the canvas was hung, so that the light fell on its back, enabling my friend and her companion to see how the picture was drawn. That window formed the upper part of a door. The canvas could not be affected from without. There was no space under the door through which anything could be passed. But in either case, any attempt from above or underneath would have been detected at once.

It must also be borne in mind that it was the side of the canvas away from the window on which the picture was precipitated. The two ladies sat before, and the medium stood on one side, touching it Immediately they saw a cloud over-spreading the canvas, and by degrees the picture was finally precipitated in the manner described by Mr Subha Rau, in the *Hindu Spiritual Magazine*, March 1909. These ladies had a watch before them, and when three raps announced the completion, they saw it was finished in exactly twenty minutes.

Any human artist would, in my opinion, take at least twenty minutes to select the colours and blend the tints. In this delicate work of art no sign of brush-work is visible, no crudities, as in portraits painted by competent artists. It was not done by the coarse hand of a material being, but by some means unknown to artists on earth. Most assuredly it was not done, drawn, or painted by the only medium present or by the witnesses.

The question arises, Was the picture a painting of my son as the subject, or was it from his photograph? It may be alleged that the medium saw the photograph clairvoyantly, and that the spirit artist saw it through her. This is supported by the fact that the picture is very much like the photograph. There is one little circumstance which suggests that the spirit of my son was the subject of the picture, and that is, *the complexion* is correctly given. The medium could not have known that from the photograph. The Hindus of the higher classes in Bengal have a peculiar complexion, which has its distinctive characteristics. Again, the sisters allege that they can get pictures precipitated in a similar fashion without a photograph. I have no reason to doubt the evidence; therefore I conclude that the painting was that of the spirit present, and not from the photograph. The evidence is also conclusive that the picture was not done by mortal hand, but was finished by occult means: by invisible intelligence or spirit.

The above account may have suffered a little by my curtailment, but the central fact stands, *i.e.* that an identifiable portrait of a departed was obtained through the agency of intelligent artists in the Invisible, by the aid of a medium. This is supported by the testimony of Mrs Adams and her lady friend. The first was doubtful of the legitimacy of the procedure and the genuineness of the mediums; and the second — if not both — was a non-believer in spiritualism. There is also the identification by the hitherto unseen photograph; that of the honoured Babu; the testimony of his son and a brother of the departed one. If this were not enough, there is the united testimony of the adult members of possibly the largest family in India, consisting of Babu Shishir Kumar Ghose's [1] immediate descendants; his brothers

---

[1] Since writing the above, Babu Shishir Kumar Ghose passed to the higher life 10th January 1911.

Although the late head of this family was a modern journalist, author, man of affairs, founder of the *The Daily Amrita Bazar, Patrika* (the most influential paper in Bengal), the head of other businesses, landed interests, and proprietor of various publica-

and their wives, children, and grandchildren; his sisters, their husbands, children, and grandchildren; together with not a few other relatives, with the servants and dependants of this great household.

My only comment is that, the fact of the painting and the manner of its accomplishment being established beyond doubt, and while it may be possible that the departed presented an image of his bodily form to the psychic artist or artists for production, the factor of the reproduction of the unseen photograph cannot well be excluded. It would still remain the portrait of an invisible produced by no mortal hand. This is the central fact, and to my mind the most important.

THE TESTIMONY OF DR AND MRS E. H. THURSTON

I give their account in full, as I consider the evidence of value, and of interest as being recent:—

HAGERSTOWN, IND., U.S.A.,
5th April 1910.

Desiring a spirit portrait of our daughter, who passed into the spirit life at the age of thirty years, and having viewed some of the results obtained for others through this remarkable phase of the Bangs Sisters' mediumship, we decided to make a test of it ourselves.

tions, he was also a patriarch. His household is a survival of the patriarchal rule which in ancient times obtained in the Orient, although now almost non-existent in India.

Honoured by the Indian Government, his reputation was of the highest; he was and is revered by his family and many people as a saint. Such is the character of the man whose testimony is given in these pages.

Visiting Chesterfield Camp, Indiana, we called upon the Bangs Sisters in their cottage and arranged the date for our sitting, the hour set being the following afternoon. At the stated time we again called at

FIG. 71.—Photograph taken by an amateur of the spirit-painted portrait of the deceased daughter of Dr and Mrs E. H. Thurston, of Hagerstown, Indiana, U.S.A.

their cottage. Entering the séance-room, and finding only three canvases, I selected two of them, took them out in the sunlight, in company with one of the Miss Bangs, exposed them for fifteen minutes to the strong rays of the noonday sun, examined the surface thoroughly to fully assure myself that they were not chemically prepared, at the same time to secretly mark them for identification.   Returning to the séance-room, I placed the canvas on the small table before a well-lighted north window, and by examination of table and surroundings convinced myself that every-thing was void of any and all mechanical apparatus.

The Bangs Sisters, seated on each side of the table, merely supported the canvas in an upright position with one hand, myself and wife being seated directly in front of, and not more than two feet from them. After sitting a very short time, a dark shadow passed over the canvas, followed by the outline of the head and body; then, to our wonderful amazement, the perfect features of our daughter appeared, with the eyes closed; a few more seconds, and the eyes opened, and before us was the beautiful spirit portrait of our deceased daughter, perfectly lifelike in every feature, and which has been instantly recognised by all who knew her when in earth-life.   When the picture was completed, the identification marks previously spoken of showed that the canvas had not been tampered with in any way.

While the portrait has much the appearance of pastel work, we have since removed particles of the material or substance of which the picture is made, and find it perfectly soluble in water, without impart-ing any colour whatever to the water, which is not the case in pastel work.

Being somewhat familiar with photography and photographic processes, especially solar print work, we are fully convinced that the picture is not the product of any photographic process, and we desire to say right here there was positively no evidence whatever of any trick, of sleight-of-hand performance; everything was perfectly straightforward and honest, as far as the physical eye could discern, and we went away from that cottage at beautiful Camp Chesterfield more con-vinced than ever before of the continuity of life after death, and the beautiful philosophy of spiritualism.

The Bangs Sisters will ever have our highest regards, for we believe they are thoroughly genuine and honest.   DR and MRS H. E. THURSTON.

Dr and Mrs H. E. Thurston did not state whether they had a photograph of their daughter taken in life, but I assume that to be possible, as the doctor was himself a photographer. It does not affect the facts stated whether they had or not.

I now give an interesting case in which no photograph had been taken. The account — which I summarise—was given by Mr George C. Holland, of Ottawa, Canada. In *Light*, 15th May 1909 (after describing procedure at the cottage of the Bangs Sisters, at Lilydale Camp, the test measures adopted, and the fact that Mrs Holland and himself had no photograph of their son in their possession), he says :—

First, a cloud seemed to roll over the face of the canvas and disappear. It was followed by other clouds, each time some of the colour remaining on the canvas, until a background was formed. Then appeared a faint outline of a human head, which disappeared and reappeared several times before remaining on the canvas. Rapidly the features seemed to grow, and finally the eyes, which for a time were indistinct and apparently closed, opened, and remained open on the canvas. In about twenty minutes the picture was completed. In a general way it resembled our son, but it was not even a fairly good portrait.

All the foregoing was carried out in a well-lighted room, and executed with the sunshine directly bearing on the canvas, which was selected by the investigators, and the mediums had no intimation of what sort of portrait was desired.   The test adopted was a remarkable one, namely, two canvases were held face to face, and the portrait of the son appeared on one of them.

The one point I wish to note was the failure to produce a good likeness of the son of Mr and Mrs Holland.   It will also be remembered that they had no photograph of their departed son with them. Possibly, too, they had not a clear mental picture of him, or, what is most likely, the mother had one conception of him and the father another; and the spirit artists produced a composite picture of the two.

An Exhibition of Spirit Paintings

I have omitted, from lack of space, Mr J. M. White's graphic report of the great exhibition of over one hundred psychic portraits, and allegorical pictures of scenes in the Invisible, done by these mediums, held last January in Kansas City.   Two of these have been held in the Galleries of Psychic Art, in the Temple of Health, corner of 12th and Washington Streets, Kansas City, Missouri—the one above mentioned in January, and the other in December 1910.   These were visited by thousands of people on both occasions. To use Dr Carson's words in his "Announcement" and invitation to the December exhibit: "Nothing before seen can compare with the marvellous beauty of these psychic pictures and creations from an unseen world.   To one interested in divine revelations, a view of these pictures would be ample reward for coming thousands of miles to attend the Convention."

As to the nature and character of this Convention, I have nothing to say in these pages except that it was a remarkable one, where highly intellectual men and women gathered together to discuss matters of health and well-being. Among the objects which were discussed was the building of the Temple of Light. In this temple a new system of education was to be carried out. What is of interest to us is that, in addition to the hundred odd pictures, done by the Bangs Sisters, adorning four art parlours in the Temple of Health, there is the psychic painting of the proposed Temple of Light.

Dr Carson says :—

The photograph is taken from the psychic painting executed in the Temple of Health. The Temple of Light will be of the Grecian - Roman - Ionian school of architecture, adhering to the beautiful lines of the ancient temples that were erected in the Old World, and which withstood the ravages of time for hundreds of years. The Temple of Light will be built in the form of a cross, with four fronts, each 210 feet long, and a dome of magnificent proportions will surmount the centre. The building will be four stories in height, and marble will be the principal material of construction Immense columns of granite, 40 feet in height, and nearly 6 feet in thickness, will be placed at the entrance on each of the four sides. Broad marble steps will lead to great bronze doors, which in themselves are beautiful works of art, reproductions of the doors of one of the ancient Grecian temples. . . .

I refrain from giving a detailed description of the internal arrangements of the proposed building. The

fact of the deepest interest to me is that the designs and
colouring, etc., of this building were obtained psychically, with strict attention to architectural technique,
from which any qualified architect could form his plans.

The Temple of Health is a large structure, occupy-

FIG. 72.—Photograph of the psychic painting and architectural design
of the Temple of Light, on canvas 4 by 6 feet, done in oil, in the
presence of the Bangs Sisters.

ing a prominent position in the city of Kansas, where
Dr C. H. Carson[1] and his assistants have been carrying on a vito-therapeutic system of medical treatment
for the last thirty years. No greater or stronger
testimony could be given to the unique gifts of the

[1] Since the foregoing was written, Dr C. H. Carson, in his letter
of the 25th February 1911, sent me corroborative evidence and
the portraits of the Carson family—among others, the mother of
Dr Carson, Mrs C. H. Carson, and a nephew, all unfortunately
too late for this book.

Bangs Sisters than the collection of paintings within its walls, where they can be seen, including the original painting of the Temple of Light.

This thing is not done in a corner, for the Society for Scientific Revelation, which is to build the great Temple of Light, consists of a quarter of a million members. No testimony within the range of psychical research will—in my opinion—be greater.

THE EVIDENCE OF DR J. M. PEEBLES

Dr Peebles, the genial veteran author and lecturer, who possesses a world-wide reputation, has on several occasions testified to the genuineness of the phenomena witnessed in the presence of these gifted psychics. He requires no introduction. I have curtailed report received, making reference only to the precipitated painting. There were obtained at this time psychographic messages, under exceptionally satisfactory conditions; but owing to limited space, and the fact that an outline of psychography is given further on, I omit these.

Journeying on our way to the Pacific Coast, we stayed overnight in Chicago, calling on the Bangs Sisters, with whom we had previously corresponded.

Though expressing their unpreparedness, they gave us a séance. We were admitted to the séance-room, which had a large window at one end, a door at the other, and two side doors.

Comfortably seated, conversation was genial and general, Dr Peebles desiring to have a spirit picture of one of his chief guides.

Mr Sudall accompanied one of the sisters to a storeroom wherein a pile of new canvases were stored. Selecting two of these from the centre, he marked them and carried them to the séance-room. We examined the room, chairs, table, window, and shutters, finding them to our satisfaction. Next, a curtain of black velvet was placed over the window, and around the edges of the canvases, thus shutting off all light, except that focussed upon the almost transparent canvas.

With the sisters occupying seats on each side of the table, holding the canvas near the window, and Dr Peebles, Mr Sudall, and a lady facing in front, the conditions necessary for this kind of phenomena were completed.

Soon the canvas assumed a gradually darker appearance around the edges. Now a change to light, and then dark again, wavering thus intermittently for a short time. Then came waves of seemingly coloured clouds passing from side to side, up and down. Dimly we perceived the outline of a human head and shoulders; clearer and clearer they came to view, until the facial outlines were distinctly visible. Slowly, surely and gradually, with persevering effort, came the clear and distinct features of a patriarchal man with snowy white hair and beard. Suddenly the form vanished; and, clouding again, the canvas was almost a blank! Patient watching revealed to us the careful unfolding of the same remarkable features; the eyes were more brilliant and the features more distinct. *But we thought the beard was short and somewhat scant; the moustache a little uneven; and so, without further ado, the eyes gradually closed and the picture again clouded, to be again restored to our sight, in all the glory and magnificence it was possible to conceive of.*[1] Brilliant and piercing were the eyes, beautifully tinted were the features, and the beard no longer scraggy, but long, wide, flowing, and profusive in snowy whiteness, a glorious picture to behold.

[1] Italics are mine.—J. C.

Later, the words, "The Apostle John," were added in one corner of the picture. So here was the Apostle John's picture, as he trod the earth, ministering to the people, teaching and being taught, emphasising the love of God to man. The whole proceeding seemed like a miracle, filling us with a feeling of awe and

Fig. 73.—Photograph of the precipitated painting of St John, obtained through the Bangs sisters.

wonder. We are grateful beyond measure in the happy possession of such a valuable work of spirit science and art.

Believing in the integrity of the Bangs Sisters, we express our sincerest thanks for their untiring efforts in the work of spiritualism, and for the comforting and inspiring messages received from our loved ones.

ROBERT PEEBLES SUDALL.
JAMES M. PEEBLES, M.D.

28th September 1910.

While it is wholly impossible from an identification point to say whether this spirit painting is a portrait of St John — in earth-life — I accept the statement over the signatures of the doctor and Mr Sudall as to the facts and manner of obtaining this picture. Whether it was a portrait of the Apostle or—more probably—that of a thought-picture in the mind of Dr Peebles, psychically discerned by the mediums, or the Intelligences controlling, I cannot say.   I, however, call attention to the fact that the beard, which was at first thought to be somewhat scant, was changed to correspond with the sitters' ideas of what the portrait of St John should be; and from this, corresponding to what I know of Dr Peebles's opinions, writings, and public addresses, I am led to the conclusion that the painting came from the spirit artists (operating through the mediumship of those remarkable psychics) as a precipitation of the doctor's ideal.   I might even go a step further and say it was a reproduction of a mental vision impressed on the subconsciousness of Dr Peebles by an Invisible.   The fact of the painting I admit, but I neither believe it to be the portrait of St John, nor can I conceive the possibility of the beloved Apostle having a distinctly American physiognomy.   The valuable evidence by the venerable lecturer is admirably sustained by the few cases selected for this book.   If the evidences given in these pages are sufficiently strong to furnish a *prima facie* case that human beings departed can be photographed, or have their portraits painted, why not St John?

But that this has been done, there is absolutely no evidence.

THE PORTRAIT OF MRS BAXTER

This painting is of spirit precipitation [says Miss

FIG. 74.—This is a photo taken from a portrait (obtained August 1910) of Mrs Lee Baxter, of 346 W. Maleon Street, Klecatur, Ill.

May Bangs], the same as all our art work, but taken from the mortal, that is, the subject is still in earth-life. It is a most excellent likeness, thus showing that if our artist guides can so closely and beautifully portray a perfect likeness of those in earth-life, why not of the spirit?

I produce—owing to their importance—the portrait (fig. 74) and extract from Miss May Bang's letter (10th October 1910) here. I cannot answer the question. It is, however, a matter of fact, and the above is not the only instance of the portraits of embodied persons being precipitated—that portraits of the living and so-called dead have been obtained in this manner through these mediums is beyond cavil.

The evidence to my mind is conclusive as to the genuineness of the phenomenon of precipitated paintings, but not that the same are the portraits of our departed—in a state discarnate—but rather of something representing them in the Akasa or thought-atmosphere of those who knew them, when the same portrait is not an idealised production of a photograph or picture in existence on earth. It may be I am wrong; I am open for further information.

Many of these precipitated pictures had been done in a remarkably short time. I have been present when direct paintings have been done by the late Mr David Duguid in two to three minutes. The Bangs Sisters have obtained complete portraits in eight minutes.

I have submitted a few portraits with actual reports and attestations, but I have on my desk at the moment of writing over sixty recent cases out of hundreds. Those which I have deliberately selected cover a sufficient period of time—five years or thereby to date—to give the reader a fair idea of what these precipitated spirit paintings are.

The half-tones which illustrate the artistic work done through the mediumship of these psychics do not do justice to the original paintings. They, however, show how lifelike the work is. A good deal of the effect, however, is lost in the half-tone process. All correspondents assure me of this fact.

There is and must be a great deal of difference between portraits precipitated in the light and photographs taken by camera of the departed; yet, while this is true, there are points of similarity. In both, the likenesses are obtained of persons *as they were once on earth.* Their features are reproduced. Recognition would be impossible otherwise.

All spirit paintings—not portraits—which I have seen, represented scenes on earth. Many direct paintings and drawings obtained through the late Mr David Duguid were of this character. Some drawings (not all) were line-for-line reproductions of drawings extant. The spirit-painted portraits of the Bangs Sisters are best obtained—

1st. When the person desiring the portrait is able to carry a clear mental picture of the departed; or

2nd. Has a photograph of the departed on his or her person, although the said photograph has neither been seen nor handled by the mediums.

Now, let it be noted :—

1st. Whoever or whatever are the subjects of these portraits, whether they are of the departed, of mental pictures psychically obtained, or of actual photographs, etc., they must have been clairvoyantly perceived either by the Bangs Sisters or by the Intelligences in the Invisible using their — the mediums' — psychic faculties.

2nd. However produced, these portraits were not painted by the hands of man, and by no process—not even solar prints—known to artists.

I therefore conclude we have reached the bed-rock fact: That these precipitated paintings and psychic photographs are the work of human intelligences operating on psychic planes, and through the agency of appropriate media. In the unique phenomenon of these remarkable spirit-produced paintings, the Bangs Sisters, in the history of the world's psychics, stand alone.

CHAPTER XV

As reference has been made to psychographs, I propose to give a few concrete cases, with illustrations, in order that the whole may be better understood by those to whom the subject is new. Extraordinary as are the claims made, that psychic images—invisible to the human eye—can be photographed, they pale into insignificance before that which claims not only that these images but written messages come on photographic plates which have never been exposed. Extraordinary claims demand extraordinary evidence, and this is given as freely as possible within my limited space. I could readily devote the entire book to psychography, but the following must suffice.

Psychography (Gr. *psuche*, soul; *graphein*, to write) means writing by soul or psychic power. The term covers a much wider range of phenomena than non-camera photography. All designs, figures, portraits, etc., written — impressed, precipitated — on papers, slates, walls, or other surfaces by spirit power are psychographs.

In the Hebrew Scriptures—Old Testament—several

instances are given. The "writing" which appeared during the impious feast of Belshazzar in Babylon, "on the plaister of the wall of the king's palace," is a striking case. Psychic writings obtained in modern times may not be so terrifically prophetic or so drastically fulfilled, but the characteristics are similar, i.e. they are produced by spirit or occult agency, and intelligence is indicated in the designs, letters, and messages given. A true psychograph is produced without the agency of mortal hands, and exhibits intelligence other than that of the investigators. Except one or two instances, I limit my cases to those of portraits or graphs obtained on photographic plates.

In our experiments with Mr David Duguid, on one occasion we obtained a satisfactory psychograph on a piece of paper which was shown, folded, and placed in a small tin box, in the presence of eleven persons. The closed box was placed on a table and the light turned out. In three minutes' time a direct painting in several colours was given, and within the folds of the paper in the closed box was written: "God bless you. Lesnith." Many things took place during the séance that night. Neither Duguid nor anyone present — except one — knew what was meant by "Lesnith." The paper was mine. Mr Auld, who folded up the paper and put it in the box, was startled with the result. "Lesnith" was one known and very dear to him, but from whom no message of any kind was expected. It was a spontaneous and striking bit of evidence. The following is of interest, and illustrates graphically what "spirit writing" is.

Mr A. Brittlebank (whose address is Salisbury

Fig. 75.—Psychograph or "direct" writing given at a séance held in Pretoria on 21st December 1908, at which the spirit of Signor Ricci drew his own picture, of which the above is a photograph, supplied by Mr George Baker, and forwarded for this book by Mr A. Brittlebank.

Hotel, Anderson Street, Johannesburg, Transvaal, United South Africa) was a guest of, and attended many séances given by, an Austrian medical man,

Dr Meyer, who resided for a time in Pretoria. As the doctor was a non-professional psychic, I do not give his address, but I give the facts.

Mr George Baker, who supplied the photograph, in his letter, dated Pretoria, 10th April 1910, says:—

When the original sketch was produced, the top of the pencil was brilliantly lit, like a small incandescent lamp, and the movements were exceedingly rapid. The whole drawing was executed in about five seconds. Please note on the right arm the name S. Ricci, which I only discovered in copying. The Italian under the drawing is: *Questo fui io un di*, meaning, "As I looked when I was."

The following remarkable psychograph was given at a séance held at Pretoria, 21st December 1908, by the spirit known as Signor Ricci, who declared himself to be a great reformer of the (Roman) Catholic Church, and said he was born at Florence, 9th June 1741, and died 27th June 1810.

Mr A. Brittlebank, who sent me the translation, made by Baron Von Ahlefeldt, Pretoria, says:—

The whole of the message was rendered in the very best Italian, legible and good penmanship. The time occupied did not exceed twenty seconds. It was given in darkness, under the same conditions as the drawing.

THE MESSAGE

Death is the separation of the immortal element of the human aggregate from the two perishable ones, life and body. The soul is both immortal and immaterial; the body both material and mortal. The soul is eternal, the life is liable to destruction. The body that was my shelter is only a temporary place of abode. The soul is immaterial, immortal, imperishable; it is endowed with intelligence, conscience, will, and is not liable to decline, decrepitude, or death. On the contrary, it is perfected through exercise, thus attaining the great end.

The life or vital principle is neither material nor immortal, thus distinguishing itself from soul and body as heat, electricity, and other powers still unknown to you. Life, an immaterial power, is perishable and dies. It is a transmissible power, an architectonic, plastic, organising power, acting instinctively and without knowledge. Life is subject to development, to a climax, and then to a gradual decline, ending with ultimate destruction.

Death is the parting of the immortal element. After death, the body, being no longer protected by the vital principle, falls under the power of the chemical forces, and life, as electricity, vanishes away. Through the dissolution of the body, the soul sets itself free from its corporeal enclosure and passes into the ether, leaving behind everything that is earthy and heavy.

The scale of perfection, from algæ and zoophyta to mollusca and up to man, goes on following the same hierarchy, and our knowledge is unlimited and our studies are incomprehensible to you. Man shall never understand such a fact, though human knowledge is destined to become wider and wider.

Use reason, observation, experience, talent; don't be afraid of new things, don't allow yourself to be ruled by neophobia; and thus you will be able to formulate laws and not simple statements.

I do not know that Signor Ricci was a priest who served before the altar in the Catholic Church. In fact, I do not know whether he ever existed, and therefore I do not know that the message given emanated from him through the mediumship of Dr Meyer; but I have every confidence in my informants that the phenomenon took place as described. Among those present at these sittings, in addition to Mr Baker, were Messrs Brett, Nicosic, Menzel, Walker, Dr Meyer, Baron von Ahlefeldt, and several others.

Mr Sidney Clarke, now sub-editor of the *Pretoria News*, in his letter to me, dated Pretoria, 12th December 1910, sent me a fully corroborated account of descriptions which have reached me from other sources, and says:—

These things I have described I can swear to. Of course I would not swear that they were brought about by spirits, but neither I nor anyone else could see how they could have been done by anyone in the circle.

THE TESTIMONY OF MADAME ST HILL, FORMERLY OF PRETORIA, TO THE SIGNOR RICCI PSYCHOGRAPHS

HAMILTON HOUSE, RISSIK STREET,
JOHANNESBURG, TRANSVAAL,
7th February 1911.

DEAR SIR,—At Mr Brittlebank's request I am sending you a short account of the message that was received from Dr Ricci at a séance held at the residence of Dr Meyer, of Pretoria, during the month of December 1909. The message was written in Italian in direct writing, and in a most beautifully clear and distinct hand, but on account of the words joining it was a little difficult to translate. During the time the message was being written the pen appeared to have an electric spark on it, and (as nearly as I can remember) it was written in about twenty or thirty seconds.

Besides myself, there were six other persons present, and including Dr Meyer, at whose house we were meeting for the purpose of psychic research.—Yours faithfully,   (Mrs) A. L. St Hill.

I have given the Ricci drawing and writing, declared by sane and reputable persons to have been received as stated.   Remarkable as the case is, still more extraordinary instances have been reported to me, but this must suffice for this phase of psychography.

Psychographs on Photographic Plates

In the notable experiments conducted by the late Mr J. Traill Taylor with Mr David Duguid, the Glasgow trance-painting medium, in 1893, two outstanding features were noted—first, the lighting of the psychic figures was (often) different from that of the material subject; second, the focussing was (often) different.   These two features were problems from the beginning of spirit photography, and the *butt* of experts.   These two points, supplemented by the evidence of the binocular stereoscopic camera, showing that the psychic figures were neither in exact relation to, nor imposed on, the plates at the same time as the subject, led the way to the discovery that these psychic figures came on the plates *outwith all known laws* of photography, therefore by other than photographic processes.

Following the discovery, Mr Andrew Glendinning was the first in Great Britain to get results without the camera.   As Mr W. T. Stead said, " No one was better qualified." It soon became clear that the *light* by which the plates were affected is other than sunlight, flashlight, electricity, incandescent gaslight. What this light is, is not as yet fully known. It

FIG. 76.—Psychic picture obtained without light or camera by Mr Andrew Glendinning and a lady.

appears allied to the violet rays of the spectrum. Whether so or not, the light is invisible which affects the plates.

The author of *The Veil Lifted*, in his lifetime, having given me permission to make certain extracts from that work, I take the above illustration from page 145. With reference to this case, Mr Glendinning experimented with a lady in private life who was a good, but non-professional, psychic. Concerning this he says:—

A dry plate from my packet of unused plates was placed in a mahogany slide. The lady held the slide in the palms of her hands. She was under continuous and close observation in a well-lighted room. One end of the slide was held by myself. On putting the plate in the developer, the child appeared on it. The plate was not tampered with by anyone, nor was there any opportunity given to do so, nor was it exposed to light until after it was developed and fixed.

Although I have no definite statements about this psychograph, as the name of the lady is withheld and particulars about the baby, I am satisfied that Mr Glendinning, *as usual*, took every precaution. Admitting the possibility of psychic photography and of Mr J. Traill Taylor's deductions, psychic pictures without the camera must also be admitted. I have obtained these too with Mr David Duguid. But even if I had not, I would not reject the word of Mr Glendinning.

Both Mr Traill Taylor and Mr Glendinning in their experiments with Mr and Mrs Duguid found that not only were the forms and faces sometimes positives and sometimes negatives, but often the same pictures came with equal facility with the camera and *without*. One gentleman (unknown) had been photographed twice by Mr J. T. Taylor and five times by Mr Glendinning. Mr Stead says:—

His general appearance—sometimes younger than at other times—is always the same. And the strange thing about him is that he is indifferent whether the plate is exposed in the camera or merely held in the hands of the medium. The name "D. G. Gosling" appears on some of the negatives. I have seen one of these. Whether anyone has been able to identify this "D. G. Gosling" I have yet to learn.

Such were some of the results obtained at this period. Before passing on to matters of interest nearer to the present time, I give one—out of several —obtained by Mr Glendinning.

In an article contributed to *Borderland* (vol. iii. p. 313, 1896), on "Some Recent Experiments in Dorchagraphy," he says:—

In some recent experiments I used, during these evenings, twenty-four plates, and obtained abnormal images on nineteen. Some of these plates were not handled at all by Mr Duguid; some he did not so much as see till I removed the black paper wrappings from them and put them into the developing tray. Sometimes he requested me to develop and fix the plates myself without any help from him, as he preferred to be merely an onlooker of my manipulations. The pictures Nos. 1, 2, and 3 were the clearest of the first night's experiments. The plates and chemicals were supplied by me.

Fig. 77 is the No. 1 to which the writer refers. From this article—which was illustrated with seven plates—I take the one mentioned, as this picture was subsequently obtained by Mr G., "Edina's" photographic expert and friend, under strict test conditions. Among the psychographs obtained was one of his brother Alexander, referred to elsewhere. On this being examined in Edinburgh, it was dis-

FIG. 77.—Psychograph of lady obtained without light or camera, April 1896. Mr David Duguid, medium.

covered that round the (psychic) neck there was seaweed. This was a remarkable test of identity. Alexander G. was drowned at sea.

The Rev. Charles Hall Cook, B.D., A.M., Ph.D., had among his many experiences evidence of the genuineness of psychography. His account is all the more

Fig. 78.—Psychograph obtained at San Diego, Cal., U.S.A., 23rd January 1905. Mr Edward Wyllie, medium.

interesting as the arrangements were spontaneous on his part, and Wyllie was not aware of the doctor's wishes till the moment the experiment was entered upon. It was the doctor's intention to further experiment with the camera—Wyllie's once more—in order that comparisons might be made with those obtained with Dr Cook's camera, as previously related in these pages.

Having purchased a fresh box of plates, 5 × 4, for this purpose, he opened the box in his dark-room at the Willard Hotel, San Diego, and marked them there. However, when he called upon Mr Wyllie at his rooms in the Albion, the doctor says :—

I changed my mind, and on entering his room I said : "Mr Wyllie, let's try without a camera." "We might try," he said.

They entered the dark-room, and the doctor, taking a plate from the box which he had in his pocket, held it at the corners at one end, never letting it for a moment out of his fingers. Mr Wyllie similarly held it firmly at the opposite end. At the expiry of about a quarter of a minute, raps—very slight—were heard. The doctor then took full charge of the plate. Taking it to the Willard, he developed it, and found the experiment was wholly successful. I produce the psychograph obtained, with the doctor's private mark, Z, proving that there had been no shifting or exchanging of plates.

The face produced has not been identified, but it looks to me very like many of the *strong* and non-spiritualised faces which crop up in Wyllie's plates when sitting or experimenting under test conditions, which are never so facile for identifiable pictures as when the medium and the subject are co-operating under more harmonious and unrestrained conditions.

Had Dr Cook's testimony been uncorroborated, his

psychograph, notwithstanding his critical and carefully detailed procedure (which I have not reproduced)
might be rejected.   Fortunately, there is no phase of
psycho-physics more fully substantiated.   Dr J. K.
Funk (of the well-known firm of Funk & Wagnalls),
author of *The Widow's Mite*, bears testimony to the
fact.   Dr H. A. Reid, of Pasadena, Cal., U.S.A., and Dr
William J. Pierce, who is as well known in London as
in New York City and San Francisco, being the managing director of business houses there, are among those
who have obtained these psychographs with Mr Wyllie.
Indeed, the latter not only obtained them with Wyllie,
but latterly succeeded in getting them himself.   Dr H.
A. Reid reports a large number of cases with the utmost
detail, coupled with evidence of the standing of the
experimenters.   Space forbids more than the mention.

The Rev. J. T. Wills, D.D., pastor of the Franklin
Street Presbyterian Church, San Francisco, Cal., is
another who experimented and obtained undeniably
good results.

Mr Arthur G. Krause, The Abbotsford, San
Francisco, also obtained pictures under test conditions,
and, writing 11th April 1903, says:—

I have never had any reason to believe Mr Wyllie
to be other than an honest man ; nothing suspicious
about his actions, and always willing to submit to any
test conditions imposed upon him.   I believe Mr
Wyllie *does not and cannot* control the power that
operates through him, as he is never positively certain
whether there is or is not anything on the plate he
places his hands upon.

I could give, in detail, quite a number of similar cases, but neither time nor my readers' patience will permit.

TESTIMONY OF MR WALTER JONES, OF STOURBRIDGE

Before giving Mr Jones's interesting account, I will state that the late Mr Lacey had a special gift or mediumship for these psychic productions. His reputation was the best. Mr Blackwell, from whom this portrait was obtained, is a gentleman of standing, whose personal worth is too well known to need any testimony from me. Mr Jones—who is less known in matters of psychical research—is a prominent man of business. He was the sole proprietor for thirty-five years, and is now the managing director, of Messrs Jones & Attwood, Ltd., heating specialists and iron-founders, Stourbridge. He is the author of *Heating by Water*, which has run through several editions, and his addresses on various technical, social, and municipal subjects have a wide circulation. As an authority on local government, as well as a practical man of affairs, no man is better known in the district in which he lives. In the iron and steel world, and in scientific, sanitary, and municipal circles, his manifest ability has long been recognised. As a correspondent I hold him in high esteem. I have found him as modest in his statements as courageous. He has not hidden the psychic facts which came to him, lest the telling of them should hurt him in trade and commerce, or give offence to his friends. Permission to publish the following is an instance of his

23

adherence to what he sincerely believes to be the truth. It is with pleasure I produce his account to me, of 12th November 1909, with the photograph (taken in life) of Mrs Jones, and what led up to obtaining the psychically produced portrait.

COINCIDENCE OR DESIGN—WHICH ? [1]

Why does a stray paragraph in an obscure journal, or a chance remark made by an ordinary individual, apparently in the most casual manner, arrest the thoughts and demand something more than a passing attention.

For some reason or other the question of psychic or spirit photography appears to have been dogging my footsteps for several months, and I have asked myself. Is it accidental, is it simply coincidence, or is it design ? What is the purpose, and how can that purpose be best served ?

On Saturday, 7th August 1909, my daughter and I went for a cruise on board the *Amazon*, in the fiords of Norway. I made the acquaintance of two youths, who were accompanied by an aunt (Miss M., of London). One of the youths (S. J. S.) stated, and his aunt confirmed the statement, that she had received a message (by automatic writing) stating that she could safely trust the lads with Mr Jones, for he was a *seeker after the light*. This struck me as somewhat remarkable. Some months previously, when presiding at a meeting at Wolverhampton, where Mr J. J. Morse gave the lecture, I stated I was not a spiritualist, but a *seeker after the truth*. I asked the lady if she was a spiritualist. She replied, " No ! " " Do you believe in spirit photography ? " " Oh, yes; a friend of mine has hundreds of them." At my request she gave me the

[1] This also appeared as an article in *The Two Worlds*, December 1909.

name and address of the gentleman, and promised an introduction.

On my return home, the first thing that arrested my attention was a short article by Mr S. Barnett, in

FIG. 79.—Portrait of the late Mrs Jones, from the latest photograph taken in life.

The Two Worlds for 20th August, entitled " Spiritual-ism on Shipboard," in which he stated that before leaving England he " spent a delightful evening with Mr H. Blackwell, the possessor of *some two thousand spirit photos.*"

My interest was aroused. I had not seen any direct

spiritphotography. On writing Mr Blackwell, he wrote to me saying that he would be pleased to see me. I called on Wednesday, 22nd September, and spent six hours with him, when he courteously showed me the greatest assortment of psychic photos in the possession of any single individual. Just before I said good-bye, he gave me one (fig. 80) out of his collection, produced without the aid of a camera. Was it merely a coincidence that this particular photograph should be recognised by myself and several intimate personal friends as that of my dear wife, who passed away on 15th February 1897.

On my return, I examined the photo, and was impressed with the striking likeness. I showed it to my son and daughter and several other intimate friends, six persons, none of them spiritualists or psychics, who entered the room without knowing what had previously transpired, and they remarked on the striking resemblance of the photo to my departed wife.

The psychic photo was posted by Mr Jones to a friend of his, Mrs Wilson, a clairvoyant spiritualist. Mr Jones, without saying of whom it was, asked: " Can you give me any information about this ? Is it the photo of someone I have personally met ? I am anxious to get at the bottom of this matter for reasons which I will explain later."

Mrs Wilson (who had never met his wife) replied: " I don't know how long Mrs Jones has been passed on, but I certainly see a likeness. I feel that it is a genuine photo of spirit production. Moreover, I cannot disconnect the influence from your surroundings. I am sure you have met and held close intercourse."

Further, in his investigations, Mr Jones sent Mrs

Wilson a photograph of Mrs Jones taken in life, and the spirit-produced photo.

On 10th October Mrs Wilson wrote as follows: " When I wrote last I felt sure it was her. However,

FIG. 80.—Psychograph of Mrs Jones, as obtained by the late Mr C. Lacey and friend, shortly after Mrs Jones's transition.

on Friday night (8th October) I asked her to visit me, and she did. I was then confident that it was her pho o. The message was that on passing out of the body she found that she had a wonderful power, and *wished to prove to you her existence.* . . . I am quite reconciled to the two photos being one. The same

influence presses me to say that it (the photo) was
given soon after her passing over."

I wish to say here that after three years' experience
of Mrs Wilson's clairvoyant powers, I am satisfied that
she would not make statements unless she was perfectly
convinced of their truthfulness. . . . It would appear
that there is much more of "design" than "coincidence" in the happenings of the past few months.

I have given, somewhat curtailed, Mr Jones's interesting revelation, but more fully than at first intended,
owing to the striking evidence therein of "design,"
and nothing of coincidence or accident. Please note
the steps which Mr Jones was led to take, and how
different persons on the earth plane, unknown to and
apart from one another, were influenced subsequently
to the passing over of Mrs Jones :—

1. Mr Jones has his attention drawn to the subject
   of spiritualism.
2. Sufficiently interested to preside at a meeting of
   spiritualists, not as a spiritualist, but as *a
   seeker after the truth.*
3. Is dogged or pursued by the subject of spirit
   photography—a fact which I knew to be true.
4. His attention is arrested by a stranger, who
   describes him as a *seeker after the light.*
5. Is assured of the genuineness of spirit photography, and given the name and address of a
   gentleman in London.
6. On returning from his trip, reads about Mr H.
   Blackwell, in the Rev. Mr Barnett's article. Is
   further interested in the subject.

7. Visits Mr Blackwell by appointment, and out of that gentleman's 2000 spirit photos is handed one.

8. It is the spirit-produced portrait of his wife, obtained without light or the camera years before.

9. Neither the late Mr Lacey, who obtained it, nor Mr Blackwell, who presented it to Mr Jones, knew the latter, or was aware of whom the psychic picture was the portrait. It was classed as " unrecognised."

10. This portrait is recognised by Mr Jones and family and by several friends—without prompting— as the likeness of the late Mrs Jones. None of these friends were spiritualists.

11. It is psychically recognised by a trusted clair-voyante, who also received and delivered a message from the original of the portrait.

12. It has, since the first recognition by the husband of the lady, been seen and recognised by many friends. This is the *crux*. There is no higher evidence than a truly identifiable portrait.

13. Out of the collection which Mr H. Blackwell purchased from the estate of the late Mr C. Lacey, this one was handed to the right person, and the only one which has been identified.

There is no " collective hallucination " here, but the most complete evidence of spirit direction, and this may be truly called a genuine portrait of spirit production.

CHAPTER XVI

PSYCHOGRAPHY—*continued*

MRS BRIGHT, the well-known editor of the *Harbinger of Light*, Melbourne, Australia, in writing to me (24th March 1910), says :—

We who have had most experience feel that nothing is known for absolute certainty about these things. A leading photographer here, now retired, devotes himself to trying to get spirit photographs. He had a curious experience a short time ago. He simply holds the plates in his hands. One day in Sydney, on a visit, he had been much interested in watching a man in a canoe in the harbour. This is not seen in Melbourne. That night he held his plate. Next day developed it. There was a small figure on the plate, and this on close examination proved to be a reproduction of the man in the canoe, of the previous day's interest.

Here—and I have no reason to doubt the report—we get at one fact, and that is that an impression—a visual one—which excited interest in one who was a suitable psychic, was conveyed to the plate, as revealed on development. It would not make the slightest difference supposing that the psychic had this actual experience and subsequently had forgotten it, if produced later by the same means. From this instance it is possible to conclude that many of the faces and forms which appear as "extras" on photographic plates or as images in psychography have either at one time been within the field of vision of the psychic, or they have been psychically impressed, and these have been subsequently reproduced by photographic or psychographic procedure.

The Colley-Hooper Psychographs

In dealing with more recent cases, I wish to mention that the Ven. Archdeacon Colley, Rector of Stockton, Rugby, was good enough to send me albums containing many of the psychographs which he obtained through the mediumship of Dr T. D'Aute-Hooper, Birmingham, at the Crewe Circle, and through the psychics of that Circle when visiting him. He favoured me with the option of producing nine cases, sending with each a full descriptive report. I should have been pleased to give these, as the evidence in their favour was of a striking character. However, for the purposes of lectures and demonstrations before the Church Congress in 1910 the blocks were returned. I am thoroughly satisfied with the evidence in the cases submitted by the Ven. gentleman, not only from his own account, but from a careful inspection of letters and testimonies in relation thereto by persons in a position to state the facts.

Mr William Marriott, in a London magazine, expressed the opinion that if it were not for the money *in it* mediumship would be non-existent. I suppose if it were not for the money *in it* many persons would not write magazine articles or give conjuring exhibitions. Whether the labourer is worthy of his hire or not, is for those who pay him to decide. There are, however, thousands of psychics who never receive payment for their services — not that they are not worthy of it, but they decline payment. I can vouch for this : that Dr Hooper has never asked or received a fee for the exercise of his mediumship. This is not all : his services have never been acknowledged by those who have had convincing proof of the genuineness of psychography through his agency. Neither, then, in money, honour, nor acknowledgment has Dr Hooper ever received compensation for his services.

In giving the following six psychographs, it will be the first time Dr Hooper's invaluable services to scientific experimentation in psychography have been acknowledged.

His photograph (fig. 81) was taken by Mr Young, photographer, Warwick, at his own suggestion and with his own plates, in Dr Hooper's consulting-room (July 1906). The " extras " are fully identified. The first is that of an uncle of the subject; the second is that of the father of Mrs Hooper. The third is the portrait of a guide of the medium, who is called "Segaske," claiming to have been a medicine man in earth-life, and is believed to be the spirit who supplies the " X force " by which these psychographs are taken, and the healing power referred to in the Ven. Archdeacon Colley's article, "Healing Mediumship in the Church of England."

Mr Young, of Warwick, has, like Mr Bailey, of

FIG. 81.—Photograph of Dr Hooper, the Birmingham psychic, through whom the Ven. Archdeacon Colley, Stockton, Rugby, obtained many of the remarkable psychographs which were and are used to illustrate the lectures delivered by the Ven. gentleman, as well as in his advocacy before Church Congresses in England, and in his contributions to the press at home and abroad.

Birmingham, considerable experience in psychic photography, and, as a reputable and practical photographer, is in a position to certify to the genuineness of many

in it mediumship would ~~ ~~ed **in the Colley-Hooper**
if it were not for the r
not write magazir
tions. Wheth~~e~~   **REMARKABLE PSYCHOGRAPHS**
not, is for t'   *..Bailey*, **who sends me the particulars for**
however   *..formerly* **a photographer, having seven-**
payme   *..experience,* **but is now, and has been for**
wor   *..years,* **a well-known art designer in the city of**
f~~e~~   *..Birmingham.* **In his letter, dated 4th October 1910,**
from **125 Westfield Road, King's Heath, he says :—**

The **facts regarding** the production of the six
marvellous psychographs are as follows :—

On August 12, the Ven. Archdeacon Colley, of
Stockton Rectory, Warwickshire, wrote to Dr Hooper,
of 159 Gooch Street, Birmingham, asking him if he
could give him a sitting on Thursday next (August
18) to (try and) get some results for a special birthday
party and lecture.   The medium had to decline, owing
to the fact that he had no one just then to take his
place in the event of suffering from the severe nervous
exhaustion which takes place at these séances.

I had been present at a number of séances when
the venerable gentleman had brought his own unopened packets and his own diamond-marked plates,
I marvelled at the results, and often thought I should
like to try a packet of my own.

I asked the medium if he was willing to try and
get results on a packet of my own plates, to which he
acquiesced.   On Tuesday, August 16, I took a packet
of ¼-plates to Dr Hooper's house.   The medium simply
placed his hands over mine while holding the packet
of plates.   No results were felt.   I then put the
packet in an inner coat pocket, intending to visit the
following evening for another experiment.   The plates
were not once out of my possession, and the pro-

dings on Wednesday were similar to those of the ing before, excepting that a short time after the im placed his hands over mine a peculiar vibra- —which increased in intensity till heat as from a urnace — was felt. This was followed by a cool breeze, which was very apparent.

I carefully guarded the box of plates, and I carried them till I should meet the Ven. Archdeacon at the medium's residence on Thursday evening at eight o'clock.

I described my procedure to the Ven. Archdeacon, and handed him the box of plates to examine, which he did through a lens, and wrote on the box to that effect. When Dr Hooper had finished with his patients, we sat in the consulting-room, Archdeacon Colley holding the still unopened box of plates, and my hands being placed over the Archdeacon's, and the medium's being placed over mine. The medium passed into the trance state. The controlling spirit told many things to the Archdeacon entirely unknown to the medium and myself, which he said were true. The controlling spirit then informed us that she was going to leave the medium and send Segaske (the Indian chief who generally takes charge during the production of psychographs).

This spirit taking control, the Ven. Archdeacon asked them [the Intelligences operating in the Invisible.—J. C.] to write if possible upon a special subject suitable for his lecture the next day; also if they could write in another language. They promised to try. We were then told to be quiet for a short time, when gradually the vibration was felt increasing in intensity, accompanied with heat. This phenomenon lasted for about three to five minutes. While this was taking place, the Ven. Archdeacon asked if his friend Samuel Wheeler could write a few words, to which no reply was given. The controlling spirit at almost the same instant said, "Finished," and told briefly what they had endeavoured to do. The medium passing from the trance state, the Ven.

Fig. 82.—Plate No. 6 of the Birmingham psychographs. The faces thereon are not known to Mr Harold Bailey. The Ven Archdeacon Colley has not stated whether he recognises the psychic figures. This is a matter of secondary importance in view of the test conditions, and the interesting material in the other five psychographs.

Archdeacon again carefully examined the box of plates, and being satisfied, cut the outer wrapper around the box, keeping the two ends intact to prove that they had not been tampered with, and removed each end as a sliding cover.

We then adjourned to the dark-room, the Ven. Archdeacon opening the box, and carefully examining the wrappings, snapping the film that hinged the plates film to film, and developed them two at a time in a half-plate dish, with pyro developer. Then after a few seconds we could see writing coming up through the developer, the writing being black on a transparent ground, *being in fact a positive instead of a negative,* which, when printed, forms mirror writing. Five plates are covered with minute, neat writing in English, and one entirely in Latin, neither of the three present knowing sufficient of Latin to translate it. Many of the things mentioned in the psychographs are known, and one circumstance has come to pass. The message from Robert I take to be from my brother, an artist, who passed away a few years ago.

It seems also that they knew of the *unexpressed wish* of the Ven. Archdeacon, for there is a note in the characteristic handwriting of his old friend, with the Greek epsilon used instead of an *e*, as, the Archdeacon pointed out, always appeared in his writing whilst on earth.

I give the other five plates and a transcript of their interesting contents, in addition to a "free" translation of the Latin, a brief note of explanation about the departed, as well as of the living persons referred to in plate No. 4.

TRANSCRIPT

PLATE 1, FIG. 83 (p. 368)

Friends, Greetings! In this my first communion through this phase of mediumship, I do not wish you to treat this as a *concio ad clerium* (1) but rather for the *commium bonum* (2) and I hope, *dei gracia*, thousands will be comforted thereby. The old saying was *de mortuis nil nisi bonum* (3), and then a more modern school of sceptics altered it to *de nihilo*

Fig. 83.—No. 1 Plate of Birmingham psychographs.

nihilum, in nihilum nil posse reverti (4) trying to prove that the dead being nothing, nothing can come from them. But it is only necessary to read history and the sacred works of antient peoples and nations to know that what is termed modern Spiritualism is as old as the world. Sacred history teems with abundant evidence of the fact. The media were Prized by the Medes and Persians. The Delphic

FIG. 84.—No. 2 Plate of Birmingham psychographs.

Oracles, the Cyprian Priestesses, who were brought forward at certain feast days that the populace could commune with their *ad patres* (5).

We live, we move, we have our being, we are only hidden by a thin veil that at times we can rend apart and

24

commune with those whom we love still in the flesh. Mediums should be cherished, for without them we are helpless. This peculiar organic fitness that is necessary, that is the very essence of our success, should receive full recognition. Investigators could not receive

PLATE 2, FIG. 84 (p. 369)

the evidence of our return if it were not for our mediums. Therefore *fiat justicia, ruat coelum* (6), for no one has the right to arrogate unto themselves that power which they have not. "Honour to whom honour is due" is a trite saying among us, therefore, be just to the worker.

You must not think, my friend, that we do not appreciate the stand you have taken in the matter, now you have come into the open and thrown down the gage to stand by the principle that you know to be true.

We are helping from our Side, and we hope before long to help in bringing about a happy condition of things and circumstances by the aid of Umbolo[1] in

(1) Archaic, signifying "discourse to the clergy." (2) The commou good. (3) Speak no evil of the dead. (4) Out of nothing, nothing comes, to nothing nothing returns. (5) To their fathers: that is, dead. (6) Let justice prevail though heavens fall.

---

[1] On plate No. 2 the name Umbolo appears. The Ven. Archdeacon Colley, when sending me the *Sapere Aude* psychograph, which he obtained through the mediumship of Dr Hooper, informed me that Umbolo was a Zulu *umfaan*, or boy servant to his (the Archdeacon's) son, Captain Colley, of the Royal Horse and Royal Field Artillery, then in Natal. Umbolo, who was very much attached to the captain, was—towards the end of his life—a Zulu chief or headman of his tribe, and therefore a "ringman," hence the allusion in this psychograph. This is not the only time Umbolo has given a message to the Archdeacon. It appears to me the assurances expressed in plate No. 2 have something to do with the gold-bearing property in the Rand, in which the Ven. gentleman possesses such a large interest, and which maturing will make him a millionaire.

the affairs in which he was known so well to you in the land of his fathers. He swears by the beard of his fathers and the honour of a ringed man to bring it to a happy termination for the combined benefit of yourself and our desire for you to spread the truth.

We wonder why that the denizens of earth will read and think contrary to the spirit of the teaching in their Holy Writ. It is only necessary to read and calmly compare the phenomena of olden days chronicled therein and modern happenings To Prove they are one and the

PLATE 3, FIG. 85 (p. 372)

same, only given in different times of the world's history.

To those who wish to know should read Deut. xviii, 15; 1 Kings xviii; Jer. xxiii; Joel ii, 28—"And it shall come to pass I will pour out my spirit upon all flesh. Your sons and your daughters shall prophesy, your old men dream dreams, your young men see visions." 1 Sam. iii, 1–2; Ezekiel xiii, 23; xii, 23–24; Mickah iii, 6; Amos viii, 11; Psalm lxxiv, 9; 1 Sam. xxviii, 6; Prov. xxix, 18.

For writing and drawing mediumship, read 1 Chron. xxviii, 12, 19; 2 Chrons. xxi, 12; Exodus xxxi, 18 and xxxiv, 1, 28; Dan. v, 5.

Materialisation, Gen. xviii, 8; Gen. xxxii, 24, 30; Ezekiel ii, 9.

Levitation, Ezekiel, iii, 12, 24; xi, 1; viii, 3.

Power to resist fire, Dan. iii, 21, 27; Heb. xi, 24.

Spirit lights, Exodus, iii, 2; xiii, 21.

Healing mediumship, Elisha, 2 Kings iv, 32; v, 14; 1 Kings, xiii, 6.

Trance and visions, 1 Sam. x, 6; Ezekiel ii, 2;

PLATE 4, FIG. 86 (p. 373)

Dan. x, 8–9; Luke i, 28; ii, 9, 13; Matt. iii, 17; Matt. iv, 11; Mark ix, 4; Luke xxii, 43; Matt. xxvi, 53; Matt. xxvii, 52; Matt. xxviii, 2; Luke xxiv, 2; John xx, 25;

Mark xvi, 9; Mark xvi, 17; John xiv, 12; Acts ii, 29; Acts iv, 31; Acts xvi, 26; Roms. i, 2.

Then carefully read 1 Cor. xii, 1-31; the exhorta-

FIG. 85.—No. 3 Plate of Birmingham psychographs.

tion to covet the best Spiritual gifts, and not be ignorant of the powers that God in his blessing has showered upon you, for those who "seek shall find, knock and it shall be opened to you (the gates of the spirit world). Listen and ye shall hear, look and ye shall see." Therefore strive to know and understand,

and when the knowledge is given unto ye pass it on, hide it not, give as freely as ye are given, for there

FIG. 86.—No. 4 Plate of Birmingham psychographs.

is no Proprietorship in the knowledge of the communion of the seen with the unseen.

It may be for a short time here, " *extinctus ambitin idem* " (7) the same as the noble Nazarene. Therefore

(7) Either bad Latin or archaic. Said to mean : " Maligned whilst living, honoured when dead."

I would exhort you let not your light grow dim.   A poor, weary soul whom you knew and gave light unto his feet, sends greetings unto you.

F. W. NEVILLE, a colleague of yours.[1]

[1] The persons mentioned on plate 4 are : the Rev. F. W. Neville, who held a living near Leamington.   He had learned a great deal about spiritualism before he passed over from John Thomas, Esq., J.P., High Sheriff of Cardiganshire, a friend of the Ven. Archdeacon.   Mr Neville's demise occurred from a fall, which took place within four months of the death of his wife, who was killed by lightning.   The sad story of these sudden deaths made a profound impression in the neighbourhood.   The rev. gentleman has frequently communicated since passing over, through Dr Hooper, and by means of psychography.   "Robert" —Mr Bailey informs me—is his late brother, who in his lifetime was an accomplished artist, and one to whom the late Sir Henry Irving was a warm friend.   "Frances Helene" is unknown.   It is surmised—owing to reference to Frances Dudley—she came for Lord Leigh, who had attended a séance the week before. "Lily" is the ascended wife of the Ven. Archdeacon.   Mrs Colley has also frequently manifested in this and in other ways. "Clarence" is the ven. gentleman's son, viz. Captain Colley, of the Royal Horse and Field Artillery.   "A. W. C." is Captain Colley's son.   He was baptised Arthur Wellesley, after the Duke of Wellington, whom the Archdeacon informs me was a Colley. "Violetta," whose bright psychic photograph I have seen, cannot be identified by the ordinary canons of evidence.   She claims to be the daughter of the (or a) Duke of Lancaster, who lived in feudal times.   Whether this is so or not, her appearance and personality are well known to the members of the Hooper Circle. Her powers of divination and of repartee—a curious combination —are noted.   "Dumpy" is her word-picture for the Archdeacon. "My Lord College" is her appellation for the medium, "who was very popular among the students and masters of Clifton College, on account of his hypnotic powers and gift of thought-reading." "Pecky" is her designation for Mrs Hooper, who had occasion to correct "Violetta" for her flippancies.   "Sad Eyes" is Mrs Sharman (a member of the Circle), who has passed through much suffering.   "Saxon Sides" admirably describes Mr Bailey, who

A spirit known as Robert wishes to make his presence known to someone here; also a spirit lady known as Frances Helene, inquires for Francis Dudley, and keeps repeating "All comes from God." Lily sends her love to A, W, C. Clarence and yourself. Violetta sends her love to "Dumpy," and says, "Don't forget your promise." Greetings to "My Lord College," "Pecky," "Sad Eyes," and "Saxon Sides." Good-bye, good-bye, *Deus dit*, you will be spared to spread the truth, is the prayer *ab imo pectore*, Ajax. Hail friends! Greetings.   SAMUEL.

PLATE 5, FIG. 87 (p. 376)

In the following several words are inaccurate, but Latin scholars will know what is meant:—

> Eheu fugaces, Posthume, Posthume,
>   Labuntur anni, nec pietus moram,
> Rugis et instanti senectae.
> Afferet, indamitalque morti,
> Non, si trecenis, quotquot eunt dies,
>   Amice, places illachrymabilem,
> Plutino tauris qui tir amphim,
>   Geryoren Tityanque tristi

is fair. "Ajax," who frequently manifests in the Colley-Hooper psychographs, was, I am informed, an American divine, who frequently controls the medium. "Samuel" was the Rev. Samuel Wheeler, who controlled and materialised through Dr Francis Monck, in the seventies. It was at Monck's séances that the Rector of Stockton obtained his first proofs of spiritualistic phenomena; and since then the ven. gentleman has proved himself both a sincere friend and resolute defender of the departed medium.

I regret the exigencies of space prevent a fuller note. The marked individuality and identity of the Invisibles are most convincing to all concerned in these investigations, which have been carried on for many years now in Birmingham and elsewhere, in which Dr Hooper has been the principal agent.

Compescit undâ, Scilicet omnibus,
  Quicunque terrae munere vescimur,

FIG. 87.—No. 5 Plate of the Birmingham psychographs.

Enavigauda, Sive reges
  Sive inopes erimus coloni.

Frustra cruento Marte carebimus
Fractisque racui fluctibus adrial;
  Frustra per autum nos nocentum

Corporibus metuemus Austiam :
  Visendus ater flumine languido
Cocytus errans, et Danae genus
  Infame, damnatusque longi
  Sisyphus Aeolides laboris,
Linquenda tellus, et dormus, et placens
Uxor; neque harum, quos colis arborum
  Te, Praeter invisus cupressos,
Ulla brevem dominum sequetur
  Absumet haeres Calcuba dignior
Servata centum clavibus, et mero
  Ting et pavimenthum superbum
  Pentificum Poture, coenis.

"Free" Translation, II. Horace, Ode XIV.

Ah, Postumus, Postumus, the fleeting years glide by, bringing in their train to just and unjust alike, wrinkled age, inexorable death.

No, my friend, not even by lavish sacrifice from day to day can you appease remorseless Pluto, who confines the monster Geryones and Tityos with sullen stream, that stream which must at last be crossed by all who enjoy earth's bounty, by prince and beggar alike.

Bootless is it to avoid the blood-stained field and the surging billows of the angry deep; of no avail to guard against noxious winds of Autumn. All must cross the dark, silent stream to join the daughters of Danaus and the son of Aeolus, doomed to everlasting toil.

Fatherland, home and loving wife must be left behind. Of all these trees which for a brief time you tend with anxious care, the hated cypress alone shall follow you. A worthier heir shall quaff the wine you so jealously guard and recklessly spill your most treasured vintage.

Archdeacon Colley, Rector of Stockton, delivered

an Easter sermon on Sunday evening, 3rd April 1910, in the parish church of Stockton.

The sermon was found written on a half-plate which had been sealed up in a light-proof packet, and was held—says the Ven. gentleman—between the hands of six Christian spiritualists for thirty-nine seconds only. I do not propose to reproduce the sermon, which was reported at length in the *Leamington Spa Courier*, 15th April 1910; as we are less concerned with the opinions expressed therein — albeit it is worthy of reproduction—than with the phenomenon described, viz. 1710 words written (by no mortal fingers) in eighty-four lines within the compass of a half-plate.

The Archdeacon says :—

The smallness of the copper-plate-like writing renders it impossible to be reproduced by any engraving; while at times, with our greatly esteemed unpaid mediums in various circles, the writing on our usual quarter-plates is so microscopic, that to enable us to read it a high-power lens is necessary; and the character of the caligraphy in English, archaic Greek, Latin, Hebrew, Italian, French, Arabic, varies continually in our several separate, devotional, and private gatherings, in places from twenty-four to seventy-seven miles apart, where—like (1), (2), (3),—we meet as directed (St Matt. vi. 6) in faith and love, knowing from long experience the inscrutable power of Almighty God, "the God of the spirits of all flesh" (Numbers xvi. 22 and xxvii. 36), who thus and in other ways permits the angel world to be operated in this, and the Kingdom of Heaven to dwell abidingly with us on earth.

I have seen an enlargement of the original psychograph which contained the sermon referred to. It was certainly a remarkable psychograph. Many— almost as phenomenal—psychographs have been and are obtained through the psychics of the Crewe Circle.

THE TESTIMONY OF MR WALKER

In giving this concluding case I wish to note that Mr W. Walker (3 Palace Road, Buxton, my correspondent, a photographer of forty years' experience, who obtained the psychic photograph of the late Mr Alfred Smedley, at Crewe) had the promise of getting next day, 8th November 1910, a message in three languages. For this purpose Mr Walker brought his own plates, and these (wrapped in light-proof paper) were not out of his possession, save for a quarter of a minute, while being impressed between the lady medium's hands. Even then the packet was never out of his sight.

He developed the plate. At my request he was good enough to enlarge the photograph for these pages. The original writing can only be read through a magnifying glass.

The above not being sufficiently clear, I give with it a rough translation of the French and Latin.

DEAR FRIENDS, — The following are a few words intended to prove an Intelligence at work far beyond the capabilities of the sitters. It is a *le chef d'œuvre* as far as they are concerned. Our advice to you at present is to *audi alteram partem de crainte que*. You may make a mistake and be misjudged. *Cedant*

A Rough Translation

DEAR FRIENDS,— The following are a few words intended to prove an Intelligence far beyond the capabilities of the sitters. It is a masterpiece as far as they are concerned. Our advice to you at present is to hear both sides, lest you make a mistake and be misjudged. Let the opponent give way to the law, and be faithful to the end, and in all you do submit to Providence.

The "a" before *le chef d'œuvre* is a slip. But inaccuracies are of no importance in the face of the manner of production. None of the sitters could have produced the message; even if they had the opportunity, which was non-existent. The message can only be read from the film side, as if taken by camera; the latter being out of the question.

Mr Walker has had a certificate signed by all present, but this is not produced, as the members of this circle have to earn their living at their respective daily employment, and are unable to give sittings to all and sundry, which further publicity would bring to them.

I have taken special pains since the Lodge-Colley controversy to acquaint myself with the *bona-fides* of the Crewe Circle, and of the mediumship of three of its members, and the excellent character which all bear. I have therefore all the more pleasure in giving the above case reported by Mr Walker.

Since the foregoing psychograph was sent me (the meaning of which at the time was not clear to Mr W.

Walker, except that the evidence of its genuineness was remarkably complete), I obtained the following on 15th January 1911 :—

DEAR MR COATES,—When I last wrote I said : " At present it is cryptic to me." Now the part of the message, " Our advice to you at present is to hear both sides lest you make a mistake and be misjudged. Let the opponent give way to the law and be faithful to the end," has become clearer to me.

A question concerning a boundary fence to property had been put into my hands to see it through. I had the matter in correspondence at the time the message was given to me. However, the owner, who is a very old person, having been annoyed by trespass, ordered a fence to be put up, and it was completed. I was not made aware of this until notice had been given to the adjoining owners to remove a portion of the fence, which is said to be on their land. On my visiting the site, I found it necessary to see the other side and to hear their version, as directed in the message. After fully considering the various points raised, it was decided to take this fence down and " give way to the law."

This I consider has a just bearing upon the case. It shows the spirit friends who gave me the message knew of the case, and knew how it stood, as well as knowing what would follow, of which I at the time was not only ignorant, but our friends at Crewe could not have known,—Yours faithfully, W. WALKER.
BUXTON.

And with this I conclude—not from want of material but want of space—my case for psychography.

In the foregoing cases, the plates were either in the usual photographic slide, or wrapped up in light-proof

material, and were held between the palms of the
hands of experimenters and psychics.   In some cases
the corners of the packet containing the plate or
plates were held only.   We reach another point,
and that is: we infer that there comes from the
hands of the psychic and experimenter an aura or
magnetism, which affects the plates, and prepares
them for the operations of the unknown—but actinic
—light.   Without repeating the evidence given in
Human Magnetism and *Seeing the Invisible*, it is
clear that the plates can be chemically altered by the
radiant rays—invisible—which proceed from the hands
of the experimenter.

What the London and provincial Press has been
pleased to call "mental photos," and the "latest
wonder of the scientific world," are of the nature of
psychographs, inasmuch as they too are effects produced on photographic plates in which the camera
and ordinary light have no part.

Recently—August 1911—Major Darget has made a
communication to the Academy of Science, Paris, in
which he claims that mental images, corresponding to
material objects, can be photographed.   As a proof
he submitted with his thesis two photographs, one
representing a bottle, and the other one a cane.   This
gentleman has been for some time making investigations in this—to him—new field of research.   He also
claims to be the discoverer of what he terms the
V-rays.   These are invisible rays radiating from the
human body.   He declares that things visualised and

intently thought of can be transferred to a photographic plate.

It is a sign of the times that a communication of this kind should be noticed in the press. There is nothing specially new in the discovery Commandant Tagred reported a series of similar experiments in thought photography in the *Messenger* (December 1900), in which he says :—

The first thought radiation was produced by me, on May 27, 1876, in the presence of M. Aviron of Tours, and it was *a bottle.*

It is just a little curious that Major Darget's discovery thirty-five years afterwards should be that the mental image of a bottle affected the plate too. To resume, Major Darget declares that the cane and the bottle were photographed from his mind or brain while he was thinking of them, his procedure being as follows :—

He was in a dark room, and for a quarter of an hour thought of a bottle — or rather he kept his mind fixed on a bottle which he could see before him. At the same time he had a photographic plate in a developing dish before him, which he held in the fluid with his fingers. At the end of a quarter of an hour the image of the bottle appeared on the photographic plate. He went through the same experiment in the presence of six witnesses, and the mental image of a cane was taken in the same way.

There is a certain appropriateness in the "cane" following the "bottle," as it generally does in ordinary life. I have not been able to verify Major Darget's procedure, but, as stated in *Seeing the Invisible*, I have reason to believe similar phenomena have taken place, the investigators being persons of repute. It is assumed, as images of external objects and persons enter and fix themselves in our brains through the retina of the eye, and that if they enter they can also leave, they may be reflected in some way on a photographic plate. As the foregoing case has been stated before the Academy, we prefer to wait for the solution before arriving at a definite conclusion. My object in noticing the report is the admission by a man of science, and soberly submitted with corroborative evidence, of the possibility of thought-radiations of an image formed in the mind chemically affecting a photographic plate. Granting the accuracy of the foregoing, that would not and could not solve the problems of psychic photography, although furnishing a possible corroboration of the facts presented in these pages.

But admitting that it is scientifically demonstrated there are light and other emanations —of a subtle and occult character—radiating from the human body, or, as believed by some, produced by spirit power, these would not account for the psychic figures, faces, and written messages which are obtained. The invisible light and the nervauric or psychic forces must be directed by intelligence. *Intelligent messages can only come 'from intellects capable of sending them.*

Whose intelligence is operative in all these cases,

capable of giving the features of departed persons, instruction by symbols, and communications clearly written? This question is not one readily answered. But as we have seen that many psychic pictures have actually come in response to the sitter's thoughts; have come in fulfilment of promises made—through psychics—from those who are no longer clothed in the flesh, it is a reasonable deduction that their thoughts, too, were operative, if not the actual cause of psychic results.

In the final analysis it is thought-power, and that only, which is operative, and thought suggests the thinker. Such is the power of thought—not ordinary everyday thoughts, but thought acting subconsciously —it is not only impressed, and our lives for good and ill affected thereby, but the photographic plates are also made the means of its transmission ; psychography, as well as spirit photography, presenting distinct evidence for the claim that "Intelligences in the Invisible are still operative in this life." We know that our thoughts — under certain conditions—have not only psychic, but motor force. The facts of psychology demand examination, and the subject is here tentatively submitted for consideration, as the whole throws an important side-light not only on telepathy, psychic force, but on the physical phenomena of Modern Spiritualism.

CHAPTER XVII

Most Favourable Conditions for Psychic Photography

In bringing my notes on spirit photography to a close, I think it appropriate to deal, first, with the best conditions under which a psychic picture can be obtained, and, secondly, to refer to "experts" and their methods.

Mr Wyllie often assured me that when he and the weather were in good condition, he was frequently more successful in getting identifiable pictures from a lock of hair than with the living subject, as the latter was too often excited, over-anxious, or perhaps suspicious. There was something lacking—harmony.

What, then, appear to be the best conditions revealed by actual experimentation? These are four in number, and there are a few accessories which seem to be helpful in obtaining psychic photographs.

1st. The first essential is the condition of the sitter. Some, impressed by the idea that psychic photographs are crystallisations of thought, and that they should desire earnestly for the appearance of some special person or relative, sit, as subjects, in a very anxious and active mental state. This is the very attitude to avoid at the time of sitting. The sitter should not have the mind fixed on any special person,

Fig. 89.—From a psychic photograph taken under best possible conditions. Subject, Elsie Reynolds, a noted American materialising medium—one giving off fine auretic conditions. Wyllie in vigorous health and harmonising power. Weather conditions of the finest; and lastly, the spirit Intelligences capable of using their powers effectively. I give the photograph as a challenge to experts.

and should avoid states of anxiety and perturbation. For instance, a widow who has lost a loved life-companion, a mother a child, and being anxious to have a portrait of husband or child, will, in consequence, bring undesirable conditions with them. Calm, pleasant, cheerful, non-anxious or non-excited state is the best possible attitude of mind for spirit photography. This calm, passive condition makes for harmony. The ultra sceptic and the person who views each action of the photographer with suspicion will also make a bad sitter. These two aspects—that of anxious, suffering mourners, and the mental attitude of the antagonistic sceptic—are alike unfavourable. Let it be at once pointed out that an equable state of mind, a willingness to take what comes, and sitting as if for an ordinary photograph, the sitter will throw off the best possible psychic and nervauric conditions, which will blend with that of the sensitive-operator. Owing to the natural excitement which overtakes many at the first sitting, "repeat sittings" are desirable, as in subsequent séances there is less mental disturbance and more harmony between sitter and sensitive. To this may be added a hint about accessories. Men generally dress in dark clothes. This is favourable for showing up faces or other "extras" which might appear. Ladies like to be well dressed, wearing light blouses, using costumes and ornaments which are meant to enhance personal appearance. This is all right in its place, but for spirit photography it is undesirable. A simple dark dress or blouse— not silk which shines—without ornaments, will serve the purpose. If "extras" appear, as they often do, they will have a dark background in the lady's dress to show up the high-lights.   So far for the first essential and accessories.   With Mr Wyllie, most of the psychic pictures, etc., appear over the vital organs of the sitter.

2nd. The next essential is the condition of the sensitive-photographer.   (That a medium is necessary is borne out by the fact that there are several thousand photographers in Great Britain alone, and probably there are not five who are able to obtain these photographs.   Such persons are endowed with certain faculties which the others do not possess.)   The sensitive requires to be in a fair state of health and in an equable state of mind, and if these are disturbed from any cause—poverty, anxiety, or harassment, unsuitable environment for his work, inconsiderate and thoughtless treatment by the self-important—then obstacles are placed in the way of successful results. It is also desirable that the sensitive's camera should be the one employed, being well charged with his nervaura, or magnetism, and whatever other influences have been drawn thereto.   All manipulations in the first instance should be done by the sensitive-photographer, whatever arrangements may be made subsequently by *mutual* consent, between sitter and medium.

3rd. The next essential is good atmospheric conditions.   These cannot be so readily controlled or defined. But extremes of heat and cold, violent storms, thundery weather, fogs and mists which rise from the ground after heavy rains, not only act unfavourably on the sitter and the medium, but are objectionable as far as photography itself is concerned. All atmospheric conditions otherwise, which are fairly clear, pleasant or tolerable, are helpful. As to accessories, a well-lit room, of comfortable temperature, in which sittings can be held, a dark closet supplied with running water. Also, if the medium's sleeping apartments and living rooms are convenient to the foregoing, so much the better for psychical results.

4th and last essential, *but first in order of importance, are the Unseen Intelligences and the X or unknown forces which operate through the medium and in conjunction with the sitter.* Whatever these are, be they intelligent beings, human but discarnate, who indicate their presence by raps, lights, and other modes directing the medium or sensitive, or forces emanating from the medium, spirits, or both, neither I nor anyone else can positively say. What we really do know is this, that there are Intelligences at work, that the light that produces the psychic pictures, signs, symbols and portraits, identifiable or not, is not the ordinary light by which the embodied sitter is taken. It is conjectured that there are spirit photographers and chemists on the other side, using not only the unknown X forces on their side, but supplying others. It may be only conjecture, but it is a reasonable hypothesis. As to the fourth essential, no psychic photograph can be taken without *its* co-operation.

To recapitulate, the four essentials for psychic photography are:—The condition of the sitter, who should present a calm, passive, cheerful attitude, and in this way throw off suitable personal magnetism; persons who are over-anxious, in pain, or suffering from serious ill-health, and sceptics who hinder, persons and mediums who expect and demand too much, do not furnish what is required. Secondly, the medium should be in a non-harassed condition, and be able to give off undisturbed magnetic vibrations. Thirdly, atmospheric and climatic conditions should be free from disagreeable extremes. And fourth, the X forces and spirit Intelligences should have their conditions, as far as we understand them, accepted. The latter can be helped or hindered, conciliated or repelled, by the attitude of the sitters, the medium, or by the state of the weather. All these essentials must blend harmoniously before a psychic effect or picture can be obtained, and most assuredly be present in all cases when an identifiable portrait has been secured. I have now pointed out the favourable conditions and, indirectly, the unfavourable, but a few direct words concerning the expert may be useful.

"The expert" is sometimes a photographer, and as frequently not. In the majority of cases he claims to be a spiritualist actuated by the highest motives, and his main object is to rid the movement of persons who indulge in fraudulent practices. The persons suspected and banned by him are usually physical mediums; of these, the few photographic mediums before the public are his special aversion. To not understand is a sufficient reason for condemnation.

He may or may not have had a sitting; possibly he has had *one*. On the strength of this, he is prepared to pose as an "expert." To that sitting he brought his doubts and suspicions. When he received his print, there was probably a face on it he did not recognise, or one which someone else had already obtained; it may have come across the plate, or actually upside down. There may have been other "things" on it which had no meaning for him. The whole looked like faking, and very badly done at that. It became an easy matter—following the line of the least resistance—to decide that this photograph was produced by misplaced ingenuity.

Another "expert," who knows seven different ways of producing bogus spirit photographs (but not one genuine one), says that almost *anything* can be done with a photographic plate, and what appears is the result of that *anything*.[1]

Another suggests that there are certain laws in photography without which nothing can take place.

---

[1] The best "faked spirit photographs" which the art of an accomplished photographer could produce are those by Mr R. Child Bayley, the well-known author, editor, and expert in photography. These appeared in the *London Magazine*, January 1910. In the following August, Mr Wm. Marriott gave a few more of his best faking, but much inferior to those of Mr R. Child Bayley. Comparing their best efforts with the work, say, of Mr Wyllie, presenting undoubted portraits of persons he never knew, demonstrates at once how little these noted experts know either of psychic photography or of its claims. Their best work, under their own conditions, furnishes the best repudiation of their own claims.—J. C.

He does not say definitely that psychic photography is fraudulent, but avers that all sitters should be photographed by two cameras, and the plates should be independently developed. Without this, all so-called investigation of psychic photography is worse than useless. This looks very fair and very formidable. Judged by the well-known laws of photography, nothing can come on the one plate which does not appear on the other. This is very plausible, and is correct as far as ordinary photography is concerned, but does not touch psychic photography at all, as it leaves out the four main conditions noted to which I have referred.

The sitter brings—in addition to his state of mind — certain psychical entities, thought-forms, and images of departed persons liable to be shattered by the fussy and dominant mannerisms of " experts," whose object is not to obtain psychic photographs, but to demonstrate a foregone theory.

I respectfully maintain that the photographic plate does faithfully record what is presented to it ; that it is an impartial witness on account of its purely mechanical processes ; that the plates are not subject to either hallucination, suggestion, or auto-suggestion, and so far can be relied upon to reproduce whatever is presented—seen and unseen, in light or in darkness —according to the laws of photography.

Opinions may be divided as to the nature of the things, objects, or persons chemically recorded on the plates ; but they are there because something from them—reflected or refracted light—has been gathered up by the lens and passed on to the plate.   Whether by accident or intention the object or subject be there, its presence is recorded all the same on the exposed plate.   This is a simple statement of fact.   When we come to psychic photography – with or without the camera—we enter into a region in which the ordinary laws of photography are not set aside, but are sub-ordinated to other laws—forces in operation—not at present fully understood.   For instance, visible objects and subjects have not been photographed, of which I have several cases ; whereas, on the other hand, that which is invisible—of no material substance and of the nature and character of thought—has been.   The operations which take place in psychic photography are not wholly chemical, as far as camera, lens, light —*phos*—and chemical results are concerned.   We have all these, plus something else.   That something is of the nature of a nervaura or vital magnetic force emanating from a peculiarly endowed individual—the medium.   This force—sometimes called " fluid "—may be enhanced by the presence of sitters similarly affected.   Under these circumstances the films are affected by ordinary light, and by a light emanating from the unseen object.   By this invisible light photographic plates—both in and out of the camera —are impressed with images, symbols, reproductions of things material, and in many cases with the faces and forms of living persons — not visible—and by portraits of the departed, but only in the presence of a medium, specially gifted, and never otherwise.

Anyone who has taken pains to study the late Mr
J. Traill Taylor's experimentations with two photographic mediums, of whom the late Mr David Duguid
was one, will find abundant material for reflection.
In the presence of Mr Duguid—with whom Mr Taylor
was in friendly sympathy — results were obtained
outwith all the known laws of photography. I have
had similar experiences with Mr Edward Wyllie.
Mr W. Walker, of Buxton, reported similar cases
obtained at Crewe recently.   But I wish to emphasise
the results obtained through the mediumship of Mr
Duguid by Mr J. Traill Taylor.   These results have
been condemned by "experts," ignorant of all the
facts, as fraudulent. This has always been the case
where experts "opinionate" without having all the
facts before them. The most, so pronounced, out-
rageously fraudulent-looking "extras," were genuinely
produced.   If not so, the evidence of the then
highest authority in the photographic world, *i.e.* Mr
J. Traill Taylor, and of competent witnesses, must
stand for naught with these "experts," who assume to
know but do not understand, and many of whom
have not seen, much less carefully investigated, that
which they so readily declare to be fraudulent.
Thus Mr Wm. Marriott, in his articles contributed to
Pearson's Magazine, condemned Mr Wyllie as a
fraud, and that without the slightest knowledge of
the man or his methods.   But this is in keeping
with the usual " evidence " of experts.

In psychic or occult photography I do not assume

that spirits can be photographed. I am content to admit, on the strength of the evidence I have collected and obtained at first hand, that some things are produced by Intelligences in the Invisible. This only happens when the mechanical, chemical, and other processes of photographic procedure are supplemented by appropriate mediumship — *and never without it.* When the camera is not employed the plates are affected by invisible light, heat, and other unknown forces emanating from mediumistic persons, plus something which proceeds from spirits said to operate within the subconscious self or selves of the mediums. "The extras" obtained through camera and the "things" impressed which appeared on plates held in the hand never appear without the presence of suitable media.

This brings me to the point overlooked by those who suggest that, for scientific investigation of photographic work of this description, it should be a *sine qua non* that in every experiment there be at least two cameras, and that the plates exposed in these be immediately and independently developed. I will admit that it is not of much importance who develops the plates. But why two cameras and not half a dozen, and each with a self-important operator deliberately antagonising the psychic effort.

Mr J. Traill Taylor employed a stereoscopic camera, which he operated himself, but not excluding the presence of Mr Duguid or the presence of sympathetic and intelligent witnesses, whose object was to get at

the truth and not to discover fraud. Mr Duguid was
treated as a medium should be, as a man, a friend, and
not as a suspect, which would be to destroy the
harmony essential to obtain successful results.   Under
careful testing, a number of "extras" were obtained,
but not one identifiable picture of a departed.   Psychic
photography was established because the medium was
not ignored.   Experts do so completely.   I can
guarantee that they can experiment day after day,
year after year, with two or more cameras, develop
the plates independently, in full distrust or in accord
with one another, and succeed in obtaining—nothing.

With a suitable psychic, properly treated, and with
whom harmonious relations have been set up, it is
probable, as with the Taylor-Duguid experiments,
something would be obtained, and that in defiance of
the very laws of photography so much talked about.

The *sine qua non* is not two cameras and independent development, but an identifiable portrait of
a departed obtained under satisfactory and harmonious
conditions.

Never in the history of psychic photography has an
identifiable portrait of a departed been obtained as
the result of this so-called scientific investigation with
one camera or several, but because of the presence of
a vitally vigorous and sufficiently imperturbed medium,
whom the Intelligences in the Invisible were able to
use, and with whom the subjects were in harmony.

Expert photographers, scientific investigators, and
the would-be dabblers who claim to be experts, start

on the wrong basis in assuming that this matter can be settled on the ordinary lines of practical photography, ignoring and condemning mediumship, without which psychic photography is impossible.

Psychic photography is a phase of physical phenomena. The mediums for this phase are very rare, and are treated by these experts with suspicion. Physical phenomena are becoming non - existent through the treatment of mediums by "experts." It would be much wiser, in my opinion, to patiently study mediumship and co-operate with the Intelligences controlling them, and in this way obtain the better results. *Then the phenomena presented would bring their own best evidences.* This has ever been the experience of those who have gone thoroughly into the matter.

FINIS

PRINTED BY NEILL AND CO., LTD., EDINBURGH.

26

BY THE SAME AUTHOR

SEEING THE INVISIBLE. Practical Studies in Psychometry, Thought Transference, Telepathy, and Allied Phenomena, with 5 plates. Crown 8vo, cloth, 5s. net. Post free 5s. 4d.

"SEEING THE INVISIBLE," ACCEPTED BY THE KING.

The Author has been honoured by the following letter from Buckingham Palace, dated 6th December 1906 :—

"The Private Secretary is commanded by the King to thank Dr Coates for his letter of the 3rd inst., with the accompanying copy of his book 'Seeing the Invisible.'"

"A deeply interesting work of 300 pages, dealing with Man's Psychical Nature, Invisible Forces and Emanations; Nature's Invisible Biograph; Psychometric Experiments and Practice; Thought-Transference and Telepathy; Psychic Faculty, Telepathy, and Modern Spiritualism."—*Two Worlds.*

"Among the many volumes that are issued from the press on the all-embracing subject of Psychology . . . . none has yet appeared of such a practical and interesting character as the volume bearing the above title, by James Coates, Ph.D., F.A.S."—*Harbinger of Light*, Melbourne Australia.

"A distinct acquisition to the literature dealing with psychic faculties." —*Light.*

HUMAN MAGNETISM: OR, How TO HYPNOTISE. With 10 plates. Fourth edition. Crown 8vo, cloth, 5s net. Post free 5s. 4d.

This is an excellent work by a master of the subject. Mr Coates is no mere theorist, but has had a long practical experience of the subject with which he deals so ably. In the introduction to the work he gives a short sketch of the progress of the science from the earliest times.

THE PRACTICAL HYPNOTIST. Concise Instruction on Hypnotism. The Art and Practice of Suggestion in the Cure of Disease, the Correction of Habits, Development of Will-Power and Self-Culture With 2 Plates. Fcap. 8vo, cloth, 1s. net. Post free 1s. 2d.

Hypnotism has come to stay, and ere long its non-employment will be esteemed little less than a criminal neglect, where patients are not amenable to medicinal substances. . . . There are thousands who are invalids to-day who can be helped to help themselves, by the way of Auto-Suggestion or "New Thought Powers," to Health of both body and mind.

"HOW-TO" MANUALS

HOW TO READ HEADS. 128 pp. Illustrated. Bound in Boards. Price 1s., post free 1s. 2d.

HOW TO READ FACES. Copiously Illustrated. 128 pp. Boards. Price 1s., post free 1s. 2d.

HOW TO MESMERISE. HOW TO THOUGHT-READ. 128 pp. Illustrated. Boards. Price 1s., post free 1s. 2d.

IMPORTANT TO CORRESPONDENTS

Readers of the above published works, desiring Professional Advice or Instruction in connection with matters dealt therein, should send all letters —with stamped and addressed envelopes—direct to author at his private address, "Glenbeg House, Rothesay, Scotland," and not to Publishers. By this procedure, unnecessary delay in getting replies will be avoided.

LIST OF BOOKS

PUBLISHED AND SOLD BY

L. N. FOWLER & CO.

7 IMPERIAL ARCADE, LUDGATE CIRCUS,

LONDON, E.C.

SEEING THE INVISIBLE. Practical Studies in Psychometry, Thought Transference, Telepathy, and Allied Phenomena. By JAMES COATES, Ph.D., F.A.S., Author of " Human Magnetism," " How to Mesmerise," " How to Thought-Read," " How to Read Heads," etc. Price 5s. net, post free 5s. 4d. With five illustrations.

CHARACTER; OR, THE POWER OF PRINCIPLES. By FRANK H. RANDALL, Author of "Your Mesmeric Forces," "Psychology," etc., etc. Showing the Importance of SELF-Development. A Stimulant to all to determine what they desire to be according to PRINCIPLES. Price 2s. 6d. net, post free 2s. 9d.

YOUR MESMERIC FORCES, AND HOW TO DEVELOP THEM. Giving Full and Comprehensive Instructions How to Mesmerise. By FRANK H. RANDALL. Crown 8vo, 150 pages. Price 2s. 6d. net, post free 2s. 9d.

BUSINESS SUCCESS THROUGH MENTAL ATTRACTION. By O HASHNU HARA. A Pocket Guide to the successful application of Suggestion and the Power of Mind to the Control of Financial Conditions, with practical Rules to ensure Business Success. Price 7d. net.

CONCENTRATION AND THE ACQUIREMENT OF PERSONAL MAGNETISM. By O HASHNU HARA. One of the most lucid, original, and complete series of letters on the difficult subjects of Mental and Spiritual Concentration yet published. Price 2s. 8d. net.

THE ROAD TO SUCCESS. By O HASHNU HARA. Teaches the laws governing the practice of Auto-Suggestion. Price 1s. 2d. net.

TELEPATHY: MENTAL TELEGRAPHIC COMMUNICATION. By R. D. STOCKER. 1s. net, post free 1s. 2d. *What it is and how it is done.*

What is Man? His Soul-Life—The Rationale of Telepathy—The Nature of the Mind—How the Mind acts—Telepathy applied—Instances of Telepathic Communications.

A Copy of this Manual was accepted by H.M. King Edward VII.

SOUL-CULTURE: SELF-DEVELOPMENT. By R. D. STOCKER. 1s. net, post free 1s. 2d. *What it is, and how it is done.*

> Life's Inequalities: Their Cause and Cure (Past)—The Mystery of Being: The Remedy of "YOGA" (Present)—The Predictive Art: The Rationale of "Fortune Telling" (Future).

CLAIRVOYANCE: CLAIRAUDIENCE, PSYCHOMETRY, AND CLAIRSEN-SCIENCE. By R. D. STOCKER. 1s net, post free 1s. 2d. *What it is, and how it is done.*

> Preliminary Observations—Clairvoyance in Theory—Clairvoyance in Practice: Positive Methods — "Mediumship," Psychometry, etc.: Negative Methods.

MENTALISM; OR, MIND AND WILL-TRAINING. By R. D. STOCKER. 1s. net, post free 1s. 2d. *What it is, and how it is done.*

> Man: His Outwardness and Inwardness—Man: The Animal and the God—Principles of Auto-Development—Simple Suggestions to Right Thinking—Advanced Hints on Health and Happiness.

PHRENOMETRY: AUTO-CULTURE AND BRAIN-BUILDING BY SUGGES-TION. By R. D. STOCKER. 1s. net, post free 1s. 2d. *What it is, and how it is done.*

> Phases of Consciousness and Brain Action—The Science of Mind, the Secret of Personal Success.

HEALING: MENTAL AND MAGNETIC. By R. D. STOCKER. 1s. net, post free 1s. 2d. *What it is, and how it is done.*

> The Rationale of Mental Healing—The Modus Operandi—Suggestions for Affirmation—Magnetic Healing, its Principles and Practice — "Local" or Specific Treatment.

THE SECRET OF MENTAL MAGIC. By WILLIAM WALKER ATKINSON. A Series of Seven Lessons combined in one Cloth-covered Volume. 380 pages. 12mo. 2s. 6d. net, post free 2s. 10d.

> This contains full information about The Nature of Mental Force; The Two Mental Poles; The Law of Mental Induction; The Laws, Theory, and Practice of Mental Suggestion; Personal Influence; Personal Magnetism; Mental Magnetism; Positive Personality; Magnetic Attraction; Fascination; Mental Currents; The Circulation of Mind; Desire Force; Will Power; The Law of Mental Attraction; The Art of Visualisation; Thought Forms and their Materialisation; Will Projection; Telementation; Telemental Influence; Mental Impression; Mental Concentration; Mental Centres; Mental Therapeutics Simplified; New Methods of Healing; Absent Treatments; Mental Architecture; Character Building; The New Discoveries of Brain Cell Culture; The Dominant Will; Individuality, and many other fascinating subjects. Full information, instruction, and exercises.

THE COMPLEXION BEAUTIFUL; OR, NEW SKINS FOR OLD. How to gain a Complexion like an Infant without taking Drugs, applying Cosmetics, undergoing painful Operations, or expending Money. By O HASHNU HARA. Price 1s. net, post free 1s. 1d.

HEALTH-BUILDING; OR, HEALTH WITHOUT FADS. By JOSEPH RALPH, Author of "Brain Building." Price 1s. net, post free 1s. 2d.

Being a working outline of the principles involved in Health Building, also a little cursory dissertation on some current fallacies.

NEVER SAY DIE. Hints, Helps, and Counsel on the Preservation of Health and the Promotion of Life. By J. WALLACE-CLARKE. Price 6d. net, post free 7d.

Accepted by H.M. King Edward VII.

COLOUR AS A CURATIVE AGENT. By R. DIMSDALE STOCKER. Price 1s. net, post free 1s. 1d.

This is an unique work on the theory and practice of Chromopathy, including seven plates illustrating the seven primary colours and their significance.

The following are the leading subjects dealt with by the Author :—Light and Life—Colour : Its Value and Importance—Colour in relation to Health and Disease—Chromopathic Methods—The Human Aura—Supplement, with Plates.

HOW TO MAKE A MAN. By ALFRED T. STORY. Price 2s. 6d. net, post free 2s. 9d.

"Messrs L. N. Fowler & Co., London, have published a book of conversational lectures on health and the formation of character, written by Alfred T. Story, and entitled 'How to Make a Man.' They are interesting and suggestive discourses in practical ethics, full of useful hints to parents and guardians and men who seek advice in the matter of self-culture."—*Scotsman.*

"So much is heard of the deterioration of the race nowadays that any writer who can put us on the right track ought to find many readers. In 'How to Make a Man,' Mr Alfred T. Story essays the task."—*Tribune.*

HOW TO ACQUIRE AND STRENGTHEN WILL-POWER. Rational Training of the Will and the Development of Energy. By Prof. R. J. EBBARD. Price 6s. 10d. net, post free.

His ingenious course of self-treatment first of all removes all impediments to energy and will-power, such as—Neurasthenia, absence of mind, insomnia, exhaustion and debility, headaches, trembling, timidity, trepidation, neuralgia, nervous pains, loss of appetite, indigestion, weak memory, confusion, fits of rage, inconstancy, alcoholism, nicotinism, hysteria, cowardice, absent-mindedness, lack of self-confidence, melancholia, stage-fright, fright of exams., bashfulness, etc.

An Appendix gives an unfailing and permanent cure of Gout and Rheumatism.

THE BEDROCK OF HEALTH. Based on the Anti-Collæmic Radical Cure of Diseases and Chronic Disorders. A Real Home Self-Doctor. Self-Treatment without Physic. By Prof. R. J. EBBARD and F. W. VOGT. Price 10s. 4d. net, post free.

Professor Ebbard's latest and largest work will open a new chapter in the lives of all those who take it up. Years of diligent study, research, experiment, and experience have at last resulted in the evolution of a system of treating and curing disease which can honestly be called one of the greatest achievements of modern times. It denotes quite a new departure in therapeutics, and may be described as—Medical Reform Science. It is a rational cure of the most stubborn and chronic diseases which the new treatment aims at and actually accomplishes.

MENTAL DEPRESSION: ITS CAUSE AND TREATMENT. By Prof. R. J. EBBARD. Based on Modern Medical Reform Science and Successful Practical Experience, lucidly explained for the purpose of Self-Treatment without Medicine. Price 2s. 6d. net, post free 2s. 9d.

DYSPEPSIA AND COSTIVENESS. By Prof. R. J. EBBARD. A Natural Treatment even of the Most Serious Cases. Based on Modern Medical Reform Science and Successful Practical Experience, lucidly explained for the purpose of SELF-TREATMENT WITHOUT MEDICINE. Price 2s. 6d. net, post free 2s. 9d.

THE HUMAN AURA AND THE SIGNIFICANCE OF COLOUR. By W. J. COLVILLE. Price 1s. net, post free 1s. 2d.

Three intensely interesting Lectures by a Master in Spiritual Science and the New Thought. The use of various colours as healing agencies, otherwise known as Chromopathy, is also fully dealt with. This is unquestionably the completest exposition of this fascinating subject ever offered to the public at a nominal price.

THE MIND'S ATTAINMENT. By URIEL BUCHANAN. The Study of Laws and Methods for obtaining individual Happiness, Success, and Power through the Silent Force of Thought. Paper, 1s. net, post free 1s. 2d.

Every reader of New Thought Literature is familiar with the charming literary style of Mr Buchanan. This book expresses more nearly the high ideals of the author than anything he has hitherto published. It gives the essence of a beautiful and uplifting philosophy that cannot fail to benefit and instruct humanity.

CONTENTS :—The Supreme Force—Man's Divinity—Mysteries—The Science of Breath—Self-Mastery—Mental Control—The Law of Suggestion—The Sovereign Will—The Power of Silence—Individual Supremacy—The Spirit of Youth—Mental Influences—Elements of Success—Demand and Supply—The Higher Life—Our Destiny—Human Progress—Divine Guidance—A Lesson from Nature—Aspiration—The Highest Goal.

THE MYSTIC SCROLL. By HELEN VAN ANDERSON. Price 4s. 6d. net, post free 4s. 10d.

This is a new book, just from the press, that tells you in a plain, simple manner : How to Heal—How to train the Mind—How to become a Master—How to be filled with Peace at all Times ; How to be free from Fear ; How to come in touch with the Unseen Helpers—About the Laws of Vibration and the Secret of Clairvoyance—About entering the Silence—How to become more Prosperous—How to treat yourself in order to throw off Undesirable Influences, etc., etc.

YOGA METHODS: HOW TO PROSPER IN MIND, BODY, AND ESTATE. By R. DIMSDALE STOCKER. Price 1s. net, post free 1s. 1d.

CONTENTS.—PART I. Occultism and High Thought. Physical Regeneration. PART II. Mental Rejuvenation. PART III. The Path of Devotion.

SUB-CONSCIOUSNESS. Studies and Lessons in the Larger Life. Being a Series of Practical Instructions in the Application of the New Psychology to Daily Life. By R. DIMSDALE STOCKER. Crown 8vo. Bound. Price 3s. 6d. net, post free 3s. 10d.

> The well-known author, whose previous efforts have been so well appreciated by the public and press, explains in eight lessons the diverse phenomena, as indicated below, and gives practical suggestions and instructions for directing them to given ends.
>
> LESSON I. Thought Currents and How to Direct Them—LESSON 2. Telepathy in its Practical Application—LESSON 3. Imagination: Its Possibilities, Scope, etc.—LESSON 4. The Sleep World—LESSON 5. Hypnotism and Suggestion—LESSON 6. The Wonders of the Will—LESSON 7. Healing, and the Law of Mental Medicine—LESSON 8. The Making of a Genius.

PRACTICAL YOGA. A Series of Thoroughly Practical Lessons upon the Philosophy and Practice of Yoga, with a chapter devoted to Persian Magic. By O HASHNU HARA. Price 1s. net, post free 1s. 2d.

PRACTICAL HYPNOTISM. By O HASHNU HARA. Price 1s. net, postage 1d. extra.

> A practical manual, clearly teaching eighteen different methods of inducing Mesmerism and Hypnotism, as practised by the great French and American Schools, and the working methods of the well-known Hypnotists.

PSYCHOLOGY. The Cultivation and Development of Mind and Will by Positive and Negative Processes. By FRANK H. RANDALL. 3s. net, post free 3s. 3d.

PRACTICAL PSYCHOMETRY: ITS VALUE, AND HOW IT IS MASTERED. By O HASHNU HARA. Price 1s. net, post free 1s. 1d.

THE LAW OF SUGGESTION. A Compendium for the People. By Rev. STANLEY LeFEVRE KREBS, A.M., Psy. Dr. Price 3s. 6d. net, post free 3s. 9d.

> FOREWORD.—*My Purpose is Three Fold:* (1) To give a bird's-eye view of the whole field for busy people—all about Suggestion, but not, of course, all of it. (2) To tear from the subject that veil of mystery, or "occultism" with which so many initiates delight to surround it before the eyes of the public. (3) To awaken, if possible, an earnest and patient study of the matter on the part of parents, business men, preceptors, preachers, and people generally, as it can be observed by them affecting the affairs, not only of common daily life, but the profoundest interests, also of health, intellect, and character—body, mind, and soul.

THE PATH TO POWER. By URIEL BUCHANAN. 1s. net, post free 1s. 2d.

> You can double your earning power with no increase of work. You can find twice as much happiness with no greater effort, and without any sacrifice.
>
> The majority work hard and accomplish little, because they do not understand themselves and the forces at their command.
>
> There are keys which unlock man's hidden energies and latent talents, just as there are keys yet undiscovered to great inventions.
>
> "The Path to Power" will tell you about your own set of keys which will open the door to your treasure-house of possibilities.
>
> CONTENTS.—Natural Breathing gives Health and Joy—A Magnetic Personality Insures Affluence and Power—Practical Methods for the Cultivation of Memory—Chart and Guide to Intuition and Genius—The Invincible Will Emancipates the Mind and Conquers Adversity—Power through Repose and Affirmations.

THE MAGIC SEVEN. By LIDA A CHURCHILL. Gives Explicit Directions for using Mental Powers which may change your whole life. 1s. net, post free 1s. 2d.

CONTENTS.—How to make a Center—How to go into the Silence—How to Concentrate the Mind—How to Command Opulence—How to Use the Will—How to Insure Perfect Health—How to Ask and Receive.

"I am recommending 'Magic Seven' to everybody."—ELLA WHEELER WILCOX.

"Its methods of concentration cannot fail to produce great results."—SARA LOCKIE BROWNE, M.D.

"In 'The Magic Seven' we have the clearest and most concise statement of the practical utilisation of mental and occult forces for business success and individual self-mastery that I am acquainted with."—B. O. FLOWER in *The Arena.*

THE MAGNET. By LIDA A. CHURCHILL. Gives clear Practical Directions for gaining whatever you wish. 1s. net, post free 1s. 2d.

CONTENTS.—How to avoid Demagnetism—How to create Inward Magnetism—How to establish Outward Magnetism—How to have a Magnetic Personality—How to Magnetise Circumstances—How to Win and Hold Love—How to remain a Magnet.

"Worth its weight in gold."—ELLA WHEELER WILCOX.

THE MASTER DEMAND. By LIDA A. CHURCHILL. 1s. net, post free 1s. 2d.

The life which is moving in the natural, which is the God-appointed way, comes in contact with, and commands the use of those high intelligences and spirit-informed and vitalised forces of both worlds, which, working with infinitely fine tools in a medium of unexplainable potency and responsiveness, bring forth mightily.

CONTENTS.—How to Speak for Power—How to Speak for Adjustment—How to Speak for Understanding—How to Speak for Force and Forces—How to Speak for Attraction—How to Speak for Plenty—How to Speak for Peace.

Note.—The only complete, authorised, and unabridged edition of Lida A. Churchill's works bear the imprint of L. N. Fowler & Co.; insist upon having this edition.

PRACTICAL METHODS TO INSURE SUCCESS. By HIRAM E. BUTLER. 1s. net, post free 1s. 2d.

This is a little book containing extraordinary facts governing human life. The methods not alone quicken body, mind, and soul, but when adopted fully they make the turning-point in one's life. If you are not the success that you wish to be; if there is something wrong and you do not know just what—perhaps a condition of mind or health that has caused years of anxious hope and disappointment—would you give One Shilling to know why? This books tells why, and how to remove difficulties.

NOTE THE CONTENTS.—Prologue—Chapter I. Change of Thought Habit—II. Methods of Obtaining Perfect Health—III. To Put the Digestion in Order—IV. Regeneration the Source of Life—V. What is to be Gained by Regeneration?—VI. The Cause of Inharmony in Marriage—VII. The Law of Association of Men and Women—VIII. Control of the Mind; Methods to Develop Concentrativeness. The New Memory. Recollection—IX. Conclusion.

THE ART OF SELF-CONTROL. By RICHARD INGALESE. A Chapter from History and Power of Mind. Paper. 6d. net, post free 7d.

CPSIA information can be obtained
at www.ICGtesting.com
Printed in the USA
BVHW092202210219
540849BV00006B/134/P